LAND OF TEARS

SANJAR ROHĀM

MILSPEAK BOOKS
An Imprint Of Milspeak Foundation, Inc.

© 2024 SANJAR ROHĀM

All rights reserved, including the right of reproduction in whole or in part in any form except in the case of brief quotations embodied in critical articles or reviews. For permission, contact publisher at the following email address: info@milspeakfoundation.org.

Sanjar Rohām is a pseudonym for the author. The publisher has verified the author's identity and his service time with the U.S. Marines in Afghanistan.

Manufactured in the United States of America
Library of Congress Cataloging-in-Publication Data
Rohām, Sanjar

Library of Congress Control Number: 2024944421
ISBN: 979-8-9911731-0-0 (hardcover)
ISBN: 979-8-9887456-6-2 (paperback)
ISBN: 978-8-9887456-7-9 (epub)

Editor: Margaret MacInnis
Designer: Michelle Bradford Art

MilSpeak Foundation, Inc.
5097 York Martin Road
Liberty, NC 27298
www.MilSpeakFoundation.org

DISCLAIMER

This is my story. It is my recollection of events that occurred but not necessarily in the original sequence of time. Names, descriptions, and dialogue may have been changed or edited. Others who were present may recall these experiences and dialogue differently.

AUTHOR'S NOTE

In Farsi, the suffix *-istan* means "the land of," and *afghan* has these connotations: lament, wail, clamor, weep. Until the horrific events of September 11, 2001, few Americans knew anything about Afghanistan. Today, they likely know more than they care to. More than two decades later, the war in Afghanistan has come to mean grief and weariness, and has left deep emotional and physical scars on America.

Afghanistan, the land of endless tears, a land with an insatiable appetite for blood.

Despite all the news, most Americans still don't understand *the land of the Afghans*. It is a mostly untamed country where self-identity is measured by tribal hierarchies and alliances of convenience. These alliances are short-lived, given the country's thirty-four provinces and some fifteen ethnic groups that include Pashtons, Tajiks, Hazaras, and a dozen others. These tribal alliances have always responded to invaders with enthusiastic violence, and have bloodied aspiring conquerors from Alexander the Great to Great Britain, the Soviet Union, and perhaps the United States.

In January of 1842, the British Empire suffered a most devastating defeat. A total of 4,500 British soldiers, along with 12,000 family members and camp followers, led by Major General Sir William Elphinstone, were massacred by Emir Dost Mohamad Barakzai's son and his native forces. The Afghans spared only one man, Dr. William Bryden, instructing him to recount the butchery to the British. Once the common enemy was routed, the Afghan factions return to their normal life, protecting their tribal turfs and fighting among themselves.

As foretold, expectedly, in the Author's Note and throughout the book, the fragile hope that I harbored for more than a decade collapsed as swiftly as the Afghan government on August 15, 2021. The rapidly decaying conditions on the ground confirmed the thoughts that I tried to suppress for all these years, unsuccessfully.

The world watched as people fell from the sky, as infants got handed off to strangers, to the infidels over the concertina wire. We watched frantic and besieged people attempt to enter the Kabul Airport, a small slowly diminishing safe heaven guarded by our sons and daughters. We watched thirteen of ours brutally cut down by a vicious enemy with the patience of Job.

This book is dedicated to all who fell on the battlefield, to those who left limbs in the arena of war, and to everyone that served honorably in any capacity in Afghanistan.

The Land of Tears is *weeping*, again.

EPIGRAPH

Walk through any cemetery. Common to every tombstone is a solitary space—a small line etched between two dates, guarding the secrets between them. No longer than an inch or two, the line speaks to a lifetime of hopes and heartaches, laughter and lamentation, pleasure and pain, triumph and tribulation. It is a line connecting the beginning of a journey to its end, a trivial symbol marking our desperate attempt to quantify and harness time. It says nothing about the journey imposed on us by our forebears. In its simplicity and graveyard solitude, the line could indicate a mundane existence filled with commonplace routine, a life of quiet desperation, as Thoreau called it. In reality, the line denotes our time spent on Earth, years filled with love and loathing, fortitude and fear, beauty and brutality, loyalty and betrayal, faith and doubt.

If only those keepers of secrets could talk.

PROLOGUE

FOB EDI: NOVEMBER 21, 2010

Seven or eight personnel, both uniformed and plainclothes, were waiting in front of a U-shaped arrangement of shipping containers at one of the Forward Operating Bases. As Captain Halloran led me toward them, I deduced that the plainclothes individuals were CIA or something similar.

One of them extended his hand and introduced himself as George. I doubted that was his real name.

I took his hand. "Sanjar Rohām, Sanj for short."

At six-four, with brown hair and a scraggly beard, George looked like a WWE Wrestlemania star. He wore a sidearm strapped to each of his muscular thighs. The M4 slung over his left shoulder looked puny for his size.

He tilted his head toward the cargo container. "The person in there has disposed of his freedom. Once inside we will tell you the questions and you will translate exactly—nothing more, nothing less."

"Understood, sir," I said.

Both doors to the container were open. A dirty white sheet hung in the front like a curtain. Captain Holleran pulled the curtain aside, and all eight or nine of us entered. Lit by a weak lightbulb, the space inside felt different, cavernous. In the middle squatted a figure wrapped in a thick, gray, burlap blanket. Only the crown of his head was visible.

Not once but several times, George ordered the person to stand up.

Finally he rose, moving unhurriedly, and the blanket slowly slid off his body until it dropped on the floor. My heart sank when I saw what stood a short step away from me. Was it man or beast? I stood face-to-face with a figure at least six-feet six-inches tall but weighing no more than 140 or 150 pounds. He wore a white sheet around his crotch much like the ones sumo wrestlers wear, and nothing else. His ankles were shackled to the floor, as were the chains around his wrists. Wavy, dull, jet-black hair flowed past his shoulders and his black beard extended to the middle of his chest. His facial hair grew above his cheekbones to almost his eye sockets. The hair under his armpits hung down to the mid-ribcage section of his torso. Black, wavy hair covered his entire body.

I had a *Twilight Zone* moment, an out-of-body experience. Reality and nightmare became indistinguishable. I felt myself hover over the scene. My eyes traveled slowly from his feet to his eyes. The detainee's deep-set eyes, honey-colored and penetrating, slapped me back to reality. I'd never seen such a malignant stare.

George broke the silence. "You ready, Sanj?"

"Good to go, sir."

"Ask his name. His real name."

"*Naamet chist?*" I asked the prisoner in Dari. "*Naame asli.*"

He gave me a venomous smile. I asked the question again, this time with more force. "*NAAMET CHIST?*"

He smiled again. "*Na po—*" he said in Pashto. "Don't und—"

I cut him off before he could finish and asked the same question in Pashto. "*Sta noom tse deh?*"

The beast examined me closely, his eyes wide.

"Why does he carry six different ID cards?" George asked. "Where did he get the bomb-making material, the material in his car?"

"Can I see the ID cards?"

Another plainclothes handed me the cards. All had different names but the same picture. I informed the group of this, and they were astonished. They had had no idea. How could they? They couldn't read Pashto.

"Can I ask him why each card has a different name?" I asked George.

George nodded.

"*Waly shpag pezhand panhi da mokhtalef noom garzawi, da pa motar ki chawdendonki toki de la koma kral?*"

The beast looked at me and smiled again. The calcium buildup on his gray teeth looked like broken pieces of oyster shell. "*Ta mor ghoti, Pakhto la koma zda kari da?"* he said. *"Mor de da Taliban fahesha da aw plar za mong chai bacha woo?"*

I translated: "You motherfucker, where did you learn to speak Pashto? Is your mother a whore for the Taliban or your father a tea boy for us?" For the benefit of the observers I added, "In Afghan culture, a 'tea boy' is a boy or a young man designated to be sodomized by other men."

The beast took half a step forward, towering over me. *"De Kafirano ta waya taso ba yaw yaw wazhnam. Kala che da dway kar khalas kar, bia pohegam ta sara tse kawam,"* he said as he stroked his filthy beard.

I was unable to feel my legs under me. "Tell these infidels I will behead them one by one. I know what to do with you when I'm done with them." I translated.

But he wasn't finished. *"Sta maray da piano mazy kha da. Sta maray ba zana de charhe landy prey kegi, tar agho che sta maray prey kawam ta be azar zala marg pa stergo wawinay."*

"Your neck is good for piano wire. Your white meat will slice open under my blade, you will die a thousand deaths before I slice your throat just enough for you to feel life flow out of your body."

A long moment of silence.

The creature looked every individual in the eyes and smiled savagely. *"Agha ta waya chi tasu de tolo sa'atuno malek yee. Kho mung tol wakhtuno laro."*

"What's this shit-breath saying now?" asked one of the plainclothes men.

"He says you own all the watches, but we have all the time." I replied without taking my eyes off the beast.

1

THE DEED

SEPTEMBER 27, 2010

The interior lights on the bus were off. The mostly young, male, and rowdy Afghan passengers had passed out cold in their seats. So had Fardad, sitting in front of me. Aside from being the only Iranians, he and I were the only Jews in the group: a fact that we'd discovered during the five months we'd spent in the Pashto language training course but kept concealed from the others. My two weeks in Baltimore with Fardad had turned our acquaintance into a friendship. It had also opened our eyes to a reality lurking below the surface. Some of the Afghan interpreters in the group disliked Iranians almost as much as they resented Pakistanis, and possibly Jews with even lesser regard. Fardad and I realized we had only each other to rely on. Two Jew-boys in a turbulent sea of Muslims.

My conversation companion, Benjoe, a black ex-Marine seated across the aisle from me, had fallen asleep as well. I'd met Benjoe just a few hours ago as we left Baltimore for Fort Benning, Georgia. He was going to Afghanistan for Global Vigilance, the same private contractor that had hired me.

Besides me, the only person not sleeping was the driver. I hoped.

My watch showed 1:13 a.m. I'd been awake for more than eighteen hours. My brain was on autopilot with no off switch. The almost fourteen-hour bus ride offered me a chance to try and arbitrate my irreconcilable internal quarrels. I could not stop punishing myself for what I'd thought was my life and reality, but had proven to be a mere fragile perception destroyed by a cyclical downturn in the economy. The sense of not belonging to any one place or group that I had felt all my life—be it as a young kid in Iran or a teenager in America—had reached desperate lows. Iran is a Muslim country, and for the most part its people looked at Iranian Jews as "Kikes." In America, Americans looked at me as a "raghead." I was torn between two cultures: not fully American, and yet an outsider to my birth culture.

These thoughts and the events of the past six months buzzed around in my head like a horde of bees trapped in a canister. There had been a time when I wanted to join the military, but going to a war-torn country as a contractor and without any proper combat training was neither on my bucket list nor any thrill I sought in life, at least not at age forty-four. It was a job, and I desperately needed a job, any job. Back in March, out of despair, I responded to an ad in a Persian newspaper looking for Farsi, Dari, Pashto speakers. The tiny ad led me to the Pashto language course in Carlsbad almost two hours south of Los Angeles, twice a week. If you'd told me in February 2010 that I would be in Afghanistan by October of the same year, I would have bet money against you. All I had going for me was the fluent Farsi I'd spoken in Iran until leaving at the age of twelve, in late 1977, a year before the Islamic Revolution. And now, the U.S. government seemed to find value in that and had sent me to language school. The military needed translators in Afghanistan and Farsi speakers made good candidates to learn Pashto since the alphabet is similar to Farsi. Aside from that, Farsi and Dari have the same alphabet and are very much alike, somewhat like Italian and Spanish. You speak one, you speak the other.

Surviving the Pashto course had been arduous. I'd butted heads with the course instructor, Dr. Rasouli, and had had to resist getting pushed out by him. Our first telephone conversation had been contentious, maybe because I was an Iranian vying for a position that could possibly be filled by an Afghan. The antagonism hadn't ended after we hung up the phone; it carried over to our first face-to-face meeting, when Rasouli told me he didn't have time to teach me Pashto and not to return to class after the first day.

I didn't oblige. For five months he demeaned me frequently in front of the other students. His favorite putdown was that I wasn't physically strong enough for the job. Some of his pet students told me he thought me a "pussy-boy."

Rasouli did everything in his power to see me flunk the program. My gut feeling told me he had had a hand in my failing the language exam *twice*. He thought my back-to-back failures would get me to drop out, but I challenged his authority and the test results. The normally fifteen-minute-long test took me more than an hour on my third try, and as it turned out, Rasouli was the one who failed.

However, the clobbering didn't end with Rasouli; it was followed by a month of wrestling with government forms, and an additional two weeks at the Pre-Deployment Processing Center in Baltimore. PDPC was a meat grinder. You went in whole and came out minced. This was how the Department of Defense turned average citizens into contractors. I'd already gone through a rigorous language testing program, medical check, and an eight-hour, dauntingly intrusive Counterintelligence Interview that must've been designed by Lucifer's proctologist. Counterintelligence Interviews are no more than four hours long at best but mine took twice as long because of my month-long vacations to travel destinations like Jordan, Turkey, and Eastern Europe. Getting my anus probed by a cold-blooded blonde displaying her ice cleavage was not my idea of foreplay.

Every aspect of my life was scrutinized. Not every candidate made it. Many were deemed a liability to the U.S. government and given the boot. I hadn't been.

A bump in the road turned my autopilot off, severing my thoughts from memories past, bringing them into the now. I glanced at my watch again. It was 2:18 a.m.; we were at the gates of Fort Benning. This was the CONUS Replacement Center or the CRC. CONUS is "military speak" for Continental United States. The military loves acronyms.

The guards at the gate waved us through. We drove slowly through the grid of darkened streets and stopped after several miles. The driver switched on the overhead lights as a young soldier came on board. He ordered us to get off, form a single file, and directed us to the "sign-in and billeting" building.

My bus companion, Benjoe, fell in ahead of me. "This brings back memories," he said in a deep, sleepy voice.

"This will make memories," I replied.

We shuffled into the billeting room. Fardad followed behind in his unhurried–as-molasses-in-wintertime attitude and movement. His face looked vacant, much like my bank account. The three of us lined up at the metal-top counter in the dismally lit billeting room across from three bleary-eyed soldiers who looked thoroughly pissed off by our wee-hour arrival. The Afghans jostled in lines behind us. The soldier handling Benjoe, though, changed his tone once he found out Benjoe was an ex-Marine. While they chatted, the soldier checked my ID, checked me in, assigned me to a barracks, and gave its entry code. He then handed me a pillow, a pillowcase, a sheet, and a blanket that felt like burlap. "Move on," he commanded. I had never been arrested, but the whole process felt like being booked into jail. Still, after the mind-numbing bus ride, this new phase began to feel exciting. Instead of a victim of the 2009 Great Recession—an outsider looking in—I began to feel like I belonged.

After our *booking*, the bus drove us to the barracks. We stumbled off and the driver dropped the cargo doors and haphazardly tossed bags onto the asphalt. Benjoe, Fardad, and I cracked smiles at each other. We each shouldered our only backpack while the others scrambled like gophers digging through the mountain of suitcases.

We walked to the cinder block single-story barracks with one bag and sleeping gear. Fardad was assigned to the barracks next to mine. Benjoe punched in the code to open the door as I stood behind him. The young Afghans lined up behind us then stampeded into the corridor first, squabbling over the choice of rooms.

Benjoe took the first room by the entrance and I took the second. They were farthest from the showers and toilets at the other end of the long hall. Each eight-by-twenty foot room had two bunk beds and four lockers. I took a lower of each. Two other inmates, Gul-Mohammad and Fazil, came after me and immediately quarreled over the remaining bottom bunk. The next day Benjoe told me that as soon as he walked into the room the Afghans shut up and offered him the bottom bed and locker. Sometimes, I guess, it just takes a Marine.

Land Of Tears

We were told by our handlers that roll call was scheduled for 5:45 a.m. under a huge canopy on the jungle-like grounds. Benjoe advised me to get up early, hit the showers and grab breakfast before the morning rush. I passed this information to Fardad, who had landed in a room with an older Somali and two Afghans.

Sleep was out of the question that night. Since we had little time between arrival and roll-call, I had just enough time to stow my gear and get my bed ready for the next night. At 04:00 a.m. I headed to the showers with my towel and shower bag. I hung my clothes on a wall hook, took my shampoo, and walked into the shower room. There were twenty-four showerheads arranged along three walls, all facing the central drain, much like those in a gym with no barriers between them. The little white tiles on the shower room emanated a frosty chill making the place feel like a meat locker as I waited for the water to warm. Others now piled into the shower room. The Afghans were unnecessarily boisterous, as always. After shampooing and washing my body, I shut the water off and turned around. The ten or twelve Afghans stood staring at me. Each was under a shower with their underwear still on. I was the only one fully naked. No one said a word. All I hard was the sound of running water. Maybe I had violated some taboo that prevents Afghan men from getting fully naked in front of each other. Whatever the reason, a naked forty-four-year-old, 147 pound, 5'7" Persian Jew with his dangling circumcised dossier succeeded in silencing a dozen Afghans. Never thought dereliction to conform would feel so good.

Benjoe, a mountain of muscle, was strolling down the hallway toward the showers, stark naked with a towel slung over one shoulder. We greeted as we passed. Afghans timidly heading to the showers ducked into any room as soon as they saw Benjoe. And it wasn't out of respect.

Outside, the frigid, foggy weather turned every shadow into a ghost. Fardad waited for me in front of his barracks. We exchanged greetings and walked over to the chow hall. The place was already packed with soldiers and contractors, a long line stretching to the door. We grabbed some utensils and trays and took our place. The servers and cooks were older black women with a mean attitude that belied their southern accent. Like drill sergeants, they yelled at us for moving too fast or too slow or for asking questions about the food. Our breakfast conversation centered on the shower situation. Fardad had had a similar experience.

Singly and in pairs and bunches, everyone assembled under the big canopy and waited for roll call. Military personnel formed columns on one side with contractors on the other. The sharp, cold, dreary October weather magnified my uncertainty about my decision to sign on and set foot on this path—a journey that could very well lead to my end. We interpreters were told to see our Point of Contact, POC, after roll-call if we didn't hear our name. Given the sheer number of people, that could take hours.

After roll call, those interpreters whose names weren't called gathered around the POC. A few were told to get their bags; they were being kicked out. Duplicitous information had been discovered during their government background check. A few others had minor physical issues that had been learnt during their medical exam. They would go back to their home state to remedy the problem, returning in two weeks. Fardad and I, however, made the cut.

Roll call consumed most of the morning. Afterward, soldiers directed us to get our military gear. We formed long lines going through the massive equipment depots: soldiers and contractors mixed.

First station was the flak vest fitting counter. As individuals walked up, a soldier handed over a vest to try on for size. I was in line behind an Afghan male in his mid-sixties, Mr. Najimi, a burly guy who looked like he had never missed a meal in his life and so had a lot of territory to protect. As he stepped up to the counter, the soldier looked him over and handed him an X-large vest. Najimi tried to put it on, unsuccessfully. The soldier then handed him an XX-large, which didn't fit either. Aggravated, the soldier went in the back to find a XXX but came back empty-handed. He told Najimi to loosen the straps on the XX-large and signaled him to move along. I walked up and the soldier handed me a medium vest. I put it on. It fit, we nodded, and I moved to the next station. That's how we spent the whole day: like a shopping spree with a sugar daddy who in this case was Uncle Sam—or "Uncle Sugar" as I called him—who dished out the dough and chose the outfits.

Flak vest, sleeping bags, winter and summer boots, gas masks, canteen---basically anything a soldier got, the contractors got. The gear totaled three sea bags weighing fifty pounds each and valued at $7,500, so we were told. The helmet and the body armor alone cost over $2,500. We knew the prices because when we signed for the gear, it amounted to a receipt and promise to compensate the government in case we lost it. Going through this process was exhilarating to the point that I wondered if it was actually happening to me or was it make believe! Standing next to soldiers some of which were deploying for their second, third, or in some cases fourth tour kindled a sense of honor within me. I was on my way to join history in the making.

The next day was a photocopy of the first, except that after inhaling greasy Southern fried chicken and mashed potato for lunch, we immediately began a crash course in first aid. Actual footage of mutilated bodies, blown-off limbs, and bullet wounds the size of a grapefruit illustrated the realities of war. Other instructions demonstrated on a human-like mannequin showed how to stop bleeding caused by gunshots and explosions, how to use a tourniquet, perform a tracheotomy, and administer other life-saving measures usually reserved for EMTs back home. The classes were condensed, monotonous, boring, and superficial, so half the people in the stuffy room dozed off. A dreamlike haze besieged my mind as I processed the realities of war displayed vividly before us. Is this where I need to be? I asked myself. I tried to stay alert and retain as much information as possible. After all, my next stop was a war zone.

After a few long days of classes and administrivia, I learned to welcome dinner time. The chow hall always clamored with hungry soldiers and civilians. One night when we grabbed our meal and a table, a man approached and asked if he could sit with us. An unspoken rule of chow hall etiquette requires everyone to allow others to share a table. As the man took the seat, I stole a peek at him. His full head of wiry hair looked like a bad toupee—not just dried pine needles, but "henna hair" with an unnatural reddish tint. His pencil-thin mustache reminded me of the unsavory characters from the 1940s film noir movies, and his shifting eyes constantly surveyed the room. He looked like a Tijuana fighting cock after a rough night in the pits.

"I am Bangosh from Pakistan." His eyes cut from side to side. "I am interpreter."

I looked at Fardad then back to our heavy–accented, cuckoo-clock-eyes-on-crack guest.

We reciprocated with just a nod.

I observed the odd-looking man closely. Was he for real? Bangosh monitored the entire room and typed on his phone as he ate his meal. After finishing his meal he went and grabbed some dessert but instead of returning to our table took a seat with some of the other interpreters. Curiously enough, that was the only time I saw Bangosh, and the run-in with him raised red flags. Was it happenstance or premeditated? Maybe he got the boot, or maybe he was a government plant placed amongst us to spy on the interpreters to identify possible traitors! Whatever the case, I learned not to trust even my own echo in this line of work. I'd been there for only a few days and the events and the curious cast of characters kept getting more interesting. First the panty-boys in the showers, then Najimi and his XX flak vest, and now the comically sinister Bangosh. If this was a predictor of what was to come, then I was in for one hell of a ride.

The next morning I awoke at 4 a.m. and walked to the showers with my towel wrapped around my waist. By now everyone had learned to wake up early if they wanted a hot shower and a breakfast not picked over by early arrivals. Some Afghans were already showering, again in their underwear, as I entered the showers wearing only a smirk. They exchanged glances and left without rinsing off the soap. I completed my John Wayne Special—shit, shower, and shave—and left the bathroom with my towel over one shoulder and shower bag in hand. Benjoe was cruising to the showers, bag in hand, towel over one shoulder, wearing only his smile. We high-fived as we passed.

"Good morning, Benjoe."

"Indeed, brother."

The Afghans looked perplexed, maybe incensed, but it didn't faze Benjoe or me. In fact, we got a kick out of it. This was the military after all.

After a quick breakfast, the day began with the usual roll call. More names were called and told to pack up and leave. Fardad and I exchanged a glance. We were safe for another day. After the roll, soldiers took us to get the rest of our gear from the massive warehouses with separate departments. From one station to the next, we collected a half dozen T-shirts, three sets of army camo uniforms, fire retardant gloves, and more. The absolute size and inventory of the U.S. military apparatus was stunning.

Next came a greasy lunch, after which the hike up a hill to attend a crash course on Improvised Explosive Devices, IEDs, and how to detect them was stomach-churning. The mid-day sun further fermented the shitty lunch sitting like a chunk of plaster in my stomach, making the hike up the steep hill an agonizing trek. Everyone peeled off layers. Najimi, the plump Afghan who had taken the post's last double-wide flack vest, walked next to me and Fardad. Most Afghans dissed him because he talked non-stop. He huffed and puffed but even that didn't shut him up. I tried to be polite and pretended to listen, but my brain shut his voice out completely. Halfway up, Najimi latched onto me for support. I helped him up the hill out of respect for his age, but his short stature and 260-pound frame made it feel as if I was pulling an ox. Fardad smiled wickedly as if to say, *You're fucked, buddy.* I knew he would be of no help.

We got to the designated area, sweat flowing from every pore, breathless. I sucked in air from every orifice, including, it seemed, cavities not designed for that purpose. My heart throbbed in my throat. Though I prided myself on my great physical shape, my smoking habit had caught up with me. I stopped and took a few deep breaths to get much-needed oxygen to my brain. Najimi detached himself and walked away. After a few steps, he turned and thanked me. Nice of him.

Soldiers steered the group of a 130 or so to a prefabricated one-story building. Inside, a sergeant ordered us to take a seat and pay attention to the big TV monitors in the front of the room. A few ex-military instructors armed with laser pointers started a slide show. They described various types of IEDs and their effectiveness in vivid detail.

"Hidden explosives go as far back as the Civil War," said the older instructor. "But it took Iraq and Afghanistan to make IEDs synonymous with terrorism."

"The effects of IEDs go beyond the battlefield," said the younger instructor, swaggering in front of the class like a real hard-ass. "The psychological impact on combatants and civilians can be worse than the explosion. Sure, we try to find solutions to counter or mitigate this, but the enemy keeps upping the game." He concluded, "IEDs are the poor man's version of a WMD—a weak enemy's response to a more powerful military. They're easy to assemble, cheap, and hard to spot. IEDs account for anywhere from half to two-thirds of Americans killed or wounded in Afghanistan and Iraq."

Most of us, aghast, stared back at him except a good number of the Afghans, who carried on with their conversations.

The instructors distributed pamphlets. I read mine intently, but most other interpreters tossed them aside with no respect for the practical wisdom they contained. The instructors and soldiers glared back at them. We were supposed to be on the same team. Maybe I just didn't understand the game.

The presentation ended and we moved to a nearby ravine. The instructors barked more information on how to spot IEDs and land-mines camouflaged by the terrain. One thing they showed us stuck in my mind like gum to my shoe. They pointed to some dinner-plate-sized rocks, some painted half-red, and others half-white. The half-red rocks indicated a minefield. Venturing beyond them almost guaranteed a wheelchair or a one-way ticket to the afterlife. The half-white rocks indicated a cleared or mine-free zone. The uniformed soldiers and ex-military contractors "in civvies" in the group listened intently and took notes. Most of the interpreters showed no interest and continued to chat casually. Pre-recorded explosions boomed from concealed loudspeakers all around us as the instructors moved us through the simulated, booby-trapped, deadly labyrinth quickly, as if they needed to put bad memories behind them.

The sun faded and everyone looked exhausted. Conversations all but died. The instructors ordered us to march downhill. Thick fog rolled in and the air became damp and cold by the time we reached the bottom. My stomach growled, background sonata for the senior instructor's voice that ran through my head like a broken record: *"Don't pick it up if you didn't put it there.*" He said that a clever enemy used women, old people, and even children to leave explosive packages anywhere—on the base, near a car, inside the mess-hall, or by the side of the road. Don't touch or pick up anything that isn't yours, anywhere, anytime. "*It could be the last thing you touch.*"

The next morning we stood under a smaller canopy, separated from other contractors and soldiers. From an initial cadre of forty-five back in Baltimore, mostly men and a few female interpreters, my group had shrunk to nineteen. Most had gotten the axe as more information came to light after their Counterintelligence Interview.

Today, we spread our GI gear over the concrete pad while an instructor showed us how to pack 150 pounds of equipment into three sea bags.

"Neatness ain't gonna cut it," he said. "Shove and push, cram, and jam. Use every inch of that space."

At first, my anal personality ignored the instructions and I took my time folding and stacking. The instructor laughed and walked over, turned my bag upside down, and dumped everything on the concrete. He then grabbed one bag and randomly stuffed it with half my gear.

"*That's* how it's done!" he said with a crooked smile.

Fardad was next to me. We exchanged furtive glances to see how the other was progressing. The instructor forced him, like others, to unpack and repack again and again. Finally, after almost four hours, we were done. Now came the hard part: how to lift and carry three bags weighing fifty pounds each. The secret, he said, is to wear one bag like a backpack and sling the second bag in front, like a papoose. The third bag could either go across the shoulder or into one hand like a suitcase. Beyond the canopy, I saw soldiers picking up their sea bags with ease and carting them off. They did in twenty seconds what had taken my ragtag group four hours. Hell, some in my group had trouble picking up *one* bag, let alone three.

Fardad squatted to pick up the second bag, and let loose a big fat fart as he struggled to stand up.

The instructor laughed and walked over. "Keep the ammunition secured, son," he said with his trademark smile.

Finally, our POC came to the canopy.

"Listen up," he barked. "You're finished here at Fort Benning. You'll be transferred to a hotel where you'll spend a few days." He paused to size up the ragged bunch. "That's your last stop before your deployment."

We breathed a collective sigh of relief. Now everything was clear sailing, right?

Our last roll call at Fort Benning happened to be on a cold foggy night. The big canopy now overflowed with personnel from all branches of the military and other groups ready to deploy. The interpreters' cadre had shrunk to fifteen people. Our POC handed out Velcro name ribbons to wear on our military uniforms. Fardad's eyes glistened as he proudly checked his out. Roll-call ended but I didn't hear my name and didn't get my ribbon. I panicked.

"Did he call me?" I asked Fardad.

Fardad's usual expressionless face also showed panic. I jogged over to the POC and asked if he had missed my name.

He looked at his clipboard. "You'll leave for the hotel with everyone else." I wasn't sure he'd answered my question. "Someone'll pick you up at 0600 and take you to the main office the day after tomorrow."

"What for?"

"Just be ready," he said. "Look for the company mini-van in the parking lot."

My energy evaporated. I couldn't believe I'd been eliminated at the eleventh hour. All I could think of was the satisfied look on Dr. Rasouli's face when he heard the news. *Rohām got the boot on the last day at Fort Benning!*

Fardad spoke with other interpreters as I stood under the fog-smothered entry light smoking a cigarette.

Benjoe came out from the barracks. "Why the serious face?" he asked.

"I just got the boot."

"You gotta be shittin' me!"

"I wish." I shook my head. "They didn't call my name. I have to report to the main office in two days."

Benjoe put his big hand on my shoulder. "Don't give up, brother," he said calmly. "Just go with the program and see what gives. I'll say a prayer for you tonight. By the way, I gotta say goodbye. Ex-military like me have a separate out-process protocol than interpreters."

We shook hands. Benjoe gave me a bear hug. I felt like a twig in a vice.

"God bless," he said. "I'll catch you on the flip side."

OCTOBER 01, 2010

The bus pulled up around 4 p.m, and the interpreters threw their sea bags in its underbelly and climbed on board with their bedding. The check-out process was much faster than checking in. As the bus pulled away from Fort Benning, I looked out the window and a vacant sadness—hollower than a hollow reed—took me over. I'd wanted to be a part of the military but had never realized how much until that moment. The opportunity had been there. After high school I'd taken the Navy Entry Exam and passed, but I chickened out. One would never think me a chicken if one knew the meaning of my name. I thought this would be my second chance—a dream realized, compliments of a stormy economy. Now that dream, too, was fading.

We pulled up to the Sun Motel, a dilapited, sordid kind of place in a suburb of Atlanta, and nearly 115 miles from Fort Benning. Everyone but I rushed to register. Let them pass, I said to myself. I dropped my bags on the sidewalk and used them as a bench. Fardad joined me for a cigarette. For an hour we had nothing to say.

Finally the line was down to one person. "We should check in," I said.

The front desk had only one clerk. The poor woman looked worn out from dealing with our boisterous crew. She was beautiful, in her mid-30s, maybe Middle Eastern, with green eyes, arched eyebrows and silky jet-black hair—and curvaceous. Fardad's usually blank eyes sparkled at the sight of her. It was obvious what he was thinking: *I want some.* He checked in and stepped aside.

The last from my group, I walked up and handed her my ID.

"Your name is Sanjar Rohām?"

I smiled. "I think so."

"I know what your name means."

"You do?"

"Yes," she said, smiling back. "It means King Warrior."

"How did you know?"

"I'm from Tunisia, but I have Iranian friends." She leaned forward. "I speak a little Farsi."

"That's nice. And what is your name?" I asked.

"Fahar." She pointed to the nametag on her blouse.

"Oh, tiger!"

"You speak Arabic?"

"Just enough to know that name," I replied. "So, do you meow like a kitten or purr like a pussy?" I said, and instantly regretted it. What an imbecile!

I saw Fardad from the corner of my eye. He grinned mischievously.

Fahar handed me my room key and pointed to the elevator.

"The bridal suite," I said, embarrassed. I couldn't get out of there fast enough.

We got out on the second floor, where our rooms were next to each other. The rowdy Afghans hung out on the hotel balconies, talking loudly.

My room was tiny, dingy, and dreary in contrast with the hotel rooms I had stayed at during my month-long vacations to Europe, the Middle East, Eastern Europe, and the Americas. I dropped my bags on the shaggy stained carpet and walked into the equally grimy bathroom. The strong bleach fumes coming from the toilet bowl that held copper-tinted water ambushed me as I lifted the lid to take a piss.

Fardad joined me on the balcony, still laughing from the episode with Fahar.

"I can't believe it." I shook my head. "The words just came out on their own."

"You nailed her pantie, man," Fardad, the old lecher, said.

At least the encounter let me forget my meeting for the next day, at least momentarily.

Fardad must have noticed the look of uncertainty on my face.

"Don't worry. All will be okay," He said, trying to hide the self-doubt in his voice. It was obvious he didn't want to make the rest of the journey alone. Now, that choice was out of my hands.

The next morning after a quick shower, I dressed and went to the lobby. The Sun Motel's all-you-can-eat breakfast looked as inviting as the toilet bowl in my room, but I knew I had to eat something. With coffee and a mini muffin in hand I went outside and sat on the bench. A van pulled into the motel and parked a few feet away as I smoked and sipped my coffee. The driver stayed behind the wheel, going through some paperwork.

I walked up to him. "Are you here to take me to the main office?"

"You Rohām?"

"Yeah."

"Get in." The driver tossed his clipboard on the passenger seat and pointed his thumb to the back seat. I climbed through the sliding side door, but we were off before I could latch it.

The ten-minute drive to the main office felt like an eternity. "Get out," the driver said as we jerked to a stop. "Suite 100, first floor."

I gave the driver a "fuck you, too," look and complied.

Inside, I introduced myself to the receptionist.

"Sit," she commanded. "Someone will come for you."

The criteria for working at Global Vigilance seemed to require having an asshole personality.

Half an hour passed and nobody came. Anxious energy built inside me. The place began to feel like a plastic bag over my head, suffocating me. I wanted to get the hell out of there.

Finally, a middle-aged black woman holding a folder showed up.

"Follow me," she ordered.

We went into her office and she sat behind her desk. "Sit." She pointed to a chair.

Like a dog, I obliged. The nameplate on her desk read "Ms. Carry." How fitting.

"Do you know why you are here?" She absently thumbed through some paperwork.

"No ma'am, I do not."

"Your security clearance has been delayed. You know why? It's because of all your previous travels and destinations." She peered coldly over her glasses. "Do you know what this means?"

"No ma'am."

"It means we can't deploy you as a Category II security clearance." She stared me down. "We can deploy you as a Category I, meaning no security clearance. Your salary will be cut to $185,000. Twenty-five thousand less than what we originally offered."

"But I have a signed contract with Global Vigilance."

"Your contract is void." She produced papers. "This is your new contract. You can sign this now or we'll send you home right away." Clearly, bargaining was not an option.

"What will happen to my security clearance?"

"We'll notify you if it's approved."

"I'm not going home, then?"

"Not if you sign the new contract," she said. "Your clearance process will continue *if* you sign."

Just like that, Global Vigilance had mugged me for $25K. What the hell. I'd made it this far. I had no intention of going back home. After skimming through the contract, I signed and returned it before she could pull another bait-and-switch. For certain, I wasn't Global Vigilance's first victim.

"Is there anything else we need to discuss?" I asked.

Ms. Carry pointed her pen to the door, Global Vigilance sign-language to *get the fuck out*.

OCTOBER 04, 2010

My last day at the Sun Motel. After three days, I was getting used to the grunge. I checked out just as a new batch of interpreters rolled in. *Sausage factory*, I grunted. My group waited in front of the motel for the bus to Atlanta airport, ATL. So this was it: the first leg of our deployment. Destination Qatar.

The bus pulled up and the driver yelled, "Load your gear and get on board."

Everyone rushed at once—I'd seen this stampede before. I kept Fardad with me on the sidewalk. "You didn't learn anything from Benning, did you?" I said. "If we check in last, our gear comes out first."

We arrived at Delta Airlines International Terminal, ATL. While the other interpreters scrambled for their gear, we checked in and went to the gate. The group trickled into the terminal area. The Afghans were as loud as usual, drawing unwelcome attention. One couldn't help but feel sorry for the other passengers. Here were a bunch of terrorist-looking fellows speaking a foreign language, waiting to get on their flight. Welcome to the global war on terror.

Once onboard, we spread out. Global Vigilance purchased tickets in bulk, so our seats were cheap: center seats in the center aisle. No two people sat together. A feeling of complete detachment from family, home, and my old self settled within me as the plane's door closed.

The terminal inside Amsterdam's Schiphol airport teemed with activity. We had an almost eight-hour layover. My group disseminated like a bunch of ants running away from DDT. Fardad and I decided to get a taste of the renowned city. We rented two lockers, shoved our backpacks in, and headed for the exit.

Some of the interpreters scrambled to catch a taxi to Amsterdam's red-light district. We contemplated if we should visit the famed borough. But as fate would have it we ended up babysitting the plump Najimi, and Nazirestani, another elderly Afghan. A far cry from spending time in the warm bosom of female companions for hire. I looked at Fardad and smiled ironically. We'd contemplated goosing, and instead we got goosed.

Our eight-hour layover felt unending. With over an hour before our flight, we grabbed yet more full-bodied Amsterdam coffee and found a table next to a white grand piano in the middle of a seating area. Travelers packed the place. After a few minutes, Fardad sat at the piano and much to my surprise began to play. I had no idea he could play the instrument, and so beautifully at that. He didn't look like the type. As I listened, images of my mother playing the piano materialized in my psyche. I had last seen her and my family just a little over three weeks before, but it felt like a lifetime ago. My family knew where I was heading. My brothers were against it and thought it madness but for whatever reason my mother supported my decision fully. Maybe she saw how unhappy I was with my life, with myself.

The plane took off for the next leg of our journey: an almost seven-hour flight to Dammam, Saudi Arabia, for a short layover, and from there to Doha, Qatar. Again, we were scattered all over the plane. Not wanting to watch a movie, I took this opportunity to get some sleep. The stress and sleepless nights of the past three weeks had caught up with me.

OCTOBER 05, 2010

We landed in Dammam around 10 p.m. local time. Half of the passengers had reached their destination and disembarked, and the rest of us sat and waited. Most of the other interpreters were in deep sleep, others fidgeted in their seats. Only a small portion of the airport was visible as I looked out from the window. The atmosphere in Dammam felt heavy and uneasy. It felt shut in and I didn't want to be there. The resentment Iranians harbor toward Saudis boiled inside me. The bad blood between the two peoples dates back 1,400 years to when the Arabs invaded Persia, destroying its flourishing culture and imposing Islam on the population by the blade's edge. I got up and walked to Fardad sitting a few seat behind me. His eyes were tense.

"You feeling what I'm feeling?" I asked.

"Yeah, I don't like this."

A stewardess hurriedly came up from the back of the plane. "You need to get back to your seat," she said politely. The discernable tension in her eyes forewarned of Saudi strictness and tight control over passengers. I returned to my seat.

A few male passengers wearing slippers and dishdash, the traditional Arab garb—or, as I call it, the Man Dress—boarded the plane. It was hard not to notice their ostentatious jewel-encrusted Rolex Presidential watches and diamond rings. They each had a couple of gold mobile phones in their hands. One for each wife to call, I assumed. I looked out the window again, at the Arabian night, quiet and depressing. Finally, we took off from Dammam and headed to Doha, Qatar.

OCTOBER 06, 2010

We landed in Doha before 1 a.m. It had been a long day for us all. The airport's immigration and customs area was devoid of other passengers except for my threadbare group. Doha International Airport was impressive in every respect, from the state-of-the-art digital information boards to the futuristic sliding glass doors and shiny, flawless marble floors.

The immigration officers took their time inspecting our passports one by one, stamping them, and handing them back for passage into the country. The male airport security personnel in their dishdash and sandals were hard to miss. All were young, tall, lean men with closely cropped, well groomed beards. It was a certainty they carried weapons under their dress.

A hard stare by the young, attractive female immigration officer in hijab was my signal to walk up to the counter. As she flipped through my passport she eyed me with suspicion, deliberately looking at every entry stamp and then matching it to a corresponding exit stamp. My smile failed to break her rigid, dissecting gaze; she would have none of it. She glanced at an airport security agent. He approached the window, followed by a second security agent. I didn't understand why at first, but then I realized: I was born in Iran, a nemesis to Qatar. Also, my passport had stamps from Israel, not necessarily a friend of the Qataris.

The young woman spoke in a hushed voice with the two agents as she flipped through my passport, pointing out the information. Now there were three sets of eyes inspecting me. I looked over at Fardad, stuck just like me. Although Fardad was Iranian, he had been born in Israel. Maybe the Qataris thought we were spies trying to infiltrate the country.

All travelers had cleared the immigration and customs area except for me and Fardad. At last, a representative from Global Vigilance showed up alongside a Qatari official, and they cleared the two of us through the immigration. We rushed to the deserted baggage claim carousel, grabbed our bags, and hurried to the bus waiting outside the terminal. The muggy air was heavy and thick; it slowed down our sprint. My glasses fogged up immediately from the humidity.

The bus moved leisurely through the empty, quiet streets of the city, its inhabitants apparently in deep slumber. The streets were spotless, not a piece of trash anywhere. The homes and buildings resembled structures from *One Thousand and One Nights* and *Shahrazad*. All brand-new, and huge by any standard. My imagination distracted me from keeping track of how long it was taking to get from the airport to Camp Al Udeid. I tried to visualize the occupants of the homes as we drove by. Who were they? What did they look like, how did they live?

We got to the gates of Camp Al Udeid, the forward headquarters for the U.S. Central Command, or CENTCOM. Al Udeid houses the Air Forces from Qatar, the U.S., and Britain. It is the largest U.S. base in the Middle East and serves as the base hub for U.S. operations in Iraq and Afghanistan. It was very exciting to go through the gates of a military base again. It felt important, at least to me.

After a long check-in process, we drove to our clean prefab aluminum air-conditioned barracks. We dropped off our gear, and our POC escorted us to the chow hall. Even though it was late, we were all still hungry. Camp Al Udeid is a desert oasis, an imposing military base with chow halls serving chef-prepared meals. The Camp offers fast-food restaurants like Arby's and Burger King. There are Jewelry shops, cell phone stores, gift shops, coffee shops, and even a Baskin Robbins. It has a huge bar and an outdoor canopied concert area with huge flat-screen TVs hanging in every corner. There is an outdoor Olympic-size swimming pool, and giant Post Exchange stores, or PX's in military lingo, resembling Walmarts. The PX's carried everything from underwear to cereal to bedding. I'd heard that out of all the branches of the military, the Air Force got the best of everything. This Camp proved the rumor right.

The large 24/7 chow hall was impressive: high ceilings, shining, stainless-steel food counters. The chefs wore clean uniforms and tall hats, and the busboys constantly picked up and cleaned. The salad bar, dessert, and fruit sections resembled an all-you-can-eat Vegas-style buffet. Uniformed and civilian personnel piled their plates high with taxpayer-supplied offerings. I grabbed some noodle Lo Mein from the self-serve section that displayed a tantalizing array of foods: steak, grilled chicken, and fish just to name a few. Fardad joined me at the table with his sandwich.

Four ex-military contractors shared the table with us. I overheard one of them tell the others that "Al Udeid houses almost 10,000 U.S. servicemen."

Maybe this was a sign of what waited ahead. Maybe Dr. Rasouli hadn't been bullshitting when he told the class there were hair salons and restaurants on the bases.

Later, the drastic difference between the indoor and outdoor air made it hard to breathe when we walked from the air-conditioned building into the hot, muggy outdoor desert air. The shapes scurrying under my feet in the dark of night grabbed my attention as we trod on the concrete pathway leading to our barracks. Initially, I thought the shapes were cockroaches or maybe even scorpions. I stopped in my tracks and knelt to take a closer look. What stood in front of me in a defensive posture was alarming: a column of black ants, each damn near half-inch long. The mighty ants looked pissed off and malicious. This was no place to instigate a confrontation, so I sidestepped to allow the stout creatures passage.

By 10 a.m. the next morning the outside temperature was already in the three-digit territory, but that didn't stop us from touring as much of the base as possible, restricted areas notwithstanding. We visited the PX with its unbelievably cheap prices. The sparkling pool hosted a group of bikini-clad women lying out in the skin-blistering desert sun, catching rays. Al Udeid could very well pass for an all-inclusive resort, but the wretchedly hot, sticky daytime weather made it impossible to do much of anything. Sitting in the shade only provided shelter from the strong UV rays but did little against the scorching hot wind. During the two days we were at the camp I took three showers a day for a mere three minutes of relief from sticky skin. The modern facilities at Al Udeid were nothing like the ones in Fort Benning.

During our second night at the Camp, a gentle breeze made the usual outdoor torrid Arabian night a bit more tolerable. Fardad and I decided to visit the bar and grab a couple of cold beers. The bar observed a strict two beers or one cocktail limit. The bouncers handed two tickets to patrons upon entry to be used for purchasing drinks. Once inside, I thought we'd walked into a bar in Los Angeles. Plush red and purple velvet couches and chairs provided plenty of seating, flat-screen TVs mounted all around showed sports, news, and the soaps, loud music played on the multi-speaker sound system. Uniformed and non-uniformed men and women mingled. We spent a couple of hours in this alternate universe, drinking beers, watching football and stale segments of *Days of Our Lives*.

OCTOBER 08, 2010

Our POC marched into the room. "Get ready," he barked. "You're flying to Bagram, Afghanistan, this afternoon."

Everyone scrambled to gather their belongings. I had only my backpack, so in a few minutes I was ready to go. From Baltimore to Fort Benning to Camp Al Udeid, I had washed and worn the same few items of clothing I had.

In late afternoon a few vans pulled up to the barracks, and another stampede erupted. Fardad and I were left behind due to a lack of space in the vans.

"Wait outside," the POC instructed us. "A van will pick you up shortly."

In the scorching heat, fifteen minutes became thirty, then an hour. Two hours later, a Suburban pulled up. A driver in a foul mood got out.

"Let's go," he said irritably. "Get your shit in the car. Pronto."

Fardad opened the tailgate, and we loaded our gear.

Inside the terminal soldiers, contractors, and others packed the place. Soldiers manned the check-in counter. A few of them carried flight manifests and called out passengers' names for boarding. Military flights are nothing like their civilian counterparts. It is possible to spend 24 hours in the terminal and not get on a flight. Personnel are boarded based on priority. Your name on a flight manifest is not a guarantee of getting on the plane. There is no complaint desk or "let me talk to your supervisor" bullshit there. Your name is either called or not.

We joined the other linguists in a corner. Piles of sea bags cluttered the congested terminal. I kept a close eye on my bags, as they could easily get mixed in with hundreds of others.

Names were called over the intercom for boarding. The military had priority, and contractors filled the leftover seats. My group shrank as names were called. Fardad got called. He grabbed his gear, waved at me, and left. Everyone from my group left except me. In the military, there are no arrival/departure boards to inform passengers when the next flight will leave. This information is closely guarded for security reasons. I dreaded being last, dreaded feeling bargain-basement. As the crowd in the terminal thinned, I sat on the floor, leaning against my gear. A pair of boots appeared in front of me. I looked up at a soldier holding a clipboard.

"What's your name?" he asked.

"Sanjar Rohām."

"Grab your gear. Follow me." He gestured quickly. "On the double."

I grabbed my three sea bags and backpack and ran after the soldier through a set of swinging doors to the palleting area where all gear got crated for the flights.

"Hand over your sea bags," the soldier said.

I handed my bags to another soldier in charge of crating.

"Let's go." The first soldier quickly escorted me onto the tarmac.

My steps slowed as I got closer to the imposing flying machine revving idle. Two rows of soldiers climbed on board through the open rear ramp of the C-130 Hercules. This plane was designed as a troop, cargo, and even medevac transport. Some C-130s are used for airborne assault or as gunships. The C-130 can land and takeoff from unprepared runways, which is especially useful in a place like Afghanistan.

The soldier walked me to the back of the line. "This is your flight." He gave me a salute and ran back.

Soldiers slowly marched into the open mouth of the plane, like a pod of alligator offsprings going into the safety of their mother's jaw. A few armored vehicles and crated sea bags sat anchored in the center section of the interior. A row of folding canvas seats was anchored to either side of the fuselage. Awestruck, I walked up the ramp. A flight crew member directed me to an open seat between two soldiers.

A jolt of energy burst through my body as I shoved my backpack under the seat and buckled my seatbelt. I sat back and took a deep breath. The plane prepared for take-off at almost midnight. Out the slowly closing ramp, I caught one last glimpse of the desert night. My journey was taking me farther and farther away from home. A sign in the distance read, "*I did the deed at Al Udeid.*"

The echoing roar of the four engines grew louder as the ramp closed. The occupants sat quietly as we taxied on the tarmac. The heavy machinery chained to the floor just a few feet away concerned me. What if one broke loose? What if we get shot by a missile?

I'd been holding my piss since the terminal at Al Udeid, and we had been in flight only a short time when I began looking around.

The soldier to my right must've noticed the urgent look on my face. "The urinal is hanging on the side," he said, pointing to something resembling a stainless steel bowl mounted on the wall in the corner. "Just wrap the shower curtain around and shake the lizard."

I returned to my seat and buckled in. Sitting there, I wondered what went through each person's mind, who would make it back home alive and in one piece, and who wouldn't.

2

BAF

OCTOBER 09, 2010

Cold air and loud engine noise flooded the fuselage as the mighty C-130 pierced through the troposphere. My jacket zipped, I shoved my frozen hands deep in its pockets. A half-hour or so into the flight, I assumed we were flying over Iran. Over the country of my birth, the country I hadn't revisited since 1977 when I, my mother, and two brothers left, two years before the Islamic Revolution. A land that was my country until the age of twelve, a land whose people had turned savagely against their own. A people that had plundered my family's effects, cutting us off from any sustenance from my father. A government that had labeled my father, a successful Jewish businessman, a Zionist accomplice, and so gave him an uncoveted place on the Radical Islamic government's "Zionist Colluders Black List." A regime that had made my father a fugitive from his own life, and ultimately the subject of a manhunt during the beginning stages of persecution and execution of the innocent.

Eventually, my father had escaped from Iran with just the clothes on his back. First to Turkey, then Israel, Germany, and finally to Los Angeles. Once in America, life had little meaning for him. He had a hard time accepting the fact that he was no longer the master of his empire. He was no longer a man, the provider that his birth culture had branded into his psyche. He woke at five every morning, showered, shaved, put on either one of his two suits and ties my mother had bought him, but he had nowhere to go. He'd lost everything tangible. His bitterness obstructed his vision of his most important treasure in front of him, his wife and kids. Eventually, my mother filed for divorce. Their split was long in the making. It did not surprise me. I had witnessed their quarrels growing up. They were just not meant for each other. But in Iran women could not get a divorce without the husband's consent, so they endured. After the divorce my father moved to Toronto, Canada, where he lived until his passing on June 28, 1994. The Islamic Revolution had condemned multitudes to death. Many were brutally butchered at the hands of hired Palestinian henchmen, while others were sent to firing squads or the gallows—yet some, like my father, had been executed by the hand of time; dying a gradual, protracted death. Prior to the revolution and the involuntary exhile that followed, and with all its challenges, my family enjoyed a blessed life in the upper echelon of the Iranian society. Multiple homes around the country, latest model cars, fashion, and private schooling

My foundation in speaking, reading, and writing the Farsi language was firm, since I'd completed the seventh grade in Iran. Plus I had a good understanding of the history, geography, and politics of the region. Besides, the ramifications of the Islamic Revolution had intensified my interest in learning and keeping up to date with the rapidly changing events of the time. Also, spending nearly six months in the Pashto class, which had been the prerequisite for securing the contract job with the DOD, had increased my consumption of everything Middle East and Afghanistan-related, and this had enhanced my knowledge of the region exponentially. Simply put, I breathed, ate, slept, and shit everything Middle East and Afghanistan.

My thoughts shifted from Iran to where I would end up once I reached Afghanistan. I would soon be touching down in a land that had been embroiled in turmoil, war, and death for eons. Would I get shipped off to the mountainous north? The barren and brown south? I knew the north was a bit friendlier toward Westerners. After all, it was Ahmad Shah Massoud's Northern Alliance who had assisted the first CIA team, code-named Jawbreaker, to enter Afghanistan through its northern border. The Northern Alliance had helped us take the fight to Al-Qaeda and the Taliban. Massoud had forewarned the U.S. about Bin Laden's imminent attack of 9/11. Sadly, Massoud did not take part in the fight against his nemesis, he was assassinated by suicide bombers on September 9, 2001.

Afghanistan's seasons and geography are well defined. Summers in southern Helmand Province are scorching, and winters in the Hindu Kush frigid and treacherous. The name of the mountain range means "the Hindu killer" for good reason. Temperatures can go as high as 120°F during the summer, and as low as 15°F in winter. Temperatures can fluctuate drastically within the same day. It could be freezing at dawn and in the nineties by midday.

The aftermath of the 1979 Islamic Revolution in Iran had reached beyond the country's borders. The ousting of the Shah, a staunch ally of the United States, or as it was known in the Middle East, the Policeman of the Region, had provided the perfect opportunity for the Soviets to invade Afghanistan in December of the same year. This invasion had led to the coming together of Shia and Sunni Muslims from all over the planet—Iran, Saudi Arabia and Chechnya to name just a few. Led by warlords, this ruthless band of militias had established the loosely formed Afghan Mujahideen. The Mujahideen had a difficult time keeping a unified front against the Soviets due to language differences, traditional rivalries between different ethnic groups, and Afghanistan's notorious mountainous terrain. The U.S. had supplied an endless quantity of weapons to the Mujahideen, who in return had rendered sheer brutality against the Soviets. By 2001 our friends the Afghan Mujahideen, had evolved into the Taliban who provided the base of operations for Osam Bin Laden and his Al-Qaeda network. An Enemy is a Friend that You Armed Yourself.

Finally, a disgraced and defeated Red Army withdrew from Afghanistan in 1989, having lost 15,000 troops. One of the psychologically devastating tactics used by the Mujahideen was the skinning of captured Russian soldiers. Salt was applied to the freshly skinned area to inflict maximum pain. This slow, deliberate process dragged on for a few days to prolong the agony.

The Unired States government didn't have much of a policy for Afghanistan once the Soviets withdrew from the ravaged land. This left neighboring Pakistan alone to deal with the war's aftereffects. The mostly

Pashton Pakistani army shares a strong religious and ethnic bond with the Pashton tribes of Afghanistan that for the most part form the Taliban, and therein lie the ties that bind. The Taliban in essence is a faction of the Mujahideen, recruited and trained by Pakistan's Inter-Services Intelligence (ISI) and its military, both of which hold extreme views of Islam.

In addition, a sizeable number of the Taliban leaders who had escaped the Soviet invasion had received their education in Pakistani refugee camps. The Pakistani military provided the Taliban with weapons, financial support, and training. This helped the Taliban to gain control of several cities in Afghanistan, and ultimately to sack Kabul, the capitol city, in September of 1996.

It was around 3:30 a.m. when we touched down in Bagram Air Field, or BAF, Afghanistan. BAF was a strategic airport because its 10,000-foot-long runway could handle our heavy planes. At the height of the operations in Afghanistan, BAF housed more than 40,000 people. For more than forty years the base had been a much-coveted rich widow chased by powerful suitors like the Russian invaders, the Taliban, Al-Qaeda, the Northern Alliance, the U.S. and our NATO partners. She flirted with many but never sealed her vows with any.

Bagram had served as the staging point for the Soviet forces from the time they invaded Afghanistan until their defeat and withdrawal in 1989. After the Soviets left, Bagram had changed hands from the Northern Alliance to its foe—namely the Taliban, Osama Bin Laden, and his Al-Qaeda network—until we moved in. After 9/11, Bagram became a base of operations for the U.S. and our NATO coalition partners, sixty-one participating countries. Operation Enduring Freedom was designed to "win the hearts and minds" of the local population by helping bring Afghanistan into the 21st century. This task has proved close to impossible to complete.

The ramp opened slowly, revealing the star-lit Afghan night. All occupants inside the plane stood in line, and then walked down the ramp and onto the tarmac in an orderly fashion. Unlike Qatar, the Afghan air was nippy. I looked around as we walked to the cargo area to collect our gear. Ghostly carcasses of former Soviet and Afghan aircraft sat on the edges of the runway, remnants of dark and bloody days.

Fardad joined me. The wait for our gear dragged on. A soldier told us we could wait at the coffee shop just outside the cargo area while pallets unloaded from the plane. Military personnel and civilians alike walked over to the coffee shop.

I tried to process the sights and sounds of Bagram. Part of me withdrew into a shell but another part fiercely looked forward to whatever the rapidly approaching future might bring. Fate had given me a second chance to experience the military, albeit as a civilian contractor.

The dinky, poorly lit coffee shop bustled with patrons, mostly soldiers. Its old wooden interior resembled a tavern in a small southern town. Fardad stood next to me outside the café as I smoked and drank coffee. He had a distant, and familiar, look on his face. Maybe he too was wondering what he'd gotten himself into.

The Afghan interpreters were in a bright, jovial mood, unlike most others. They had returned to their motherland after all. Some of them talked about parents, siblings, and relatives who still lived in various cities in Afghanistan. Observing the young men and women in uniform pass by made the whole idea of being in a war-torn country surreal, as if my brain hadn't caught up with reality just yet.

Most Afghans are Sunni Muslims, except the Hazara who are mostly Shiite and the third-largest of some fifteen ethnic groups in the country, with their lineage tracing back to Central Asian Turks and Mongolians. Life seems to have little to no meaning in this land. The average life expectancy is just under fifty-two years, with men on the lower end of this scale. Hidden within this land is an estimated trillion dollars' worth of uranium, lithium, natural gas, gold, silver, petroleum, copper, coal, chromite, and a few other natural resources. Poppy fields are almost everywhere, especially in the Helmand Province. This piece of real estate is responsible for forty-two percent of the world's total opium production, making Afghanistan the second largest opium producer. The opium derived from the poppy help sustain the nefarious activities of the tribal mafia groups and terrorist organizations. Most times, both groups are one and the same. It has been said that the processed opium makes its way through the Western Province of Herat in Afghanistan to the holy city of Qom in Iran. The opium is then forwarded to Iranian government-run labs in Azerbaijan where it is processed from opium gum into heroin before it is shipped to Eastern and Western Europe.

The call came to pick up our equipment. Everyone hustled to locate their gear, which was darn difficult since all sea bags looked the same. Some soldiers tied yellow ribbons or made markings on their bags for easy identification. Mine were the only bags with a blue nylon cord tied to the straps. "Here. Better tie this to your bags for easy ID," Benjoe had advised me back at Fort Benning as he handed me the cord.

Finally, everyone collected their bags. Three short-tempered POCs from Global Vigilance herded us into a bus, much like cattle. I didn't have a good visual of Bagram while at the cargo area, but I grasped the enormity of the place as the bus slowly drove through the base. The streets of Bagram stirred with activity even at that late hour. All makes and models of SUVs moved about on the narrow dirt roads. It took us about fifteen or twenty minutes to get to the transit tent. The bus stopped and we got off.

"Bring it in," the POC barked.

We gathered around on the gravel-covered ground.

"The nearest chow hall is that way." The POC pointed in one direction. "The PX and bazaar this way." He pointed in the opposite direction. "Barbershops, nail salons, and a bunch of other stores are over there." He pointed yet again in a different direction.

I had zero idea which direction was which and didn't pay any attention. Instead, I surveyed the other linguists hanging out outside the so-called transit tents. Men and women had segregated, adjacent tents. The transit tents were used by twenty or so contracting companies and the military. Global Vigilance happened to be the largest and the main government contractor for providing linguists to the Department of Defense. The DOD and GV handled the entire linguist operation in Afghanistan. All other companies sub-contracted from Global Vigilance.

The POC finished giving instructions. Carrying my bags, I crossed the threshold and entered the transit tent. A few half-juiced fluorescent lights lit the bleak interior of the incomprehensible scene. Three parallel rows of bunk beds ran the length of the tent, one on the right, one left, and one in the middle. I separated from Fardad to find an empty bed. The tent must have housed at least 200 people. It resembled the prisons in third-world countries that I'd seen in documentaries. Palpable foul odors permeated the tent—old dirty socks, unwashed clothes, timeworn filthy cum-stained mattresses, dust, and pungent body odor. It was the kind of smell you can taste in the back of your throat. The tent floor was grainy and looked as if it hadn't been cleaned since the tent was erected. Piles of trash enhanced the Third World feel of the interior.

I caught glimpses of unfriendly, wasted, distant faces on the top bunks quietly scanning the new arrivals. Some of the lower bunks had sheets or blankets wrapped around them to provide privacy for their occupants. Other beds had piles of unwashed clothes scattered all over them.

I walked slowly down the length of one aisle and up the other, finally stopping next to a lower bunk with a pile of dirty clothes and trash on it. A face slowly emerged from behind a thick black blanket wrapped around the neighboring bunk. Mid-forties, black disheveled hair, thick mustache, unshaven, sunken black eyes.

"*Salaam-Alaikum. Ba kheimah khosh amadid*," he said in Dari. "Peace be upon you. Welcome to the tent."

"*Alaikum-As-Salaam. In takht-e kesist?*" I asked in Dari. "And peace be upon you. Is this anyone's bed?"

The man gazed at me for a long minute. "No one," he said in a muffled voice. "I put my stuff there so people think it's taken."

"Can I use it?" I asked. "There are no empty beds."

The man slowly pushed aside the blanket and stepped out from his inner sanctum, giving me a clear view of his cluttered bed with papers scattered all over it. The untidy condition of his cocoon suggested he hadn't left the place in a long time. He slowly stepped out. His sweat pants were stained and pockmarked with holes. His white T-shirt had turned grayish-yellow, its collar stretched out of shape; old, dark sweat stains patched the underarms. He walked over to the bed barefooted on the filthy floor.

In one sweep, he grabbed his belongings from the bed and threw them under his bed.

"The bed is yours."

"*Mehrbani*," I replied. "Thank you."

The man sat on his bed, pulled out a bunch of papers and held them up. "Letters of appreciation from military." He slowly lowered his hand. "I'm here three years. Going home soon." He fell silent.

I studied the man carefully. He looked defeated, his soul conquered. "You've done more than your share, you deserve to go home," I said.

Although I wasn't soliciting a conversation, the man must have recognized my FOB—fresh off the boat—look, because he kept talking. He asked questions as I shoved my bags under the bed and sat on the filthy and with no bounce mattress that felt as rock-hard as the morgue stone slab my grandfathered laid on the last time I saw him.

"*Namat Chist? Bache koja asti?*" he asked. "What's your name? Where are you from?"

The man's inquisitiveness didn't sit well with me. We'd just met and he was asking questions I wasn't about to answer. Abruptly, I excused myself and walked away.

A few interpreters hung outside in front of the tent.

"Where's the toilet?" I asked.

They pointed to an actual concrete block, mortar, and brick building about fifteen yards away. I walked in. The place reeked of decomposing roadkill. I closed my mouth as not to breathe in the noxious air. The place was a germ incubator. An inch or more of water sat on its grimy, slippery tile floor, all toilets were backed up, with shit flowing out. The urinals were clogged, emitting the revolting smell of aged urine. I found the "cleanest" stall and went in. I was about to learn my first lesson in gorilla shit-taking. Little did I know I would master this skill in the near future. Afterward I rushed out of the shithole and ran into Fardad and a few others from my group getting ready to walk to the chow hall.

The activity in Bagram was non-stop. I guess one could call it the New York City of Afghanistan. The place never slept. We walked a good fifteen minutes before we found a chow hall, or I should say chow tent.

This was my first taste of the war-zone military lifestyle. With a cardboard tray and plastic utensils in hand, I proceeded to get some grilled chicken and vegetables from the self-serve counter. I walked to the connecting tent which served as the seating area. It was packed. On to the next connecting tent I went. This was no Al Audeid.

Fardad and a few Afghans joined me as I sat down on the high-school-type bench. On the bench next to us was a group of female Polish soldiers with messy, dirty, short blond hair, and weapons slung over one shoulder. They resembled runway models in military uniform. The smell of deliciously aromatic rice carried by an Indian kitchen worker tickled my nostrils. Swiftly, I jumped to my feet and followed him.

"Where did you get that rice?" I asked.

"The kitchen staff makes rice for themselves," he said in a heavy Indian accent and with a bobbing head. "Wait please, okay?"

The man came back with two plates filled with berms of rice.

"For you, sir." He offered the rice with a smile.

"Wow, for me?"

"Your eyes looked at the rice with such appetite my duty is to offer you." He smiled.

I thanked him and took the plates back to the tables. We devoured them.

Going back to the tent and getting much-needed sleep was essential after the heavy meal. Jetlag had a tight grip on me and I passed out cold, fully clothed, on my bed.

Someone's alarm clock woke me a short time later, and by second nature, I grabbed my towel and shower bag and rushed to the showers in the grey morning light. The already-busy showers were in the fetid toilet building but separated by a wall. I found an empty shower stall, and hung my clothes on the hook next to the door-less shower cubicle. The shower tiles were covered with green-colored shaggy carpet—except this was no carpet, it was a thick layer of sludge. I didn't dare take my slippers off, not that I would anyway. I took a quick shower, brushed my teeth, and left.

At 8 a.m. a POC stopped by the tent for roll call. He ordered us to grab breakfast and show up at a building on the other side of the base. According to the Afghan interpreters, it was the much-dreaded "assignment day." We were about to find out which region would be our new home—the front line or a relatively safe zone. Either way, I was uneasy since I didn't know which was what. Walking to the chow hall in daytime exposed the real Bagram. The streets teemed with military and civilian personnel and vehicles. I heard multiple languages as I passed soldiers in their respective countries' uniforms. The place felt like the gun-toting Dodge City, its energy undeniably contagious.

Something on the other side of the road caught my eye. A group of soldiers in protective heavy gear were on their knees in a field separated by Concertina wire, and yes, outlined with red-painted rocks. It was hard to believe that minefields could still be found in the middle of this fortified city. I stopped for a minute to watch.

"Those guys probe the ground with rods inch-by-inch," a booming voice said from behind us.

I turned around. Benjoe stood there.

"Great to see you here," I said as we shook hands. The rest of the group stopped.

"Great to see you, brother," Benjoe smiled. "Bagram is still peppered with minefields; the de-mining process has been ongoing for years, mostly by folks from India. God bless 'em."

I looked at the mine-clearing crew with amazement.

"What's your plan for today?" Benjoe asked.

"They're handing out assignments after breakfast," I replied.

"I'm getting my assignment, too."

After breakfast, Fardad and I with a few other linguists found our way to the designated building. About ninety linguists from various companies waited in the gravel-covered courtyard of a single-storey building sandwiched between two two-storey buildings. A few GV employees herded everyone inside what seemed to be a performance hall of sorts.

"Sit," barked one of the men.

A half-dozen staffers, each looking nastier than the next, stood in front of the room.

After roll-call, a red-haired, red-goateed guy with a clipboard stepped forward. "When you hear your name, come up and get your Assignment Letter," he said harshly. "ALL ASSIGNMENTS ARE FINAL. There is no negotiating for another assignment. If you refuse your assignment you'll be sent home immediately. We will not babysit you." He clearly enunciated every word.

The room fell silent.

The Afghans exchanged distressed looks. It seemed like the Afghan linguists understood what the ginger boy meant, but not me or Fardad. I watched the reaction on my colleagues' faces as they got handed their assignments. Fear was displayed prominently, mouths gaped, eyes widened, complexions flushed. Some of the women cried.

Ginger Boy called my name. I walked up, got my assignment sheet, and looked at it. "Location: LNK, Assignment: IMEF." I didn't understand all the acronyms. My stomach churned. I was about to venture deeper into unknown territory.

Fardad got his assignment sheet. We compared them. This was the end of the line for us as a team.

The session concluded. Some linguists begged the staff to be reassigned, to no avail. As people exited the hall, mayhem broke out in the courtyard. Some male linguists argued with the staff and swore at them. The staff reacted swiftly and ruthlessly, ordering them to pack their bags. They were fired on the spot. Fardad and I stood in the courtyard like two idiots, not knowing what to do next.

"*Shoma koja wazife gerefti?*" an Afghan man in his mid-fifties asked me in Dari. "Where is your assignment?"

We compared assignment sheets. Same place.

"*Midooni koja rawan mishim?*" The man recoiled. "You know where we're going?"

"*Koja?*" I asked as my heart pounded hastily. "Where?"

"*Rahi jahanam, ba haywanat.* We are going to hell, to animals."

"What—"

"*Man estefa mikonam, tosieh mikonam estefa koni.* I'm resigning; I suggest you resign." Life drained from the man's face. The tips of his bushy mustache drooped. "*Unja koshta mishim. Kate haywanat-o qatelan.*" His voice quivered. "We will get killed there. By animals and killers."

Fright turned the man's olive-toned complexion yogurt white, accentuating the deep pockmarks on his face. I took in the pandemonium around me. My fellow translators were frantic. Several resigned on the spot. I spotted Benjoe. He motioned me over. Mindlessly, I walked over.

"Where you going?" Benjoe asked.

I handed him my LOA.

Benjoe's eyes lit up. He showed the paper to another contractor standing next to him.

"Congratulations, brother," they said almost in unison.

I still had no idea what I had gotten myself into. "What's LNK, what's IMEF?" I asked.

"You're assigned to the One Marine Expeditionary Forces," Benjoe said.

"Camp Leatherneck, brother," the other said. "The tip of the spear."

"Leatherneck is in Helmand Province near Kandahar," Benjoe said. "That's where the Marines are."

"That's where all the action is," the other guy said.

The Taliban considered Kandahar their spiritual capital. Helmand Province was a Pashton tribal region, and one of the most dangerous places on the planet.

"Others are resigning," I gestured to the turmoil around us. "They don't wanna go to LNK. They say they don't wanna work with animals, the Marines."

"Don't listen to anyone." Benjoe glanced over. "Just go there and decide for yourself. Don't let anyone make your decision for you. You've come this far. Go all the way. You can always resign later. Don't give up now, brother."

Benjoe had given me sound advice in Fort Benning. I shouldn't allow others to deter me. Hell, I hadn't let Rasouli do it. Why start now?

"Wish the Marines a Happy Birthday on November 10th," said the other contractor.

"Just remember this, there's no better friend, or worse foe, than a Marine," Benjoe added.

I shook hands with Benjoe, not knowing that it would be our last encounter.

The day started with a group of almost ninety interpreters, which shrank to fifty-four by the end of the afternoon. I was assigned to the Marines at LNK, and Fardad to the Army in Sharana. He would eventually be sent to Zoroukh. Soon we would part ways.

We went through our routine over the next few agonizing days. Roll call twice a day followed by mind-diverting exploration of BAF the rest of the time. Distractions were many in Bagram: multiple bazaars, Burger King, Subway, massage parlors, nail salon, and many others. I guess that fucker Rasouli hadn't been lying about nail salons and such when he made one of his many sleazy used-car-salesman pitches to the class. Yeah, right.

I ran into Murad Khan, a Pakistani guy I'd met in passing while going through the medical phase of deployment in Georgia. He'd arrived in BAF a day or so after me. I got to know him a bit more, and liked his somewhat warped sense of humor.

We had no idea when we would get shipped off. Everyone kept up a good front so as to not show fear. In the meantime, a few more linguists resigned.

OCTOBER 20, 2010

My strange neighbor from the transit tent was still waiting to be processed out. He blabbered as I lay on my bed, but I paid him no attention. Then someone called out my name, along with Khan's and a few others.

We met a POC outside the tent in the cloudy, cold wintry night with temperature in the low forties.

"Grab your gear and wait out here," the POC said.

Fardad ran up and helped me carry my gear. We'd been each other's safety blankets up to that point, but the time had come to step out and step up. There were eight of us, all men, getting shipped off. We waited outside the tent. A van pulled up. Fardad helped put my bags in the van. We shook hands, said goodbye, and I joined the others in the van. I felt exposed and volnurable as I sat in the van with the others. A stranger among strangers.

Almost all flights left under cover of darkness to avoid small-arms fire or shoulder-fired rockets. We dropped our gear off at the palleting and waited for over two hours for our names to be called for boarding. We joined a group of soldiers on the tarmac where another C-130 sat waiting. This time there were two M1 Abrams tanks fastened to the floor in the middle section of the fuselage. The tanks looked indestructible. The sight of them emboldened me. If only my family and friends could see me now.

3
OLD CHERRY

OCTOBER 20, 2010

The two Marines sitting next to me on the flight engaged in a conversation. While eavesdropping, I heard the older of the two, back for his second deployment, brief the younger Marine, who couldn't have been more than nineteen years old.

"The airfield in Bastion is sizable. Its long airstrips can handle heavy payloads. That's where we keep all our fixed-wing and rotary contingencies," he said.

"Leatherneck must be small, then, if it don't have an airfield!" said the young Marine.

"Hah. LNK is 1600 acres of sprawling real estate," said the older Marine.

"For real, Staff Sarge? I hear there's more than just us and the Brits there."

"Yeah, we're in Leatherneck. Bastion 0, I, and II house mainly the Brits," the older Marine said, taking out a Skoal chewing tobacco canister from his pant cargo pocket. He took a dip and shoved it in the corner of his lower lip. "Estonia and Denmark are there too."

"No Afghan military there?" asked the younger.

"Shorabak is the Afghan National Army base. It sits adjacent to Leatherneck." He pushed the tobacco deeper inside his lip with his tongue. "A smaller camp, Camp Tombstone, is shared between us, the Army and coalition forces." He spat brown saliva into an empty water bottle.

"That's a fucked-up name, ain't it?" said the younger Marine.

"It's named after the gun-slinging town of the Old American West," said the older Marine with a sinister smirk.

The flight from BAF to LNK, or Leatherneck, didn't take long, at most forty minutes. The plane landed in Bastion I, the British base containing the airfields. Camp Leatherneck had been assembled in the fall of 2008 by the U.S. Army Corps of Engineers. Our military had needed a suitable location in Helmand Province to handle between 2,000 and 15,000 troops, but conditions necessitated expanding the base to house almost 26,000 coalition forces. Before Leatherneck was built, smaller bases in southern Afghanistan overflowed and couldn't accommodate the surge in forces.

In a land where roads and infrastructure are rare, the choice for erecting Leatherneck in Helmand Province was strategic. LNK flanked the British Camp Bastion and its airfield, and provided necessary protection to the primary east-west corridor of Highway 1 in Helmand Province, which connected the adjacent Taliban stronghold of Kandahar to Herat and Zaranj, bordering Iran. The mainly Pashton region is one of the most dangerous neighborhoods on the planet. Before our offensive, Kandahar had been the spiritual capital of the tyrannical Taliban, under whose rule women and ordinary folks had been executed in the soccer stadium on an almost daily basis.

Helmand Province, where unforgivingly hot, dusty and arid summers give rise to blinding sandstorms, and winters bear frigid downpours. The weather in Helmand is ruthless and acts as a force multiplier for the Taliban. Camp Leatherneck, Helmand Province, home to the Marines and now my new residence, at least for the time being, is a massive tent city in the middle of nowhere with sparse one-storey plywood buildings here and there. I would soon discover that Helmand's weather pattern is as radical and punishing as the enemy we were fighting.

Benjoe had briefed me to some degree about LNK the day I got my assignment location. He told me that the rap sheet for this place displayed a prominent blood stain in Marine Corps history, and that the blood of more than 350 Marines quenched the parched earth of this region. Numerous other Marines left limbs on the battlefields in this merciless land. He said that the Battle for Jackson/Sangin was one of the bloodiest fought by the U.S. Marines in Helmand. My nickname for this place was "The Leveler": It killed indiscriminately, regardless of a person's ethnicity, religion, color; whether they were insider or outsider, young, old, man, woman, rich or poor.

While in BAF I researched Helmand online to learn more about the place. The Helmand River is the lifeline for this arid land, and the Kajaki Dam in Kajaki District is a major water reservoir. The Taliban had tried to destroy the dam on numerous occasions to inflict as much pain as possible on the local population and then blame the infidels for its destruction.

The ramp slowly opened. A cold, uncomfortable breeze greeted us as we got off. Again, we waited at the gear collection area. My group was quiet. It wasn't difficult to guess what was going through everyone's mind: *What did I get myself into?*

Our welcoming committee, a POC, or should I say another asshole from Global Vigilance, waited for us along with two mammoth-looking Fijians. The eight of us grabbed our gear and got into a waiting van, which drove away from the airfield into complete darkness. The only light on the road came from our headlights. The drive to LNK felt longer than the flight, even though the trip took no more than twenty minutes.

A lone minibus drove by.

"There are buses here?" I asked the POC.

"Yeah, they run 24/7. Some go between all the camps, except Shorabak."

The van pulled up next to a tent and stopped.

"Grab your shit and follow me." The POC motioned.

We entered a huge, well-lit, empty tent with at least one hundred cots in it.

"You'll stay here for now until you get assigned to a team," he said. "Come on out."

We followed him outside. He pointed out the big chow hall, and the small chow hall in the opposite direction. "Shower tents are on the other side." He pointed toward a group of tents across the dirt road from us surrounded by concrete T-walls, then gestured at a couple of porta potties next to the tent: "Your toilets."

The porta potties were anchored to the ground with straps to prevent them from tipping over in storms or if a vehicle ran into them. Later on, I learned to keep a few empty Gatorade bottles next to my bed. This was standard procedure: we used them as piss bottles instead of leaving the tent at night.

"I say again," said the POC, somewhat annoyed, "DO NOT relocate to any other tent. Stay put." He left the eight of us in the huge tent.

Apparently some interpreters had gone missing in the past and hid in other tents, and it took a while before anyone could locate them. In the meantime, the interpreter collected a handsome paycheck without having to work for it. So we had to stay put.

I walked outside to smoke a cigarette. Soon after, Khan joined me. Inhaling the nicotine deep into my lungs helped take the edge off.

Khan held his cigarette between his fingertips like an English aristocrat. He chuckled. "What the fuck," he said in his Pakistani accent. "This is fucked up."

I smiled, not at what he said, rather at my uncertain fate. I looked around to find a landmark to use as a direction finder. LNK was kept semi-dark at night for security reasons. The Taliban were notorious for firing rockets into the bases, and the military did not want to provide lit targets.

The others came out of the tent. It was almost 2 a.m. Since we hadn't had dinner, we decided to walk over to the small chow hall to get a bite.

The small chow hall was nothing more than two small connecting tents. One had a sandwich bar with a limited self-serve counter; the other was the sitting area with a few racks of chips, cookies, beef jerky, and light snacks. All the meals and accouterments were compliments of the American taxpayer. The DOD kept track of how many meals were served daily through a sign-in sheet and a quick scan of military ID. At first, the soldier at the check-in table refused us entry because we didn't have LNK ID, but then he reluctantly allowed us passage after seeing our LOAs.

The seating tent was furnished with six benches. My group took over two of them. A few Air Force personnel and some Marines occupied the other benches. After inhaling my meal, I left the tent and entered into the heavy blanket of darkness outside.

The semilit dirt road was quiet and the air chilly as I walked alone back to my new temporary home. Inside, the massive emptiness and stillness of the big tent felt eerie. The florescent lights glowed brightly, illuminating the trace energy of all who had passed through the place. For sure, some of them were no longer on this planet. I spread my sleeping bag over a corner cot, took off my boots, and slid into the bag fully clothed. My scrunched jacket was my pillow. It hadn't been that long ago when I'd slept in my goose down featherbed in my fancy bachelor pad in a plush LA neighborhood, albeit on the verge of foreclosure.

The tent swayed back and forth gently as the wind picked up outside. Cold air infiltrated the tent through open gaps. But jet-lag still had a tight grip on me; I could hardly keep my eyes open. *Is this really me here, alone?* I asked myself.

Slumber conquered me before I could contemplate the question.

The eight of us lingered on in the tent for a couple of weeks. For security reasons, contracting companies limited the amount of information they provided. All we knew was that we would be assigned either to the Marines, the Army, or the Air Force based on the needs of the military. All questions went unanswered. This only compounded our stress and anxiety.

My six Afghan tent mates left the tent one morning and went AWOL for a few days. They probably stayed in their Afghan friend's tents already there. Khan met with other Pakistanis, and he too went missing from time to time.

My companions' absence gave me a chance to CONFRONT my internal irreconcilable differences. The solitude allowed my mind to journey back in time to when my family arrived in U.S. Thirty-three years of memories came crashing down on me. The monumental hardships, the small victories. Unlike many Jewish Iranians in Los Angeles, my family hadn't inherited anything from my father, even though he had once had enough to last for generations. The bearded bastard, Ayatollah Khomeini, and his goons had collected my father's fortune. My only inheritance from my father was his shaving brush, his tweed trilby hat, and a dash of his unmitigated charm. Thanks to my mother's hard work the three of us—my brothers, twins, older by four years, and I—were able to get advanced educations. Both my brothers graduated from the New York University Dental School. One became a periodontist and the other a prosthodontist. I got my MBA from Pepperdine University. What else would you expect from any good mother? The three of us formed a management company and through it, we purchased dental offices. My brothers handled the dental aspect, and I, the day-to-day business operations.

The pressure exerted on my brothers by their wives, who thought I was leeching off my brothers along with the economic crash, devastated our dental management and my business consulting firm. It all came to a halt when I decided to leave the partnership for the sake of saving the oath of brotherhood. Until then, nothing could break our bonds. Prior to the crash and the breakup my annual earnings from both my businesses averaged in the high six digits. But my lavish lifestyle kept my bank accounts on a lean diet to the point of starvation. After the crash my finances went into a downward spiral. My anemic cash reserve did not cover my constant monthly minimum overhead. The three of us tried to keep our business disunion veiled from our mother but her motherly intuition made that next to impossible The brotherly breakup inflicted an abundance of pain and worry on Mini who thought our business separation was an end to our brotherhood. My mother, a petite woman in her mid-sixties, just over five-feet-four, and weighing 110 pounds was more distressed about her sons circumstance than when she decided to divorce my father. Don't be fooled by her small stature, she is one of the toughest people I've ever known. A true testament to her Kurdish heritage.

I remembered our first few years in America. The absence of a husband and a father figure, and the ensuing financial hardship, thrust my mother into the position of protector and provider. She gracefully made the transition from the lady of the house who had never worked a day in her life to long days working at two menial cashier jobs. The first was in a donut shop from 4:30 to 9:00 a.m., after which she headed to a fast-food restaurant where she worked an eight-hour shift. As for the three of us boys, we managed to get small jobs to contribute to our survival. My brothers worked as dishwashers in Sambo's, now Denny's, and I mowed the neighbors' lawns for five dollars a pop.

Mini pulled herself through countless adversities thrown at her by life. She was eighteen when she married my father, who was twice her age. That's the culture she and countless others like her come from. She walked away from my father at the age of thirty-four and prior to the Islamic Revolution. She left my father and a life of opulence when he was at the height of success and migrated to a foreign country with us three boys without taking a penny from my father. Strong female role models have always played a central role in my life. My maternal grandmother was one of the first women employed by the Iranian Oil Company as a cartographer in a completely chauvinistic world. There she was, a ninety-five-pound woman teaching men the art of cartography. My maternal aunt rode suicide-clutch Harley-Davidson motorcycles in Iran at a time when no woman dared to do so. She taught me and my brothers how to ride when I was eight. That's Kurdish women for you, they are fighters and a force to be reckoned with. Maybe this is why I gravitate toward women who display mental fortitude and determination. Conversely, I understand the plight of women in a male-dominated culture such as the one I come from.

About a week into our arrival at LNK a POC took us to get our LNK ID card. The LNK military police had detained me and members of my group on a few occasions because we didn't display the ID as required. After all, they had to ensure the safety and security of everyone on the base. Besides, the USO, the MWR, the gym, the PX, and the chow hall all required ID to allow entry.

One afternoon after lunch, Khan and I enjoyed a cigarette at the smoke pit near the big chow hall. An intersection of sorts, this area was always busy with high-volume foot traffic as personnel moved about.

"Rohām. You want to know what I just discovered?" Khan took a deep drag.

"What's that, Khan?"

"Look around. There are no beautiful women here."

I looked at the passing female population. Khan was right; most looked plain, maybe because none wore makeup or walked around dressed up and in high heels. We were on a military base in the middle of a war zone, after all.

I smiled. "Give it some time, Khan. Even the K9s will start looking attractive after a while."

NOVEMBER 10, 2010

We went to the big chow hall for dinner. The place was overflowing with Marines celebrating the Corps' 235th Birthday. A massive five-tier cake was displayed prominently in the middle of the open space.

I made sure to congratulate any Marine who would acknowledge me.

NOVEMBER 12, 2010

A POC picked up the eight of us early in the evening and drove us to the Global Vigilance office. The site office consisted of four small shipping containers, or "conexes," organized in a square. The containers didn't touch one another, but sat about 30 feet apart. The center patio area contained probably 800 square feet of space. A camouflage net tarp covered the patio area. A high-profile wooden table jerry-rigged from pallets dominated the center. Two wooden benches and a bunch of broken office chairs sat randomly here and there. This was *Home and Garden Magazine's* war zone edition.

My group joined the rest of the linguists already there. Together we numbered about twenty-three or so, including eight female linguists of varying ages. The rest were men, also of varying ages. All the seats and benches were already taken, so I sat on the dirt floor and leaned against one of the containers. Khan sat next to me, others grabbed any open space they found. The wind gust kicked up sand and dust, adding more distress to the misery of the moment. All our waiting came down to this juncture when we would get assigned to a specific task in a particular branch of the military.

The site manager walked out of one of the containers which appeared to be the main office. He was accompanied by the mammoth menacing-looking Fijians. The sad-looking site manager looked to be in his sixties. His gray hair failed to bring life to his pasty face, and his slouch made his belly look bigger than its actual size. He spoke in a soft but no-nonsense voice. You could tell he didn't take shit from anyone.

"My name is Mathers. I am your site manager. I am in charge of linguist allocation in the southern corridor." Mathers did a 360-degree turn and looked at all the interpreters. "You report to me. Any concerns, you come to me."

He seemed like a decent man. He didn't display the same shitty attitude as the other staff members.

"Teams will arrive here soon." Mathers shoved his hands deep in his tactical pant pockets. "Linguists will be assigned to each team. He or she will then be taken to a tent designated by the team. That will be your home unless told otherwise."

I monitored the other linguists' anxiety-ridden faces. Surely, mine looked worse. The thought of getting assigned to the animals, the Marines, made my butthole pucker up and quiver.

"Some teams are here from other FOBs (Forward Operating Bases), COBs (Combat Operating Bases), or OPs (Observation Post or Outposts) in the region."

"Where are these places?" a female linguist asked.

"Jackson/Sangin, Kajaki, Nolay, Edinburgh, Shamshir, Marja, Shir-Ghazi, Shindand, Dwyer, Delaram and a few others."

Chatter ignited between the Afghan linguists. This was their country and they knew where all the shit places were.

The name Jackson/Sangin got the most reaction by far. This place was synonymous with death.

"These are all dangerous, full of Taliban," said one interpreter.

Khan and I were the only two not talking. I tried to anticipate my fast-approaching future as I remembered the bloody films from the training days: severed limbs, mutilated bodies, mass executions in the soccer field at the hands of the Taliban.

We listened to Mathers for a couple of long, miserable hours as he spoke and answered repetitive and senseless questions by the linguists. With the night came the frigid air. I smoked nervously. It calmed and warmed me, or at least I felt it did.

The first team of army soldiers arrived. Three names got called, the linguists were handed over to their assigned teams, and off they went.

The second team of army soldiers arrived. A few more names got called. Off they went.

Everyone looked uneasy. The process felt the way I imagined a slave market might feel, like what I'd read in the history books or seen in the movies. A few linguists resigned right then and there and were escorted away by one of the Fijians. By the end of the first hour, more than half the group had either left with a team or quit.

Khan lit a cigarette and offered me one. One positive aspect for smokers in a war zone: cigarettes are plentiful and cheap. The PX sold a carton of Marlboros for twenty dollars. I once bought a carton of Japanese Seven Stars cigarettes for five dollars. Of course, one puff and I nearly choked and coughed up a lung. That whole carton ended up in the garbage.

While I waited, one voice in my head screamed at me to quit, resign right now and go home, I didn't need this shit, while the other voice pressed me to hold fast.

Another army team showed up. Khan and three others from my tent were assigned to their team. We shook hands and wished each other good luck. I became more anxious. My heart pounded like a jackhammer against my ribcage, rocking me back and forth. Everyone I knew had left. I had only myself to have faith in now.

A Marine showed up as I nervously sucked on a cigarette. About six feet tall, he looked proud, confident, and in great physical shape. His boyish face was friendly and relaxed. He couldn't have been more than twenty-four or twenty-five. I remembered Bagram again on the day assignments had been handed out—how the Afghans said the Marines were animals, and refused to work with them and resigned instead.

Mathers called my name along with two others, Samir and Ajmal. I put out my cigarette, jumped to my feet, walked over to the Marine, introduced myself, and shook hands. The other two linguists didn't make eye contact or shake hands with the young soldier.

"I'm Sergeant Thomas Kent," he said with his boyish smile.

Kent signed some paperwork with Mathers.

"Follow me to my gator," he said.

A gator is a utility vehicle used on farms or for off-roading; it resembles a golf cart.

"Sit in the front," Kent said to me. "Get in the back." He pointed the other two.

Kent's smile did little to calm my jittery nerves.

"May I smoke?" I asked.

"Only if you share."

I handed him a cigarette and held up my lighter for him.

"Thanks." Kent held up the cigarette. "If the Taliban don't kill you, these will."

We drove back to the transit tent, grabbed our gear, and drove a short distance down the dusty road until we reached a row of tents.

"Grab your gear," Kent said.

He led us into the tent. The light inside was hazy. Four Afghans sat on folding camping chairs around a wooden chest they were using as a table, playing cards. A depressing Indian song played on a laptop. One didn't need to speak Hindi to understand the burden in the female singer's voice as it quivered from heartache and lamented in pain.

I took a quick survey of the tent. Ten bunk beds, the best ones already taken by the four inhabitants. They had curtained off the four corners of the tent, creating a small private retreat for themselves, and used the top bunks as storage space. Flak vests and other military gear had been thrown on the top beds haphazardly.

The four men ignored us at first as they played and laughed.

"Listen up," Sgt. Kent said. "These are your new teammates."

Three of the four stood and introduced themselves. Shafi, sleepy-eyed, a friendly guy in his early thirties. Mujib, mid-forties, the oldest of the group, mustached, and friendly but not a friend. Sami, mid-twenties with a wannabe cool machismo attitude, a typical Middle Eastern chauvinist. The fourth, Ziar, in his mid-twenties, short jet-black hair, dark complexion, a set of devious eyes, and a smug attitude. He looked to be the type who is always rather impressed with himself. His stumpy, five-foot-seven or so physique couldn't compensate for his screechy, annoying voice. He sounded hoarse, as if constantly needing to clear his throat, which spoiled his attempt at looking tough. He stayed seated and didn't shake hands with any of us. I looked at his dirty and probably smelly bare feet. He emanated bad vibes from the minute I laid eyes on him.

"Get situated," Kent said. "Expect to get your first assignment in a few days." He left the tent.

I grabbed a bed in the far left corner. The other two took the beds opposite me.

Shafi offered us tea and welcomed us.

"Did they tell you anything about the work with this team?" Mujib asked.

I shook my head.

Sami spoke to the other linguist in Dari. He ate half his words, making it hard to understand him.

"Where you from?" Ziar asked me in English as he played with a small cardboard cookie container, flipping it over and over again on the floor.

In his tone I heard malintent.

"From L.A."

"Where was you born?"

"Iran."

Ziar laughed, exposing the cookie crumbs in his mouth as he chomped away. "Oh, so you a Shia," he said. "You are the worst of all, you Irani *and* Shia." He looked at the others and said, "We don't like either," with an acerbic smile.

Everyone stopped talking and exchanged uncomfortable looks. Shafi and Mujib jumped in and told Ziar to be more welcoming and respectful. Shafi handed me a cup of tea and offered me some sweets.

Ziar didn't let up. "Irani, you have no place here. This isn't your country. Go sit on Ahmadinejad lap," he said in his imperfect English. He laughed at his own joke, and he and I exchanged visual daggers. I knew he would walk all over me if I showed any weakness. Everyone waited to see my reaction.

But Mujib injected himself: *"Tawajoh be in bacha nakon,"* he said to me in Dari. "Don't pay attention to this guy."

My stare didn't leave Ziar's. I raised my teacup in a toast. "Here's to your filthy feet," I said in Dari. "They're cleaner than your big mouth."

The others laughed uncomfortably. Ziar looked confused.

"He doesn't understand Dari," Shafi said. "He is full Pashton. Talks only Pashto and English."

Ziar jumped to his feet. "What everyone laughing at?"

Sami told him what I'd said. Ziar's anger turned his dark complexion purple. He stormed toward me, but Mujib and Shafi stopped him from getting close.

Ziar shook the cookie box he was holding. The sound of tiny screams came from inside it. He had captured two or three mice, which were clawing desperately to get out. Ziar took the lit candle from the makeshift table, tilted it, and doused the helpless creatures with dripping hot wax.

"In Allah's name, *stop*," Shafi said as painful tortured sounds poured out of the box.

No one made a move to save the poor critters, myself included.

"*Zalem, Zalem*," Ziar sang as he smiled. "Tyrant, Tyrant." He gave me a hard look as if to convey a message.

Finally, the scratching and screaming from inside the box stopped.

Like an encounter between a mongoose and a snake, my first meeting with Ziar had been contentious; instantaneous mutual loathing flourished. Maybe Ziar was Dr. Rasouli's curse on me! I thought. I grabbed my sleeping bag and spread it on top of the filthy, stiff mattress, then took my army-issued poncho and draped my bed to provide a bit of privacy. I threw my sea bags on the top bunk, took off my boots, tied their laces loosely together, and hung them on the bunk post. We had been told that scorpions, tarantulas, camel spiders, or snakes could crawl into our boots if we left them on the floor. This was the desert, after all.

Without having a place to get undressed for bed, I disrobed in front of the others. The group stared at me just like the Afghans in the showers at Fort Benning had. At least this time I kept my underwear on. I slid into the sleeping bag. Ziar talked shit about me in English and Pashto. Honestly, I didn't give a musty rat's ass. This was prison, and I had to get with the system.

I closed my eyes and fell asleep.

Over the next couple of days, Shafi and Mujib explained what my job entailed. I had been assigned to a CLB, or Combat Logistic Battalion. CLB teams were tasked with delivering vital provisions ranging from food, water and fuel, and other critical and secret supplies to FOBs, COBs, and OPs near and far. According to Shafi and Mujib, Leatherneck was the main hub for supplying the posts peppered around the countryside.

"I'm done with my contract, going home to Sacramento," Mujib said happily.

"I have a few months to go," Shafi said.

"How difficult and dangerous is this job?" I asked, naïvely.

"FOB Nolay and FOB Jackson/Sangin are very dangerous," Shafi said.

Mujib confirmed with a nod. "Many Marines died to capture those locations."

"Be ready for ambush every time you go outside," Shafi added.

"Did anyone tell you about how much the Taliban pay for a captured tarjoman?" Mujib asked.

"Interpreters have a bounty on their heads?" I asked, alarmed.

"The Taliban pay up to 40,000 dollars for us," Shafi said.

"Have they captured any?" I asked.

"We've heard of local boy getting captured, but no one from America," Mujib said.

"The Taliban hacked a young boy to death and sent the pieces back to the base where he worked with the soldiers," Shafi added.

This was startling news. Pure panic rattled my testicles. I went silent as the two told stories from their own experience and those they'd heard from other interpreters. Stories of ambushes, of trucks getting blown up by IEDs, and raging gun battles between the Marines and the Taliban. I listened to their stories carefully and heeded their advice, even though I sensed a bit of exaggeration. But what did I know? I had just arrived on the scene, a newcomer; these guys were veterans. Still, I tried to separate truth from embellishment.

One afternoon I stopped by the Morale, Welfare, and Recreation tent, MWR, to check my emails. An email from Fardad waited in my inbox. The message was much welcomed since I hadn't heard from him in a while and wanted to know his status. Much to my surprise, Fardad had resigned and gone back home to Los Angeles. This news depressed me. The thought of quitting zipped through my mind but I suppressed the idea before it grew tentacles and got a grip in my head. I'd promised myself to endure no matter what. Cut and run was not an option, not this time. The divine hand of providence had set me on this path, and I had to see it through to the end. Growing up, religion provided me with a foundation but in my adult life it did not play a pivotal role. My faith in the Higher Power did not require a middleman or a designated place to worship. My creator was with me in my internal solitude, always.

NOVEMBER 14, 2010

Sgt. Kent came by the tent early that evening and took me and the other two newcomers to get Marine-issued gear. I told Kent about the three bags of brand-new equipment, uniforms, boots, sleeping bags, plus all I had brought.

"You're with the Marines now," he said proudly. "You'll wear our uniform and use our equipment." He pointed me to the front seat and the other two to the back.

The two Afghans exchanged looks. Their rumblings betrayed their inner feelings disdain. As we rode on the gator to the equipment depot, dusk set in and the Muslim call to prayer rose in the desert air. That sound never ceased to depress the hell out of me, even as a boy in Iran. I battled feelings of apprehension as the gloomy autumn sunset further depressed me. The cold, unfriendly wind provided more anguish to my already shitty mood.

"Got a cigarette?" Kent asked.

I gladly handed him one and took one myself.

"Where're you from?" he asked.

"Los Angeles," I said as I held up my lighter.

Kent looked at me. "You crazy to come to this hellhole?"

I had no intention of disclosing the dire circumstance I faced back home. I simply diverted the conversation. I studied the surroundings, taking note of landmarks for reference as we drove to the depot, since my habitat was still somewhat unknown to me. Everything had a dull khaki look to it. LNK lacked trees or vegetation. The air above looked heavy, a mixture of khaki and ash.

"What's up with the color of the sky here?" I asked.

"That's moondust for you," Kent said.

"Moondust?"

"The soil here is like powdered sugar. Fine-grained and lightweight." He pointed to the sky. "There's always a hue of moondust hanging over the base. We inhale this shit constantly."

I looked at the cigarette between my fingers.

"Don't think of quitting now." Kent took a puff. "It's a useful addiction for this place."

We arrived at the depot, an area of a dozen full-size shipping containers set up like a corral with an improvised chicken-wire entry gate. Night had arrived, too. A couple of powerful spotlights lit the equipment depot area. We walked into a tent and met three young Marines.

"These are the new terps. Get 'em geared up," Kent said.

What the hell is a "Terp"? I wondered.

One of the Marines darted a look at me and the other two. "Hey Sarge," he snickered, "You think this batch of terps will stick around or run away?"

The Marines laughed.

Sgt. Kent must have noticed the perplexed look on my face.

"The military abbreviates everything." Kent smiled. "Interpreters are 'terps' for short."

I smiled back and nodded.

One of the Marines walked us over to a container and gave each of us two sets of new Marine uniforms, a backpack, a day bag, which is smaller and meant for short journeys, and two sleeping bags, one for winter and one for summer. The summer sleeping bag was thinner and lighter, and snapped into the thicker heavier winter bag to create an extra layer of insulation from frigid winter weather. We got T-shirts, fire-resistant gloves, hats, flak vests, helmet, and a bunch of other items. The clothing we received was brand new, but the other gear was used. The Marines recycle and get the leftovers or used equipment from the other branches of the military, perhaps by design, to keep them hungry and resourceful.

We walked back to the original tent and signed a chit just like we did in Fort Benning; the only difference was what we got here didn't cost anywhere near as much as the new Army gear, three grand at best.

Outside, the weather got colder, windier, and drearier as we drove back to the tent.

Mujib packed for his trip back home the next day. Shafi, Sami, and Ziar drank tea and yapped. As I put my new gear away, I noticed dried blood splatter on my day bag and wondered about the fate of its previous owner.

Shafi noticed my bag. "You have to return that to the depot," he said. "Any item with blood is burned, that's the rule."

"*Haqa hamjensbaz dai.*" Ziar ran his mouth and gave me dirty looks. "He is a homosexual. *Muzhsa leh wini wireh lari.* The rat is afraid of blood."

I had no desire to confront him, so I took a cup of tea and stepped outside. The small empty ammunition canister wedged next to the T-wall wasn't the most comfortable seat, but I sat on it. It took a minute for my ass to warm the cold metal canister. The wintry breeze weather had forced everyone else inside. I leaned back against the concrete T-wall, lit a cigarette, and looked up at the sky. The haze from the moondust opaqued the moonlight and diminished the stars' luster. I wondered what my family and friends were up to back home. They could never imagine this place. I couldn't believe I was there myself, but believe it or not, I was glad to be away from L.A., away from fake friendships of convenience and the decadent lifestyle.

Inside, I said goodbye to Mujib and wished him a safe trip home. Mujib reciprocated. Others stared, again, as I disrobed for bed.

"Look at that fag," Ziar said to the others in Pashto.

I fully understood his words but didn't respond, instead I climbed into my bed, and pulled the poncho down to block the light and the view. As the minutes passed, Ziar bad-mouthed me and purposely laughed out loud to keep me from sleeping. Mujib and Shafi tried to get him to ease up, but none of the others said a word or defended me. The quality of people I had been teamed up with was evident. None could be counted on, except maybe Shafi.

NOVEMBER 17, 2010

Mujib left in the early morning, and I moved my gear to his private corner and claimed it for myself. Then I headed over to the shower tent with shower gear in hand. The tent's heater warmed the space inside in contrast with the dry-cold dusty weather outside. All showers and some toilets were in tents on LNK. The sixteen small shower cubicles, eight stalls on each side, and partitioned with heavy yellow plastic were situated in the middle of the tent. They sat on a platform to allow the water to run into a reservoir tank below. The plastic divider was missing between some cubicles, making them the deluxe luxury version. The showers backed to a row of eight stainless steel sinks that looked like restaurant kitchen sinks. The mirrors above the sinks were polished sheets of aluminum. Two multi-thousand-gallon plastic tanks sat outside next to the tent. One tank contained gray-water—recycled wastewater—for showering only, not for consumption. Prominently posted signs gave sufficient warning not to drink it. The other was the black-water tank, containing wastewater used in showers and toilets.

After a quick shave and shower, I headed to the big chow hall to grab breakfast. This eatery consisted of three massive tents, each as big as a neighborhood supermarket. The place could probably accommodate 1,000 diners, if not more. The entry tent served food, fruit, and dessert,. The other two provided seating with high-school cafeteria-style benches.

After breakfast, I set out to explore the colossal 1,600-acre base, most of which was either inaccessible or restricted. Even at that, there was plenty I hadn't seen yet. The PX on LNK was small in comparison with the size of the camp. The base had a couple of gym tents, and USOs where all could make free calls home and use the computers. Leatherneck didn't provide Wi-Fi service inside the residential tents; one had to visit the USO or one of the MWR tents scattered around the base to access the internet.

The USOs had a "hangout joint" feel to them, most with a pool table, and a small movie theater with a large movie library.

I walked a dirt road congested with traffic, maybe three cars. Two vast, empty fields flanked the road as it passed through an area featuring two forty-foot-tall concrete watchtowers. Twenty-foot-high concrete walls extended to either side and abruptly ended nowhere in particular. This was the demarcation line between LNK and Bastion I.

Once on the British soil, I approached a one-storey building with a bunch of two-wheel carts and a few military Land Rover ambulances parked in front. The hospital, I assumed. A helicopter descended from the sky and landed in the field across from the hospital. A group of soldiers ran out of the one-storey building, jumped in ambulances, and rushed to the helicopter. The distance from the hospital to the landing zone couldn't have been more than 120 yards. Paramedics quickly grabbed two field gurneys from the helicopters, moved the wounded to the waiting ambulances, and rushed them to the hospital.

I'd just witnessed how the injured in action were transported. The wounded were eclipsed from eyesight. Nevertheless, I prayed for them. Then I realized they could have been Taliban fighters, who received the same care as our soldiers! In time I would learn that some of the best American and British doctors in the world worked in that hospital.

At the bus stop, a group of Marines got off the bus and went around the bend. Like an investigator, I followed. Hah, a Pizza Hut; albeit not an actual restaurant but a Pizza Hut in a can, a cargo container. Three canopies covered the open space in front of the pizza parlor, about ten yards away. Three rows of one-piece wood picnic-style benches ran the length of the covered area. Some twenty or so soldiers were hanging out, enjoying the fat, doughy pizza.

A one-storey prefab building sat next to the pizzeria, a café. In I went, as this required a closer inspection. Large flat-screen TVs on the walls showed soccer games and British game shows. The high tables with bar stools, the fake leather couches and chairs added a nice touch to the place. The sturdy imitation dark hardwood floor was scuffed up. A long display case offered an array of tasty-looking pastries. The board hanging behind the counter listed the drinks: tea, coffee, cappuccinos, frappes, juices, and British energy drinks. A stack of board games sat on a corner shelf for anyone who cared to play. The adjacent room had a couple of snooker and pool tables. Such a place in the middle of a war zone was an unexpected bonus.

I went next door to the British PX. The market had shelf after shelf of chocolate, cigarettes, chips, sleeping bags, toothpaste, magazines, and cameras, all kinds of non-alcoholic beverages, canned foods, hygiene products, underwear, and what have you. The smell of cardboard boxes and freshly stacked magazines meshed with the sharp scent of cheap aftershave as I walked down the aisle. The sight of British After Eight dark chocolate mints instantaneously brought back memories. I used to eat this chocolate in Iran. I grabbed a box.

With coffee and chocolate in hand, I went outside and sat in a corner under the canopy. After eagerly opening the chocolates, I shoved two pieces in my mouth. The taste took me back to 1974. I was nine years old, and my brothers had left Iran to attend boarding school in England. They would send me the latest toys, clothing, chewing gum, skate board, and of course, my favorite, After Eight chocolate mints. It was truly a wonderful time, when I received undivided attention from my parents and siblings. It was a time of abundance.

I finished the whole box with my coffee, lit a cigarette, and walked around the concrete T-walls to the bazaar. A row of Afghan-owned shops teemed with activity. The shops sold rugs of various sizes, trinkets, shoes, pirated movies, counterfeit money, figurines, Afghan clothes, and a bunch of other useless widgets that soldiers and contractors bought as souvenirs for folks back home. The MPs raided the shops now and then and confiscated the pirated movies and software programs for sale, but that didn't stop the shop owners from bringing a new batch the next day to display and sell. No shop owner ever got in trouble for this.

As I browsed the dusty glass displays and tables of junk, an announcement sounded off on the PA loudspeakers: "Op Minimize, Op Minimize, Op Minimize," the British female voice said.

I overheard one Afghan shopkeeper tell the other, "Another dead infidel." They smiled.

Although I was puzzled about the broadcast, I walked away. "Do not answer or ask questions of strangers, no matter uniformed or not. Op Sec, Operational Security, is paramount," had been drilled into our heads during training.

A group of British soldiers browsing the display counters talked about going over to Bastion II for some KFC. I decided to trail them. For about twenty minutes, they walked through rows of tents housing British soldiers, the military fire department, and other British contingencies with me in tow. We got to another café and PX very much like the one I'd just left. Here, instead of a Pizza Hut, there was a Kentucky Fried Chicken in a can. A half-dozen Afghan-owned shops lined the flip side of the café and the KFC.

I went over to the shops and chatted with a young shopkeeper who spoke broken English. At first, I didn't divulge my knowledge of Dari and Pashto. Seeing how hard the young shopkeeper was struggling with his English made me feel bad, so I engaged him in Dari. The young man said most shop owners on Leatherneck and both Bastions were from the nearby city of Lashkar Gah or a few small villages in the area. Shop owners and their employees went through a comprehensive background check before getting permission to open a shop and work on the base. They had to close shop by 6 p.m. every day and leave the base no later than 7 p.m.. They went through a rigorous search, body and vehicle alike, every day before entering the base. Talking to the young Afghan hipster wearing skin-tight jeans and cockroach-killing pointed shoes made me appreciate my freedoms back home. His questions about life in America and how he wished to live there conveyed his thirst for what we take for granted.

A couple of Marines stood in front of my tent talking to Shafi when I got back.

"You're going on your first mission tonight," Shafi said, catching me by surprise.

"Report to the battalion compound for the pre-mission briefing," said a Marine.

Shafi must have noticed the look of concern on my face. "Don't worry, I'm on the mission, I show you everything," he said, leaving out the part about Ziar and Sami going with us as well.

Inside the tent, Shafi told me what to pack in my day bag. We had a few hours before the briefing. My anxiety made me jittery. I put on my Marine uniform with great care, blousing my pants—tucking the trouser legs using green blousing rubbers with little hooked ends. Putting on the Marine uniform gave me a profound sense of belonging, one I'd never before experienced. My soul made a fervid connection with the uniform, as if it had slipped into its skin. My posture changed subconsciously: upright, straighter, poised. I wished I could turn back the hands of time to when I was eighteen, to the time when I took the Navy exam and passed but chickened out at the last minute and didn't enlist.

Shafi stepped out from his private area dressed in his uniform.

"Oh, Mr. Rohām, you look like a real Marine," he said.

Ziar and Sami stepped out from their enclosures. Sami gave me thumbs up. Ziar looked at me with disdain written all over his face. Ziar had put on the uniform carelessly, with the utmost disrespect. He looked tousled.

Minutes passed. I walked in and out of the tent to smoke. Between cigarettes I ran to one of the two porta potties next to my tent. I wore a Marine uniform but I was no soldier, had no formal training, and had no idea how I would react in a gun battle. Every sensation I felt was brand new to me, from putting on the uniform and getting geared up to marching into possible battle, unarmed.

Ziar ran his mouth the whole time. "*Mezha feker kawi chi da Iran di. De Afghanistan khalk doi tah sakht dars tadris ki,*" he said, cracking a spiteful smile at me. "The rat thinks this is Iran. The Afghan people will teach him a hard lesson." He placed his right hand on his ass. "*Da ahmagh napohigi chi delta zeh mesher yom. Agha bayad zma kenati machah ki.* This idiot doesn't know I'm the boss here. He must kiss my ass."

Clearly, he thought I couldn't understand Pashto. I understood every word. Ziar was the kind of guy that farts from his mouth and burps from his ass. Because hanging around the tent would further aggravate me, I walked over to the plywood USO building to check my emails and maybe call home.

Talking to my mother, I said I wouldn't be able to call for a few days because the phone and computer lines on the base were scheduled for maintenance. A complete lie, of course. I didn't want to share any information, for security reasons, and I didn't want her to worry about me. I spoke with Jimmy, and repeated the same lie. Jimmy knew damn well I was bullshitting.

"Never volunteer for anything," he advised me.

Minibuses weren't operating that afternoon for some reason, so at 1600 hours the four of us walked a mile to the battalion compound. The compound housed all the vehicles, ammunition, and office tents for the higher-ups and those in charge of the logistics operations.

The guard at the gate pointed us to the pre-mission briefing tent, which was small and tightly packed with Marines. A good portion of the interior space was taken up by a large wooden table with maps and a slide projector on it. A white screen hung at the far end of the tent.

Sgt. Kent called roll. "We have a new terp joining us on this mission," he said at the end as he pointed to me. "Stand up, please."

I got up. The crowd in the tent was composed of mere kids.

"This is our new terp straight from Hollywood, Sanjar Rohām."

The Marines sized me up. By the looks on their faces, I knew my name sounded strange to them.

"SANJ," Kent said, "That'll be his call name."

Some of the Marines nodded in agreement. I took my seat.

The briefing began, but the information went over my head. I understood ten percent of it, at best. The Marines were assigned designated tasks. Each vehicle had a given position in the convoy. Radio frequencies were called out, followed by exact instructions for alternate channels and frequencies. Sgt. Kent finished with the technical aspects of the mission. He then introduced Lt. Laramy, a female Marine in charge of planning the mission and choosing the route for the convoy.

The lights went off and the slide projector turned on. Black and white satellite images bounced off the screen and onto the Marines who listened intently as they took notes. Lt. Laramy described the route and alternate trail should it be needed. I paid close attention, even though I didn't understand all the military jargon. The projector light lit a third of Laramy's face and her tightly-wrapped bun. She spoke with authority and perfect elocution as the higher-ups watched and analyzed her presentation. I'm sure the mission plan had been approved in advance by the high brass. Looking at the slides, I tried to identify landmarks so that I could gauge our position once we were on the move. Not an easy task since everything looked the same—desert, mountains, and dried-up riverbeds.

The briefing concluded, the lights came back on, and the Marines began exiting the tent.

"Wait for me outside," Sgt. Kent told me.

Ziar and Sami joked around with some of the Marines, trying to show off in front of me. Shafi and I waited by the side of the tent near a few wooden benches, smoking.

Sgt. Kent walked out accompanied with two Marines. They joined us for a smoke.

"You're riding with me," Kent said to me.

"Okay."

Kent introduced the two Marines. "This is Cpl. Jordon Smitts and Pfc. Kevin Gospol. We ride rear security in the convoy."

I shook hands with both. Their smiles were friendly and welcoming. Cpl. Smitts was almost my height but had at least twenty pounds on me. That would be twenty pounds in muscle mass. Smitts was in his mid-twenties, with dark hair, dark eyes, a round face, and a friendly voice.

"So, you're from Hollywood?" he asked playfully. "This ain't no movie set, bro; you gotta keep your eyes open and your balls tucked, and watch where you step. But as long as you're with us, you got nothin' to worry about. We got you covered." He patted me on the back.

Pfc. Gospol didn't say much, just smiled. A lanky kid in his late teens or early twenties, he was over six feet tall, blond and blue-eyed, an all-American kid from the Midwest, shy and awkward because of his youth and inexperience. He weighed maybe 140 pounds soaking wet.

"Hey, get the truck ready," Sgt. Kent ordered Smitts and Gospol, and off they went.

"Can I help you with the prep?" I asked Kent.

Kent smiled. "That's the Marines' job. Terps have no obligation to help us before or after the mission."

"Don't volunteer to help," Shafi told me in Dari.

His words came as a surprise. In my mind, team members stepped up and contributed.

"Can I go?" Shafi asked Kent.

"You can leave, but Sanj has to stay and meet his POC."

Shafi hightailed it out of there, leaving me with the Marines.

Lt. Laramy emerged from the tent and walked over, a folder under one arm, a green notebook and her hat—or "cover," as it is called in the military—in her other hand. I saw for the first time what she looked like. She carried herself with poise and authority. In her early thirties, about 5'8", she had a charismatic if non-traditional face, gelled chestnut brown hair pulled back tightly into a bun, same color full eyebrows, and a set of steadfast blue-green eyes. Her suntanned skin was tight and smooth. Her uniform accentuated her flat stomach and great physical condition. Her arresting quality was unmistakable.

Sgt. Kent introduced me. We shook hands. Lt. Laramy had a firm handshake. She met my smile with a stone look. "Welcome to the team," she said sternly. "I am your POC; you will report to me any concerns or questions." She pointed to a tent. "My office is there."

I gladly accepted her offer with a flirty smile. She wouldn't have any of it, and walked away. I got the feeling Laramy came from a military lineage.

When Ziar and Sami walked up to Lt. Laramy they were met with a smile. I stepped back and watched Ziar and Sami salivate at the mouth, trying to outdo the other for Laramy's attention as they joked around with each other.

"Push-off is at 0200 hours," Kent said. "Be back here by 0100."

Like the flights, most, if not all, missions departed from the base in the dark of night. I walked the mile alone back to my tent in cold dusk, since I had no desire to accompany Ziar and Sami.

Ziar sat in his usual spot in the tent eating a bag of potato chips. Everything about him rubbed me the wrong way—the way he talked, the way he laughed, the way he ate food with his mouth open, making smacking sounds. My tentmates' loud conversation prevented me from gathering my thoughts as I lay in bed, so I got up and ran to the toilet one more time even though my bowels were completely empty. My first mission had left me with a bad case of jitters.

1215 HOURS / NOVEMBER 18, 2010

Shafi, Sami, and Ziar geared up to leave. One would think they were in the Special Forces from the way they'd prepared. Elbow and knee pads, goggles, water canister. And here I stood with a simple day bag containing some nutrition bars, a couple of T-shirts, underwear, socks, my shower bag and my Marine fleece jacket. I strapped my sleeping bag sack to my backpack, put my fleece and flak jacket on over it, clipped my Helmet to the flak, and threw my backpack on. The four of us left the tent.

My teammates didn't include me in their three-way conversation while we waited at the bus stop. And honestly, I didn't care. The anticipation of the moment was sufficient diversion. Darkness enveloped the quiet, chilly night. The moondust layer had settled, in contrast with my spiked anxiety. "Scared shitless" doesn't come close to describing how I felt. My internal organs shuddered!

A minibus approached, meaning the bus service was back on. We climbed on board the bus. Its inside light glowed brightly. The young Indian or Pakistani driver played great techno music by David Guetta on the mp3 player he had connected to two small speakers. The club music gave a different feel to the moment, a strange juxtaposition—war on one side, club music on the other. The few Marines and soldiers on the bus were going to their shift. They sat silently, lost in thought, staring at their own reflections in the glass as the bus drove the 5-mph speed limit.

Shafi signaled me to be ready as the bus pulled up to a stop. We stepped off and walked about fifty yards to the compound. The place pulsated with activity as Marines sprinted from one end to the other, carrying heavy loads. My three teammates disappeared as soon as we walked in. I was standing there with no idea where to go when I heard someone call out.

"Hey, Sanj, Sanj! Over here." Smitts was waving from top of an LVSR,

Logistics Vehicle System Replacement, the most powerful heavy-duty all-purpose ten-wheel military truck with a long flatbed and plenty of towing power.

I walked over swiftly. "Is this our truck?"

"Yeah, this is it," Smitts said. "We're gonna sit on each other's lap!"

I looked at the LVSR, a two-passenger truck, maybe three with a gunner in the turret.

Smitts jumped down from the bed. "We gotta go all the way to the end of the line," he said.

We walked to the last vehicle in the column: an MATV, Military All-Terrain Vehicle, a mean-looking fighting truck with an aggressive design and a roaring engine that shook the ground I stood on.

Smitts opened the passenger door behind the driver. "Not much room back here," he said. "This is where you'll sit." He grabbed my day bag and threw it on the adjacent passenger seat, which already had a shitload of stuff on it: cases of MREs (meals ready-to-eat), bottled water, and the gear from the others.

"Try it on for size," Smitts said.

I climbed in the cramped space. It was tight even for me.

"Can you pull up the driver's seat?" I asked.

Smitts smiled. "This ain't no fancy car, Sanj. This here is a mean fighting machine."

The seats were immovable.

"Can I help with anything?" I asked.

"Just hang and relax."

I jumped down from the truck, lit a cigarette, and had the urge to use the toilet again. Spotting a porta potty, I ran in. My ass hovered over the seat since I didn't dare to sit down. God knows what kind of germs crawled on that surface, not to mention ageless piss stains from other visitors. After a few minutes of unsuccessful squeezing, I pulled up my pants and went back to the truck.

I watched with admiration as the young male and female Marines geared up, mounting the big 50-caliber guns in the turrets, joking with one another and working in unison getting ready for what could be their last hours on this planet. They lived in the moment; no past, no future, not the slightest hint of fear. Watching them reminded me of what my father used to tell me and my brothers when we were kids, "*Know the splendor of the present, enjoy your youth. It's a fleeting moment not to be repeated.*" It took more than thirty years for me to comprehend his words and realize that I'd pissed my life away without much gratitude. Chasing momentarily pleasures and instant gratifications, be it with people or possessions, had yielded wasted treasure, time. My father had passed away sixteen years earlier, but I could still smell the distinctive, spicy scent of his cologne: Givenchy Musk.

At about 0130 we were summoned to the front of the convoy for one last manifest check and confirmation of personnel to their assigned vehicles. Names were called out, weapons checked. I stood next to Ziar, Shafi, and Sami, not knowing which vehicle they would be riding in.

"I'm a few trucks ahead of you," Shafi said. "Sami is a few trucks ahead of the convoy commander."

"I'm ride with convoy commander," Ziar said. "My place is always with leader."

I gave Ziar a "Who gives a fuck?" look. Everyone headed to their respective vehicles.

Kent and Smitts tended to last-minute checks. Gospol got the 50-caliber gun in the turret ready for action. He'd hooked a wide canvas strap—like a swing or a miniature hammock—from the ceiling of the truck to sit on during the mission.

Orders came for all trucks to start their engines. The rumbling of the diesels made it difficult to even hear yourself breathe.

"Hey, put on your flak and helmet before you get in," Kent said.

"Yeah, regulations require'em to be on at all times while inside the truck and on a mission," Smitts added.

We slipped on our vests, put on our helmets, climbed on board, and closed the heavy- armored doors. Sitting in the MATV with three Marines as a part of a mission in a war zone felt purposeful, something I hadn't felt for the longest time. I latched my door from the inside so it couldn't be opened from the outside. I thought—naively—of the Taliban sneaking up, opening the door and snatching me. Or worse, throwing a grenade inside the truck, or simply opening fire. Ricocheting bullets would wreak havoc. For the first time since my father's passing, I recited the Hebrew prayer he always recited before trips, and asked God to keep the convoy in his sight.

B'shem Hashem, elohei Yisrael,
B'yumini Michael umismoli Gavriel,
Umilfanai Uriel, ume'acharai Raphael,
V'al roshi, v'al roshi, Shechinat-El

I didn't understand Hebrew even though I had attended a private Jewish school in Iran, but I remembered my father telling me what the prayer meant.

"Four angels lead us in four directions. To our right is Michael, the archangel who defeated evil. He is the angel of mercy and justice. To our left is Gabriel, defender of Jews and executor of judgment. In front is Uriel, the angel of light, he illuminates the darkness before us. And behind us is Raphael, he takes in our pain, despair, and sickness; and above our head the devine presence of God."

4
WAG BAG

0230 HOURS / NOVEMBER 18, 2010

The convoy inched slowly ahead. The vibration of the roaring engines rebounded from the dry, hard-packed surface of the earth, working its way up from my cramped seat all the way to the tips of the cropped hair on my head.

We drove for a good thirty minutes before arriving at the main gates of Bastion I. It took another thirty minutes until authorization descended from the proper channels, granting us permission to leave the base. The protocol involved layers of calculated measures, all for good reason.

Once outside the gates, we drove slowly through the Serpentine—the slalom formation of concrete barriers meant to slow down possible suicide bombers' vehicles from driving head-on into the gates, giving the guards ample time to mitigate the threat, hopefully blowing it to smithereens. Flickering campfires and small shimmering lights were the only things visible in the pitch-black velvet night as I looked out the small window to get a glimpse of the country beyond the gates.

"Our guys are camping out here?" I asked.

"Nah. Those are Afghan nationals." Kent turned in his seat to look at me. "They camp outside the gates looking for work or to pick up scraps to sell in the bazaars."

"Taliban spies hang out here to monitor the infidels' movements," Smitts added.

His words both excited and alarmed me. What if the Taliban attacked us right then and there? That would be suicide for them. But, then again, it's the Taliban! I answered my question before blurting it out.

Cigarettes were lit. Gospol's hand dropped down from the turret. I lit a cigarette and passed it up to him.

Sgt. Kent turned to me. "Hey, Sanj, welcome to your first mission with the Marines." He seemed as excited as I was. "Remember, if there's a need for us to step out, I want you to shadow me. Step where I step, always stay behind me unless I tell you differently."

I nodded.

"You're a vital asset, we won't compromise you; your safety is paramount," he added.

So much for "animals," I thought. These guys had been nothing less than professional so far.

"Hey Sanj, you're getting your cherry popped," Smitts said. "If only folks back home could experience what you gonna experience."

"I'm afraid you're not gonna get much pop out of a forty-four-year-old cherry," I replied.

After what seemed to be an eternity of driving at a very slow speed on the dirt road, I felt paved road under the tires.

"We made it to Highway 1," Smitts said. "The Ring Road connecting major cities of Afghanistan."

"We're gonna drive down Highway 1 for about 20 klicks, then go off-road to FOB Edinburgh," Kent said.

"From Leatherneck to Edi is less than a hundred miles, but 'cause of the bullshit stuff it'll take us about 72 hours to get there." Smitts added.

"He means if we're lucky not to get ambushed or hit any IEDs," Kent translated with a confident smile.

I wiggled in my tight quarters to find some comfort. No chance. My knees were damn near my ears and my asshole dangerously close to my nose. My first mission in Afghanistan was bringing me intimately close to that often unacknowledged but vital orifice.

Eventually, we went off-road. The humdrum rocking motion of the truck powering through the rough desert terrain accompanied by the roar of the engine put me in a trance.

A loud *boom* shook us, followed by what sounded like ball bearings hitting the truck's armor.

Ta, ta, ta, ta. Ping, ping, ping.

Radio chatter erupted instantaneously.

"IED, repeat IED, lead vic down..." the voice on the radio said urgently.

The radio chatter was loud, staticky, and mixed. It was tough to understand. Vehicles communicated with one another, calling out enemy positions.

"Permission to open fire if you have PID (Positive ID)," the convoy commander barked.

"PID, Sarge," Gospol yelled as he stood up from his hammock seat.

"Give 'em a lead shower, Gos," Kent replied.

Thump, thump, thump, thump. Gospol opened fire. The excitement of the moment got the best of the young soldier. Farts bolted out of his ass as rapidly as bullets left the gun. He was firing on all cylinders. My seat was right under the gun turret. The empty 50-caliber shells rained down on my helmet and bounced off. One of the hot shells found its way down my shirt, and got lodged between my upper back and the flack vest. The flack limited my range of motion, and I couldn't reach back to take out the scalding shell. My flesh sizzled, but the intensity of the action and the adrenalin rush dulled the pain, eclipsing the sensation of my burning flesh. The smell of gunpowder permeated the inside of the MATV. Although my space was confined, I moved agilely, rubbernecking to look out the dust-covered bulletproof windows. A slug struck the thick bulletproof glass and made a *thud*, chipping a piece off. My initial instinct was to duck but I was exhilarated and frightened at the same time, and had to see what was happening around me.

The radio was on fire as Marines called out enemy positions. We were in a full-on ambush. The AK47 rounds bounced off the armored trucks like BB gun pellets off a rhino's hide. While Kent communicated on the radio with other trucks and the convoy commander, Smitts peered outside with his night-vision goggles to identify enemy positions. Red and green tracer rounds from our guns and the enemy's dashed through the darkness like small meteors.

Gospol dropped his head in. "Ammo!" he yelled. "HURRY!"

I reached over to the passenger side, yanked out the almost thirty-five-pound ammo box with one hand, and passed it to Gospol in a single swipe. The adrenalin had given me superpowers.

Gospol reloaded the 50-cal in a snap and opened fire again, cocking the gun every few rounds. *Thump, thump, thump.* The sound of the gun alone could scare the shit out of anyone. Enemy bullets recoiled off the heavy armor on our truck. *Ping, ping, ping.* The ambush raged on for a half-hour or so—and then stopped as quickly as it had begun.

Dead silence. Radio traffic subsided. Thankfully no one from our side had gotten hurt, including the people in the truck that hit the IED. The floorboard under my feet was littered with empty shells. Staring at them, I imagined what kind of damage the rounds could inflict on the enemy. A 50-cal can devastate even if it hits within twelve inches of the intended target.

A call came over the radio instructing my truck to escort a tow truck to the disabled vehicle to get it hitched for a tow. This task was a part of the rear security responsibilities.

"Sit tight, we're goin' off path," Smitts said as he buckled his seatbelt. "Fuckin' Tali love this tactic, get us off path and blow us up!"

Gospol dropped down from the turret and braced himself. I buckled my seatbelt. We slowly drove up the side of the convoy. All gunners ducked as we passed by to avoid getting hit by shrapnel in case we hit an IED. My knuckles turned pinkish-white as I hung on tight to the handle on the back of Smitts' seat. Finally, we reached one of the LVSRs. Smitts cracked his door open and so did the passenger of the LVSR.

"Stay on my tracks. Keep a twenty-yard distance," Smitts shouted to the LVSR crew.

Kent got on the radio. "No boots on deck," he told the occupants of the blown-up truck.

That meant everyone had to stay inside their vehicle. We finally reached the damaged truck. The front passenger axle was a mangled piece of iron.

"Dismount the gun, get all the ammo," Kent ordered the occupants of the damaged truck.

He then called a third vehicle to come and pick up the 3-pack from the downed truck. Marines call individuals "Pack."

I watched from the small cracked bulletproof porthole as the third truck arrived to load up the 3-pack. That truck was equipped with a mine roller, which looks a bit like a reverse farming plow. Mounted in front of the armored truck, it has either eight or ten tires spanning the track's width. Heavy flat steel sheets are mounted on top make it weighty enough to detonate IEDs concealed underground.

The truck went around in circles to discover secondary IEDs, each time making the circle smaller and tighter. Better for a hundred-thousand-dollar mine roller to blow up than one of us getting hurt.

The all-clear signal came from the mine roller, and the LVSR backed up to the damaged truck. The Marines dismounted and began moving ammo boxes and gear to the third truck as others hitched the downed truck to the LVSR.

"Gunners, watch for enemy snipers," said the convoy commander on the radio.

The Marines executed everything smoothly. Watching their impressive performance made me forget how badly I had to piss.

"Sarge, can I step out for a leak?" I asked.

Smitts and Kent responded collectively in the affirmative; they had to take a leak also.

Kent opened his door and stood on the truck's side-step. "No one move until all boots are off deck," he barked.

"Let's hit it, Sanj," Smitts said. "Gotta piss out the adrenaline." He smiled.

I stood between Kent and Smitts facing the truck. The sound of forceful streams of urine hitting the powdery moondust was loud. Small piss mud-puddles formed in the parched desert floor.

I took out a cigarette and lit it.

"Gimme a drag," Smitts said.

I passed the cigarette over.

"Send it," Kent said.

I took the cigarette from Smitts and passed it to Kent.

"Hey Sanj, don't panic at the sight of my pipe." Smitts grinned.

My mind was still trying to digest the whole ambush episode, so it took me a second to comprehend his words. "What, you mean that slow-drip irrigation straw?" I replied.

A low, funky chuckle came from the gun turret, then a similar chuckle from Kent, followed by one from me and eventually Smitts. We burst out laughing as the other Marines waited for us to finish and mount up.

I tried to remove the 50-caliber shell from my shirt, but couldn't.

"You okay?" Kent asked.

"I got a shell stuck back there."

"Let me see." Kent reached inside my FROG top and pulled out the shell. FROG top is a combat shirt sewn to U.S. Marine Corps specifications. It stands for Fire Resistant Organizational Gear.

"Fuck, this musta burned like a son of a bitch," Kent held up the large shell. "Lemme get the medic to take a look; you're gonna blister."

I appreciated Kent's concern but felt guilty to hold up the convoy and put everyone in further danger.

"I'm okay," I said.

The convoy was on the move again. Our conversation revolved around the ambush for a short while as we journeyed along our path, then we went silent. We were present in body, but our souls had drifted away.

I looked up. Gospol was slouched over. He'd fallen asleep. His sling rocked back and forth like a swing. The adrenalin rush had left him exhausted. This seemed to apply to everyone in the convoy. My hand reached into my pocket and took out a cigarette. I lit up again. Smitts turned on his MP3 player, which he'd hooked up to a small speaker. He played a soft Latin tune; *Dos Locos*, a duet, a man and a woman sang together.

"That's a beautiful song," I said, having no idea what the lyrics meant.

"This is the first song my wife and I danced to in our wedding," Smitts replied.

"Hey Sanj, pass me a cig, will ya?" Kent asked. "It's a nice tune."

I lit two cigarettes and passed them over to Kent and Smitts. Smoke filled the interior of the truck and slowly drifted out from the turret like a chimney. We went silent again. The humming of the engine faded into the background. The realization that I'd just been a part of a small battle in a big war, a war that most likely wouldn't end in my lifetime, reminded me of my mortality. I thought of my family. Their images appeared as pale silhouettes as if they were part of a dream or another lifetime. Had I betrayed them because I couldn't remember them vividly? I took a long, deep drag from my cigarette, and looked over at Kent, Smitts and Gospol. They were my family now. Here we were, four strangers, and yet I trusted them with my life.

Daybreak. The convoy came to a halt due to some mechanical issues with a couple of the trucks. Smitts jumped out and walked over to the passenger side and grabbed a case of MREs. Each Meal Ready to Eat case contains a dozen different meals. I'd never eaten an MRE and didn't know how to prepare one.

Gospol dropped down from the turret, "Got any meatballs in there?" he asked.

Smitts looked through the case, handed me the meatballs pack, and I passed it to Gospol.

"What's your flavor?" Kent asked me.

"Meatballs, breakfast? " I sounded like a spoiled L.A. douchebag.

Kent pulled out a chicken fajita and handed it to me. "You gonna either get butt-choke or the shits." He smiled. "I get choked."

The package contained a pouch with pre-cooked sliced chicken, a couple of small doughy tortillas, and a bag of Skittles for dessert.

Smitts noticed my ineptitude. "Let me show you how it's done, Hollywood Sanj. Fill the heater bag with water and let it sit for a minute. The water activates whatever chemical shit is inside to almost scalding hot." He demonstrated as he explained. "Put the unopened entrée pouch in the heater bag and wait for a few minutes for it to warm up."

The heater bag emanated a distinct acidic odor, somewhat like an overheated car radiator.

After a couple of hours we were on the move again. Cigarettes got lit, music played, and a light conversation ensued.

"You married, Sanj?" Smitts asked.

"Nope."

"My wife is a Marine too, but our deployment is staggered," Smitts said. "One stays home, one deploys."

"Kids?" I asked.

"No intention of havin' 'em while we're in the Corps," he replied.

Kent said he was married also. He showed me a picture of his wife, a beautiful young southern belle. They didn't have any children either.

"I wanna stay on with the Marines as a career military guy," Kent said.

The conversation turned to me.

"How old are you, Sanj?" Smitts asked.

"Forty-four."

"You said that before," Kent said, "but I didn't believe you."

"I have no reason to lie to you, not in the middle of this place."

Smitts smiled. "Hey Sanj, you're an old man in a young guy's body."

Gospol dropped down as if to examine me closely. He didn't say a word, just shook his head and slowly went back up in the turret.

The convoy moved slowly but steadily through the desert. It snaked around the naked terrain, in and out, up and down dried-up river beds. My stomach felt uneasy; something ominous was cooking in the basement. Could it be what Kent had said at breakfast, diarrhea? I kept to myself and concentrated on puckering up my butt cheeks, but the bouncing motion made the circumstance very challenging. I shifted from side to side in my tight seat. Not ever having experienced such a circumstance before, I felt embarrassed to voice my predicament to my companions. My flack vest put pressure on my stomach. My helmet felt like a ton of bricks on my head as beads of sweat ran down the sides of my face. I prayed to God for some kind of relief.

What does God have to do with this? I wondered.

My prayers were answered. The convoy stopped. We had been driving through a patch of soft sandy terrain, and some of the trucks had gotten stuck in the soft moondust. The LVSR's had to tow them across the area one at a time. My rear security truck was the last in the convoy, which gave me the chance to address the state of affairs. I took advantage of the situation and told the guys I had to step out. They thought I had to piss. I knew better.

I jumped down and frantically looked around for a place to take a shit. But we were in the middle of nowhere and I didn't dare venture off the tracks because of possible IEDs. I paced back and forth, trying to think of something. I noticed the driver of an empty personnel carrier running around. The situation with the convoy and the tow looked hectic, moondust rising through the air as trucks tried to get out of the quicksand terrain. A few Marines on deck were organizing and coordinating the movement of the LVSRs and the rest of the convoy. The Marine from the personnel carrier ran up to me. There he stood in his abbreviated height, a man shorter than me.

"You got a wag bag?" he asked with a harried look on his face.

I realized I hadn't brought a wag bag with me. A wag bag, also known as shit bag, is a compact, heavy-duty human-waste sanitary bag that contains a biodegradable solution for trapping, encapsulating, deodorizing, and breaking down shit. The bag can be pulled over a bucket or used in makeshift field toilets. Each pack contains baby wipes for obvious reasons.

We had a bunch of shit bags in my truck. The young Marine and I noticed the despair written on each other's faces.

"You gotta take a shit too?" he asked.

I responded with a solid nod.

"Got an extra shit bag?" he asked again.

"Yeah, in the truck, but where to shit?"

"Get me a shit bag." He pointed to his truck. "You can get in the back of my truck and take a shit there."

Before he could finish his sentence I was running back with two shit bags. He opened the back gate of the personnel carrier and I climbed up. My hands shook as I ripped open the packaging. I spread the shit bag on the floor, pulled my pants down, squatted, and leaned against the bench seat for support. Taking a shit while wearing a flack vest is not an easy task. Liquids discharged from me non-stop. I thought of the poor Marine waiting outside. I squeezed out as much as I could in as short a time as possible, then quickly used the wet wipes, pulled my pants up, closed the shit bag, opened the gate, and jumped down from the back of the truck.

"You done?" he asked desperately.

"Yeah, thanks, but what to do with this?" I held up the bag.

The Marine swiped it out my hand, threw it in the back of his truck and disappeared behind its gates.

I climbed back in my truck.

"Hey Sanj, don't be bashful out here with the Marines. If you gotta take a shit, then take a shit—ain't no crime to dump a lump." Smitts smiled.

"Just so you know, it wasn't a lump," I said.

"Oh, shit, you got the shits, bro?" Kent asked.

"Guess I'm not one of the lucky ones to get butt-choke from MREs."

The convoy crawled over the arid landscape, slowly and methodically. There were moments of conversation in the truck followed by moments of complete silence.

We stopped at the outskirts of Nawzad, a village sixty-five or so kilometers north of Leatherneck.

"You know anything about Nawzad?" Smitts asked.

"I know the name means 'New Born' in Farsi and Dari," I replied.

"All the villagers ran away from here in 2008. This place was a Taliban headquarters and retreat whenever they weren't in Musa Qala next door." Kent said.

"Yeah, bro, FOB Cafareta in Nawzad is a tactical location for us," Smitts added.

The main road in Nawzad ran through the bazaar, with narrow alleys branching off into a maze of compounds and mud houses. Poppy fields and other vegetable farmlands spread out on the outskirts of the village. The coalition forces, also known as ISAF, had helped build a couple of schools for the children in Nawzad. We'd provided all the textbooks, notepads, and school supplies, and handed out orange and blue winter jackets to the kids, somewhat like a uniform. No sooner had our guys left the camoflauged Taliban portion of the local population resurfaced and collected all the supplies and books and burned them, along with the school structures themselves, threatening to kill any kid wearing the jackets or wanting to attend school. I did see a few kids wearing the jackets, however. Maybe having our guys in Cafareta provided some degree of protection for the population, a portion of which wanted us dead.

The convoy commander gave instructions on the radio: We had to stay outside the village until darkness fell. Our route went through the main dirt road and the bazaar that bustled with foot, donkey, bicycle, motorcycle, and some automobile traffic during the day. The dirt passageway provided the perfect opportunity for a suicide bomber or an ambush. We had a couple of hours till sundown. Everyone got out of their trucks to stretch their legs.

Kent came to my side. "Come on out, stretch your legs. Stay close to us."

Kent and Smitts had their M4 carbines at the ready, hanging from their shoulders. Above us, Gospol kept a sharp lookout as did all the gunners.

"Gospol's M4 is right by your seat." Kent pointed. "Push comes to shove, use it!"

"You know how to use a big-boy toy, Sanj?" Smitts asked playfully.

"Sure I do, Mr. Slow Drip," I replied.

Smitts smiled. "The man knows how to shoot, Sarge."

We weren't out for a minute before a stampede of young children, teenage boys and men came running from the village. The kids begged for pencils and notebooks, which were rarities thanks to the Taliban. Young and old pleaded for food, candy, money, soldier gear, anything and everything. I kept a keen eye on the locals, partly because it was my first such encounter and partly because we were in enemy territory. I zeroed in on the younger boys. They were tricky little bastards. They surrounded the Marines and picked their pockets with their quick little hands. The older teenagers and the men weren't much better. For sure there were Taliban, Taliban sympathizers, and spies concealed amongst them. Their eyes told me all I needed to know. If a newcomer like me could pick up this vibe from some of the locals, imagine what a seasoned veteran noticed that I didn't. Some of the Marines were mere kids themselves, simple Midwestern kids, farm-raised, naive to the ways of the world, especially the ways of the world in this region. I watched the Marines' interactions with the kids. They displayed great compassion and generosity, handing out money, candy, pens and so much more to the youngest Afghans.

A few kids came up to us and begged for stuff. Kent and Smitts asked me to translate for them.

"Ask 'em what they want," Smitts said.

"*Tse ghuari, bachem?*" I asked the boys in Pashto.

The children became wide-eyed when they heard me talk to them in their native tongue. They had taken me as a Marine and didn't expect me to understand what they were saying. I'd caught the little devils in their scheme to nab a case of MRE. In a way, I felt bad for them. They were children of war and didn't know anything else. What a fucked-up existence.

A boy of maybe ten came closer. "*Kafira, ta pa Pakhto tsanga pohegi?*" he asked. "Infidel, how do you know Pashto?"

I smiled at him and took out a cigarette.

"*Ma ta cekrette dar ki.*" The boy asked for a cigarette.

I looked at this little man. "*Cekrette tsakawal to tah kha na di*," I said. "Smoking isn't good for you."

The boy kept begging. I handed him a cigarette.

"*Orlageet ra krah,*" he said.

"He's asking for a light," I translated.

Smitts took out his lighter and handed it to him. The boy lit the cigarette, took a few professional puffs, stuck Smitts' lighter in his pocket, and took off running.

The wait dragged on. At some point near dusk, the sound of evening prayer rose from the village. The village's dirt streets would soon be devoid of all activity, as I knew from the villages back in Iran. We broke out some MREs— meatballs, tuna, hamburger—and had our dinner as we waited for orders to move out. Kent and I stood outside the truck, quietly eating and watching the sunset. The sun's blood-red color stained the sky, the floating clouds, and the round moon on the horizon. The moment reflected the burden of all the souls who had fallen in this ancient battlefield. As the sun descended, so did the temperature. The cold breeze delivered the smell of freshly baked bread, *naan*, from the village. I am sure the scene would have been spectacular under different circumstances, but at that moment it felt lonely, desperate.

Kent put his food down and lit a cigarette. "That's the most brilliantly cheerless sunset I've ever seen. It's as if heaven is bleeding."

His words stopped me from eating. I guess I'd prejudged him as a simple, naive soldier. He'd proved me wrong. "What made you join the Marines?" I asked.

"Life on its own has no significance," he said as he took a drag. "It's what you choose to do with it that gives it meaning."

His words steered me deep into my own thoughts. What had I done with my own life?

Before long, orders came to move out. Everyone was relieved to hear those words. The convoy moved slowly, making its way through the village. The mud walls on either side of the narrow dirt road vibrated from the echoes of the rumbling engines and mufflers. I looked out the window at the dilapidated mud huts and shops. Most of the trees in the village had shrunk, dried up and died. Only a handful displayed some remnant of life. The convoy moved ever-so slowly through the village. Most of the trucks cleared the village on the other end. Ours was halfway through the village when the radio lid up. A truck ahead of us had lost control, run into a small mud-wood-and-tin shop, and flipped over on its side.

Our position couldn't be more precarious. We were sitting ducks stuck between the mud walls, boxed in from all sides. Half of the convoy had already gone through the village and the rest hadn't. It was the perfect opportunity for the Taliban to attack.

"Gunners keep 360," the commander barked on the radio.

By now male villagers had spilled onto the street, watching and snooping around. The situation got heated when the owner of the destroyed shop arrived on the scene, screaming and swearing at the Marines. Orders came on the radio for Kent to investigate and remedy the problem.

"Time to earn our paycheck, Sanj." Kent gestured for me to join him as he grabbed his M4.

I tightened my helmet chin strap.

"Shadow me," Kent said.

My nerves fired at a rapid pace. I jumped down and joined Kent. We squeezed past a few trucks on the downsloping dirt road until we got to the scene. What a mess. A truck's brakes had given out, and the vehicle had slammed into the mud-brick shop and overturned, destroying it. I looked around for any of the other three terps. I didn't see them in the dark crazed environment.

"Let's get the shop owner," Kent said. "We need to take a report. The military pays good money for any damages caused by coalition forces to locals or locally owned businesses."

Another Marine joined us to write the report. Kent ordered two more Marines to stay with me as I translated between the shop owner and the Marine taking the report. Around us the crowd swelled and tensions ran high. My fear mounted. I'd never been in such a life–or-death situation before. The thought of getting killed or, worse yet, kidnapped, mortified me. I remembered the Taliban's bounty on the linguists and their torture techniques. Immediately, I suppressed the fear and took a bold stance, however tentative.

The agitated crowd pressed in. We were getting sandwiched between all-male mobs. I juggled between translating and pushing the unruly crowd away from us. The Marines shoved back the angry wall of people, but there were just too many of them and not enough of us. I told the two Marines to keep an eye on the villagers' hands, especially the teenage boys, knowing they could easily shank us or even slit our throats in the dark, confused atmosphere.

My primal instincts were on fire, giving me a heightened state of awareness. I felt light on my feet and took inventory of everything around me. Never in my life had I experienced such a sensation. My abdominal muscles tightened, my biceps bulged, and my butt cheeks puckered as my balls retreated. My heart pounded, blood flowed through my veins with intensity, and my body felt on fire. My spine elongated, making me feel six feet tall. The circle around me and the three Marines tightened by the second.

"*Koor ta lar sha!*" I yelled at the crowd to go home with no success.

"*Kos madar, khar kos!*" The shop owner called me a motherfucker asshole for helping the infidels.

I wanted to punch him in the face and break his hooked nose just to shut him up. My fingers clenched into a fist, which felt strong as if made of concrete, but I knew one punch would end up costing lives. Instead, I grabbed the shop owner by his shirt and shoved him through a gap between two mud shops to separate him from the angry mob.

The three young Marines followed behind and guarded the opening.

"*Chop sha!*" I yelled at the shop keeper to shut up.

Instead, the man hit himself on the head.

"*Amrikayan sta tawan darkawi,*" I said, assuring him that the Americans would pay for his damages, trying to calm him down.

Finally Kent came back with a dozen Marines and took charge of the situation. Shafi accompanied the group. No sign of Ziar or Sami. Kent told Shafi to help with the report.

"Sanj, come with me," he said.

Back at the accident site, some of the Marines hooked the truck to an LVSR with chains. Their plan was to drag the truck on its side out of the village and then turn it right side up.

The hodgepodge content of the shop littered the narrow street: packs of biscuits, chips, canned foods, soap, hairbrushes, and batteries strewn all over. The little boys eagerly grabbed anything they could and disappeared in the dark.

Finally, the Marines finished hooking up the overturned truck and began pulling it away on its side. They hauled the truck out of the shop, further destroying what was left of it, but there was no other choice. I walked next to Kent, slowly chaperoning the procession outside the confines of the village, although villagers followed.

Once we cleared the village, another truck came over to help turn the heavy armored vehicle right side up.

The Marine taking the report handed the shop owner a slip to take to the nearest military base in order to collect monies for the damages.

Shafi walked over. "It was getting crazy," he said, smiling.

I nodded. Shafi walked back to his truck with a group of Marines. I looked at my watch: 0315 a.m. The ordeal had taken more than five hours to remedy.

The village became a ghost town as all the trucks in the convoy pulled out.

0424 HOURS / NOVEMBER 20, 2010

Inside the truck, we lit cigarettes. I still felt my Superman sensations at such an intense level that I finished my cigarette in four or five puffs and lit up another one.

Kent looked back. "Sanj, you rocked back there. Taking charge of the situation and the Marines, I'm impressed."

The recognition was priceless to me. My smile released my tense jaw muscles and the stiffness on my face.

"Yeah, Sanj, I was keeping an eye on you. You rocked," Smitts chimed in.

A tap on my helmet drew my eyes to Gospol's thumbs-up sign.

I sat quietly, sucked on my cigarette, and thought about what had just happened. The sense of pride and self-worth I felt was inestimable, especially the thumbs up affirmation from Gospol, a Marine who could have been my son's age if I had a son.

NOVEMBER 21, 2010

The following day passed without incident. We made it to FOB Edi late in the afternoon. I lifted myself off my seat to get a look at this place. Edi sat on a plateau with nothing around but barren land. Six-foot-high dirt berms surrounded its outer perimeter, while a few yards further in, dirt-filled hescos (burlap-lined wire containers of varying sizes used as perimeter fencing) offered a secondary layer of protection. Watchtowers accentuated the corners of the perimeter.

Orders came for all weapons to be emptied and magazines removed, even the mounted guns in the turrets, standard procedure for any convoy entering a base. We inched up to the FOB until all vehicles were inside the hesco corral area. Everyone dismounted and gathered around for roll-call. After that the Marines went to work, unloading the provisions for occupants of FOB Edi.

"Can I help with anything?" I asked Kent.

"Just relax, Sanj," he said.

I took off my gear and left it inside the truck, grabbed a Gatorade bottle, and walked over to a dirt pile and sat down. Shafi, Sami, and Ziar walked over. They planted themselves next to me. Shafi told Sami and Ziar about the village incident.

"How was it, dealing with Afghans?" Sami asked.

"Like dealing with any other people," I replied, even though I had mixed emotions about the locals. I didn't want to instigate a negative reaction. Besides, being the only Iranian there, I didn't want to be singled out amongst the terps. In this way I adopted the approach of telling other terps what they wanted to hear. Ziar tracked me with his beady eyes as I talked. I avoided eye contact.

Kent approached with another Marine. "This is Captain Holleran."

I got up, introduced myself, and shook hands. The other three stayed seated.

"Captain needs a volunteer to help with some translations," Kent said.

I looked over to the other three. This was their turf, after all. Instead, I saw three heads drop down, looking at the ground. None of them made eye contact with Kent or the Captain. This angered me.

"I'll go, sir," I said.

"Thank you," Captain Holleran said.

"This is my terp, Sanj," Kent said.

The Captain asked me to follow him. He, Kent and I began walking, but Holleran stopped short. "Sarge Kent, I need your terp *only*."

The Captain and I walked to another part of the FOB. I looked around as we walked through the uneven terrain, trying to get a read on the size of the place or the number of servicemen stationed there, but I couldn't. If I had to guess, the place was probably the size of six football fields stacked next to each other in two rows, and probably housed 300 to 400 personnel.

We walked by the helicopter LZ (landing zone) to a U-shaped formation of cargo containers. A small group of uniformed and plain-clothed personnel stood in front of one of the containers, talking. The Captain introduced me as the terp. I looked at the group and deduced that the plainclothes individuals were CIA or something similar. A couple of the guys had imposing physiques. As large as I had felt during the village incident, I now felt like a mouse in a herd of rhinos.

One of the plainclothes men extended his hand and introduced himself as George.

I doubted that was his real name. I took his hand. "Sanjar Rohām, Sanj for short."

At six-four, with brown hair and a scraggly beard, George looked like a WWE Wrestlemania star. He wore a sidearm strapped to each of his muscular thighs. The M4 slung over his left shoulder looked puny for his size.

He tilted his head toward the cargo container. "The person in there has disposed of his freedom. Once inside we will tell you the questions and you will translate exactly—nothing more, nothing less."

"Understood, sir," I said.

Both doors to the container were open. A dirty white sheet hung in the front like a curtain. Captain Holleran pulled the curtain aside, and all eight or nine of us entered. Lit by a weak lightbulb, the space inside felt different, cavernous. In the middle squatted a figure wrapped in a thick, gray, burlap blanket. Only the crown of his head was visible.

Not once but several times, George ordered the person to stand up.

Finally he rose, moving unhurriedly, and the blanket slowly slid off his body until it dropped on the floor. My heart sank when I saw what stood a short step away from me. Was it man or beast? I stood face-to-face with a figure at least six-feet six-inches tall but weighing no more than 140 or 150 pounds. He wore a white sheet around his crotch much like the ones sumo wrestlers wear, and nothing else. His ankles were shackled to the floor, as were the chains around his wrists. Wavy, dull, jet-black hair flowed past his shoulders and his black beard extended to the middle of his chest. His facial hair grew above his cheekbones to almost his eye sockets. The hair under his armpits hung down to the mid-ribcage section of his torso. Black, wavy hair covered his entire body.

I had a *Twilight Zone* moment, an out-of-body experience. Reality and nightmare became indistinguishable. I felt myself hover over the scene. My eyes traveled slowly from his feet to his eyes. The detainee's deep-set eyes, honey-colored and penetrating, slapped me back to reality. I'd never seen such a malignant stare.

George broke the silence. "You ready, Sanj?"

"Good to go, sir."

"Ask his name. His real name."

"*Naamet chist?*" I asked the prisoner in Dari. "*Naame asli.*"

He gave me a venomous smile. I asked the question again, this time with more force. "*NAAMET CHIST?*"

He smiled again. "*Na po*—" he said in Pashto. "Don't und—"

I cut him off before he could finish and asked the same question in Pashto. "*Sta noom tse deh?*"

The beast examined me closely, his eyes wide.

"Why does he carry six different ID cards?" George asked. "Where did he get the bomb-making material, the material in his car?"

"Can I see the ID cards?"

Another plainclothes handed me the cards. All had different names but the same picture. I informed the group of this, and they were astonished. They had had no idea. How could they? They couldn't read Pashto.

"Can I ask him why each card has a different name?" I asked George.

George nodded.

"*Waly shpag pezhand panhi da mokhtalef noom garzawi, da pa motar ki chawdendonki toki de la koma kral?*"

The beast looked at me and smiled again. The calcium buildup on his gray teeth looked like broken pieces of oyster shell. "*Ta mor ghoti, Pakhto la koma zda kari da?*" he said. "*Mor de da Taliban fahesha da aw plar za mong chai bacha woo?*"

I translated: "You motherfucker, where did you learn to speak Pashto? Is your mother a whore for the Taliban or your father a tea boy for us?" For the benefit of the observers I added, "In Afghan culture, a 'tea boy' is a boy or a young man designated to be sodomized by other men."

The beast took half a step forward, towering over me. "*De Kafirano ta waya taso ba yaw yaw wazhnam. Kala che da dway kar khalas kar, bia pohegam ta sara tse kawam,*" he said as he stroked his filthy beard.

I was unable to feel my legs under me. "Tell these infidels I will behead them one by one. I know what to do with you when I'm done with them." I translated.

But he wasn't finished. "*Sta maray da piano mazy kha da. Sta maray ba zana de charhe landy prey kegi, tar agho che sta maray prey kawam ta be azar zala marg pa stergo wawinay.*"

"Your neck is good for piano wire. Your white meat will slice open under my blade, you will die a thousand deaths before I slice your throat just enough for you to feel life flow out of your body."

A long moment of silence.

The creature looked every individual in the eyes and smiled savagely. "*Agha ta waya chi tasu de tolo sa'atuno malek yee. Kho mung tol wakhtuno laro.*"

"What's this shit-breath saying now?" asked one of the plainclothes men.

"He says you own all the watches, but we have all the time." I replied without taking my eyes off the beast.

Outside of the shipping container, I took out a cigarette and searched my pockets for matches. Captain Holleran flicked his lighter and lit my cigarette. My hands were unsteady. George noticed.

"Hey Sanj, don't let this get to you, brother," he said with unshakable confidence. "Now you know what kind of animals we're up against."

I looked at the group. "I'm sorry if I've let you down," I said with all sincerity.

They assured me I hadn't. "It's the nature of the beast we're dealing with," said one.

We stood there in silence for a minute, smoking.

"Keep this encounter strictly confidential," George said with a stern look. "Do not discuss it with anyone, not even your team."

Captain Holleran told the group I had volunteered to help them out. One by one they shook hands with me and thanked me for being a part of the fight.

The next couple of days at FOB Edi were spent unloading provisions and repairing mechanical issues with the trucks. I offered to help on multiple occasions, and got the same answer every time: "This is not a part of your job description."

Shafi, Sami, and Ziar hung out with the local terps and slept in their tent. I stayed close to my team and slept inside the frigid truck. Besides, rain began falling and I was a city boy; sleeping under a poncho in the damp cold was more than I'd bargained for. To add to that, the fear of Taliban sneaking up on us had a stranglehold on my imagination, especially after my encounter with the chained animal.

NOVEMBER 24, 2010

On the third day, the convoy commander summoned us four terps. This time he asked for a volunteer to fly back to Leatherneck on a helicopter to join Bravo Company on a mission. Two of Bravo Company's terps had reported in sick—a technique often used by terps any time they didn't want to go on a dangerous mission. Right away conversation broke out between Shafi, Sami, and Ziar. They didn't want to fly on a helicopter—they were afraid of getting shot down by a heat-seeking shoulder-mounted rocket fired from the ground.

It was true that helicopters made relatively easy targets for small arms fire and rockets. In the end, Shafi, Sami, and Ziar flat-out refused to fly. I stepped forward and volunteered.

Ziar giggled like a schoolgirl.

"Grab your gear and be at the LZ by 0200 hours," the commander instructed me.

Kent and Smitts walked up as I gathered my gear.

"We just heard you volunteered to fly back," Smitts said.

"Yeah," I replied as I grabbed my day bag. "Hope that's okay with you guys."

"We're gonna miss you," Smitts said sarcastically.

He and Kent helped me get my things together. We shook hands and they joined the other members of the convoy sitting around a bonfire in the muddy field.

I had a few hours till the flight, so I decided to check my emails, maybe send one to my family. A line of Marines and others had gathered ahead of me at the MWR tent. I put my name on the waiting list and sat outside in the chilled air and lit up again.

It was completely dark outside by the time I left the computer tent. Lights were rare on Edi at night, making it very difficult to find my way around the unfamiliar grounds. I didn't have a flashlight and wandered blindly in the dark until I ran into the short Marine who had let me use the back of his truck as my personal lavatory. He had a flashlight and offered to walk me to the LZ.

It was 1205 when I entered the flight room and checked in. I had at least a two-hour wait ahead of me, and unfortunately there were no waiting area tents in FOB Edi. Passengers waiting for flights had to hang outside in the elements until their flight arrived. To keep warm, I packed myself into a corner of a bench placed between some sand-bags near a group of eight or ten Marines who traded stories as they waited for the same flight. I looked up at the cloudless sky. The constellations shined brightly on the black velvet canvas. Too bad I didn't know their names. Nights in the Afghan desert are brilliantly beautiful in contrast with the evil that lurked in the dark just beyond the couple of dirt mounds that separated us from it. The faint, eerie barking of dogs came from some distance away. The wind picked up. The chill in the air banded with my imagination and sent shivers down my spine. I zipped my fleece all the way up to my nose and pulled my Marine beanie low on my forehead to keep my hairless head warm. Closing my eyes, I daydreamed of the good things back home. My family, my cozy place.

Minutes ticked away like hours. 0200 hours came and went: no flight. My toes were frozen, and I couldn't feel my nose.

Finally, at 0530 a Marine came out of the flight room, "The bird is inbound." He pointed to a white line on the ground. "Line up on the stripe and wait for my signal. Put on your helmet and flak before boarding."

The sound of thumping helicopter rotors reverberated in the darkness. In the blink of an eye, a CH-53 swooped in out of nowhere and landed a few yards away from us. It was hard to stand in the turbulence of the powerful rotors that made the cold night even colder. The tailgate of the bird was open. A group of Marines poured out, carrying their gear.

We formed a single file and boarded the big bird. It was exhilarating. First the C-130, and now this. I looked at my Marine companions and envied their youth and experience. A sliver of sunlight cut through the thick blanket of night as I buckled in. I surveyed the helicopter. It contained three M134 guns, one on either side behind the pilot compartment and one mounted on the floor of the open tailgate. The gunners' helmets had skulls painted on them, giving them a menacing look; they reminded me of the alien in *Predator*. The tailgate gunner sat on a small camping-style folding stool behind his gun. A cable anchored him to the floor to keep him from falling out since the tailgate would stay open. Oil drops on my pants got my attention. I looked up and saw fluid dripping, which concerned me.

The Marine next to me elbowed me. "You should worry if oil *isn't* dripping. That's when you know you're in real trouble."

Apparently, no leakage meant no hydraulic fluids, which meant trouble.

The heavy bird took to the skies. The sun peaked through as we gained altitude. The open tailgate provided a bird's-eye view of the land. The sun climbed from behind the mountains and banished the secrets that fell on this land at every sunset. My unobstructed view of the farmlands and clusters of green trees that broke the monotonous khaki theme of the arid landscape was spectacular, but the imposing vastness of the harsh backdrop served as a sobering reminder that *I was not in charge*.

Much to my surprise, we were in flight for some time before we got to Bastion I. Once outside the airport, I looked around to find my ride. No one was there to collect me. I walked over to the bus stop and waited. An hour passed. Other soldiers got picked up by their units while I waited. At one point I thought of walking to Leatherneck, but quickly changed my mind. The walk from the airfield would take a good hour, plus I had no idea if walking was even permitted from the airfield.

A few Marines walked up to the bus stop, dropped their gear on the ground and lit up cigarettes. My stomach growled. I had starved myself to get rid of the diarrhea situation. A van drove up after a few minutes, and the Marines next to me piled in. The van pulled away and stopped after a few yards.

The Marine in the passenger seat opened his door. "Where're you going?" he asked.

"CLB compound," I said.

He signaled me to jump in.

The Marines dropped me off by my team's compound. I thanked them for the ride and walked over to the tent housing my POC to report in.

When I entered, I saw Lt. Laramy. "Hello, Lieutenant," I said with a smile.

She greeted me with a stiff-lipped nod.

5
AUTUMN OF HOPE

0729 HOURS / NOVEMBER 25, 2010

The mile-long walk from the compound to my tent served as a sort of decompression. I threw my day pack on top of my bunkbed and laid down for a few minutes. The quietness of the tent felt good. After a short time, I grabbed my shower gear and headed to the shower tent. The tent was empty. I went into one of the cubicles, wet myself down, shampooed, soaped my body, and jerked off. Shooting the load deflated my tense muscles like a punctured tire and released the high-revving tension left over from my first time outside the wire.

After a nice cold shower in the wintry weather I put on my civilian clothes and walked over to Bastion I for coffee and donuts. I had about sixteen hours before going on my second mission. The hot coffee and English-style jam-filled donut hit the spot.

Unhurriedly, and after having indulged in two rounds of coffee and donuts, I headed to the USO, checked my emails, and called my family—especially my mom—to reassure them I was okay. The movie in the USO large screen TV theater room had just begun: *From Paris with Love*, a John Travolta action flick. The bulky, tattered leather sofa had my name on it, so I took it. A few soldiers and Marines watched the movie absorbedly. They cheered every time Travolta kicked ass or killed someone, which was almost every minute of the movie.

I left the USO feeling exhausted, not from the movie but the pressure of my first mission. My first time out had exposed me to the high levels of physical and mental stresses exerted on a person in a war zone. Back in my tent I hit the sack for some much needed shuteye. The hard mattress felt like a cloud compared to my makeshift MATV seat-bed of the past few nights.

It was dinnertime when I woke up. I got my gear ready, put my uniform on, and headed to the chow hall for a bite. The diarrhea situation, though, worried me. The chow hall was decorated for the day of giving thanks and was bursting at the seams with patrons. I had completely lost track of time. The mood inside was festive and energized. Depending on the day of the week, the main chow hall offered steak, hamburger, grilled chicken, and a few different kinds of Indian foods—tandoori chicken, naan and lentil—and on occasion crab legs or even lobster, albeit miniature. Not on this day, however. This was turkey day. The high brass had traded their rank for aprons. They stood behind the food counters and served turkey meals to everyone with a smile and a warm welcome. I grabbed some turkey, mashed potatoes, gravy, and cranberry sauce. The terps who had claimed to be ill were hanging out in the chow hall, laughing and gorging themselves. So much for being sick.

At around midnight I grabbed my gear and, deciding not to wait for the minibus, began walking toward the compound staging area. Once there I checked to see which vehicle I'd been assigned to. Much to my surprise, it was the convoy commander's vehicle, a 4x4 MRAP, or Mine-Resistant Ambush Protected—a much bigger and roomier truck than the MATV I'd ridden in on my first mission. The convoy commander was Lt. Maddox, a female.

With gear in hand I climbed in through the open rear gate of the MRAP. The two female Marines inside were busy getting the truck prepared, one setting up the turret gun while the other worked on the radio frequencies. They both stopped to give me a *"Who the fuck are you?"* look.

"I've been assigned to ride with Lt. Maddox," I said. "I'm the terp."

"I'm Cpl. Whipple," said the blonde Marine working on the radio. She was wearing gloves with cutout fingertips, and looked like the outdoorsy type from a small Midwest town.

"I'm Sgt. Moore," said the brunette in the turret. She wore her green Marine T-shirt and no fleece even though the temperature outside was uncomfortably cold, and ignored the goosebumps on her toned arms as she got the rooftop gun ready. She seemed street-smart, edgy. Maybe from the inner city. "You're Sanj, the Hollywood guy," Moore said.

With a nod and a smile I asked, "Can I help with anything?"

My question came as a surprise to the two Marines.

"Terps usually don't offer to help," Whipple said.

"I'm the new and improved version," I replied.

Both cracked a smile.

"Can you pass the ammo boxes?" Moore asked.

I handed her the ammo boxes for the M240 machine gun mounted in the turret, then Whipple pointed to a haphazardly placed pile of objects. "You can arrange the MRE, water cases, and everyone's gear for easy access."

"Yes. ma'am." I took the orders and got to work. As I worked, I observed my new team members. They couldn't be more than twenty-one or twenty-two years old. Both had their hair pulled back in tight buns. Both were in great shape and physically strong. They worked with poise and undivided concentration as they handled the weaponry and communication devices. It was hard to hide my smile because I felt like a wimp next to them. Either one could drop-kick my ass and not break a sweat.

Then another female Marine climbed on board. She looked at me.

"Is he the terp?" she asked the other two.

Moore and Whipple replied yes.

"I'm Sanjar Rohām, Ma'am."

"I'm Lt. Maddox. You're Sanj, the terp from Hollywood. I remember you from the briefing when Sarge Kent introduced you."

I smiled.

Maddox smiled back. "Just remember this isn't Hollywood."

Maybe they all thought I was some kind of haughty douchebag.

Maddox's smile was friendly but unyielding. She had to be in her early thirties, slenderly-built with mousy-brown hair, brown, methodical eyes and a few freckles on her face. I noticed her hands: they were rough, as if she'd been doing manual labor. She shared some of Laramy's mannerisms: confident, poised, no-nonsense. Maybe because they were both lieutenants. Whatever the case, these women were impressive.

0217 HOURS / NOVEMBER 26, 2010

After roll-call and weapons check we geared up, and got on board our trucks. We followed the same protocol as a few days earlier: a slow crawl through Leatherneck and Camp Bastion, wait at the gates for clearance, then out. Thankfully, this time I had more room and could stretch out my legs.

Our destination was Shir-Ghazi, a small FOB manned by the Marines and the Georgian military (Georgia of the former Soviet Republic, now the country).

We got to Highway 1 and drove on the paved road for five kilometers before veering off-road into the desert.

"Have you been to Shir-Ghazi?" Maddox asked.

"No, Ma'am, this is my second mission."

"By the way, thanks for volunteering and flying back from Edi." Maddox turned and looked at me.

"No need to thank me, Lieutenant," I replied. "I go where I'm directed."

Maddox nodded. "Let me brief you a bit about where we're going. Shir-Ghazi is nasty. The Georgians suffer daily casualties there." She locked eyes with me.

"The Georgians are crazy reckless," Whipple, who drove the big truck, added. "They don't observe the coalition's rules of engagement, but they're good fighters."

Moore dropped down from the turret. "Be ready for some action."

I got the feeling I was being tested by my courageous companions. So I recounted the ambush from a few days earlier just to let the women know I was no rose petal.

"You don't look like the rest of the terps, Sanj," Maddox said as she turned around in her seat. "Your English is much better, too."

Initially, Maddox looked a bit uncomfortable about my Iranian background as I gave her a quick rundown of my profile, but that quickly dissipated when we exchanged opinions and outlooks about the region and its history. For the most part, Whipple and Moore just listened.

We rolled slowly across the desert. The sun came up lazily, giving slow warmth to the outside temperature.

"Breakfast, anyone?" I asked.

They all nodded and placed their orders. I passed the MRE boxes out and took a hamburger MRE for myself, praying I wouldn't get hit with backdoor trots again. It would be very embarrassing in front of the women. The so-called hamburger looked and smelled like paté-style cat food, but smothering it with the barbecue sauce included in the packet awakened its flavor. It was actually tasty, I must admit.

We reached the outskirts of a small village by midday and had to stop due to engine problems with one of the trucks. Everyone was on high alert. The village was a mere cluster of 20 or 30 mud-brick dwellings, a mundane community in the middle of nowhere inhabited by peoples left behind by the rest of the world. Ditches lined the wide dirt path leading to the village. They provided good hiding places for the enemy, I thought in my civilian mind. I endeavored to teach myself how to spot potential crises each step of the way. It could be the difference between life and death.

As we waited, a call came on the radio: "Person walking toward the convoy, ignoring warnings and the dazzler."

"Dazzler" is a green laser light used to temporarily blind a target. Afghans were horrified by it because it was the last warning by U.S. forces before the use of deadly force.

Lt. Maddox got on the radio. "Who's the person?"

"Possibly a female, hard to tell 'cause of the burqa," the voice on the radio replied.

It could very well have been a man under the burqa. Maybe a suicide bomber or a trap.

"Eyes on 360," Maddox said on the radio, then ordered Whipple: "Drive up the column."

We edged slowly up until our truck came face-to-face with the figure under the burqa.

"Keep your gun on the subject, neutralize if necessary," Maddox told Moore. "C'mon, Sanj," Maddox said as she racked her sidearm. She handled the weapon with ease and composure.

The tension in the truck was palpable. My heart raced ahead of me.

Maddox dismounted from the passenger door up front, and me from the back gate. Three male Marines were already on deck, holding their positions on the sides of their armored vehicles with weapons trained on the subject. Maddox and I stood about ten yards away from the person.

"Tell her not to move," Maddox directed me to say.

"*Harakat ma kawa*," I said in Pashto.

The person stopped.

"Ask her what she wants," Maddox said.

"*Tse ghuwari?*"

The person took a few steps forward. I heard weapons cock. Maddox put her hand on the Sig M18 pistol attached to her flak chestplate.

The person stopped and slowly lifted the blue burqa, exposing her face. She raised her hands in the air. "*Marasti ta ertia laram.*"

"She needs help," I translated.

"Tell her to turn around," Maddox said.

"*Wogarzah*," I ordered the young woman.

She heeded my order and slowly turned 360 degrees.

Maddox gestured for me to walk up to the girl with her. We moved slowly, my gaze monitoring the ditches for any movement. As we approached the young woman, it hit me: she had unveiled her face to male infidels, a major taboo. In hyper-male-dominant cultures, a woman exposing her face to men outside the immediate family carries severe punishment. When we were a few short feet away from her, I quickly analyzed her. She couldn't have been more than sixteen or seventeen years old. There was a grippingly beautiful, yet hauntingly sad, quality about her, with her unwashed skin and gentle face adorned with pain. Her tear-filled eyes reminded me of my most coveted boyhood possessions, my colored marbles: a mixture of gray, green, and gold.

Before I could ask anything, the girl began talking, and talking fast.

"*Ta bayad qarar qarar khabari ki, poshui?*" I said. "You must speak slowly, understand?"

The girl stopped talking.

"What does she want?" Maddox asked.

"*Sta noom tse de, moong te tsang ta marastah kwaley shu?*" I asked. "What's your name, how can we help you?"

"*Zma noom Hila de,*" she said.

"Her name is Hila. It means 'hope' in Pashto." I translated.

"I was forced to marry an evil man from another village a few months ago, but I want to divorce him." Hila wiped away tears as she spoke. "I want you to take me away from this village, help me get away from him, from this life of misery."

Maddox listened intently as I translated Hila's request.

"We have no authority to help you get a divorce. That is the village elders' job," I said to Hila. In village culture, the elders oversee all internal affairs of their community and acted as mediator, judge, and jury among the villagers.

Hila persisted, begging us to help her.

"Ask her why she wants a divorce," Maddox said.

I did.

"My husband lives in another village; he is a Talib," Hila said as she wept.

The word "Talib" got my attention, so I asked Hila to tell me everything in full detail.

Maddox was getting impatient.

"Take a more relaxed posture to make the girl at ease," I told Maddox. "She could have useful intel, her husband is a Taliban."

Maddox's posture changed right away.

"Tell me your story," I said to Hila.

"I am forbidden by him to leave the one room I live in. I am a prisoner. My husband has a boy." Hila looked down. Teardrops fell from her long eyelashes and quenched the parched earth, kicking up small plumes of moondust. "My husband's boy is not his son. He is a nine-year-old concubine."

That didn't come as a surprise to me. Sodomy is a part of daily life in the Kandahar region. Growing up in Iran, I had heard stories about Kandahar and its reputation for man-to-boy and man-to-man sexual associations. The main contributing factor to this interaction came from illiteracy. Religious restrictions propagandized by superstition forbade relations between men and unmarried or single women, and this led to male-to-male or even male-to-beast coupling.

"My husband only couples with me from behind and brutalizes me in the act," she said, ashamed.

Maddox must have noticed the look on my face. "What did she just say?"

Anguish displayed on Maddox's face as I translated the words. She took a few seconds to collect her thoughts, then told me to translate: "There's nothing we can do for her. We're not allowed to get involved in such issues."

I could tell she hated saying those words. No amount of training could prepare a soldier for something like this.

"All we can do is to take her name and pass it on to the FETs," Maddox's voice shook. "They can check on her from time to time."

FETs are Female Engagement Teams designed to engage local women and children. FETs are tasked with providing basic healthcare needs for women and children, in addition to conducting physical searches of women in cultures where male personnel are forbidden from interacting with the female population.

I translated Maddox's words for Hila. I felt helpless, much like Maddox did, but there was absolutely nothing either of us could do.

Hila didn't lift her face. The shame she felt from disclosing such intimate information to the infidels, especially a male stranger, must have been devastating. A feeling of despair consumed me. I reached inside my pocket and took out a bunch of Afghani, the Afghan money, and a couple of $20 bills. I put the money in Hila's hand. Maybe I was hoping she would use the money to get away from the village.

Hila looked up. There was an unwavering look in her tear-washed eyes as they reflected the light of the afternoon sun.

"Where do infidels look when they pray to their God?" she asked.

"Where do you look, outlander?"

Slowly I pointed to the sky.

Maddox watched me closely.

"Is there more than one God up there?" Hila asked.

A few long, silent, and uncomfortable seconds passed. Maddox gestured to walk back to the truck. We took a few slow steps backward, looking at Hila and then at each other, then turned and walked back to our truck.

Hila stood alone in the middle of the dirt road. I watched her through the rear window as we drove away until she became a blue speck in the distance and eventually disappeared in the desert mirage. Life had robbed Hila of her smile, and fate had embezzled her of her youth. She symbolized the suffering women experienced daily in this merciless, male-dominated land. Nevertheless, at the same time she signified bravery, strength, and determination. Her predicament reminded me of my great-grandmother, who lived to the age of 101. In the 1880s she had been married off at the age of nine to a forty-four-year-old successful merchant. At thirteen she became a mother—and a widow when a sniper's bullet found her husband's heart as he walked on the beach in Baku. By the time she was eighteen, she was widowed twice over and had three children.

Our team was introspective for the rest of the trip. The rocking of the truck put me to sleep. I had one arm resting on the gear and the other under my chin, supporting my head.

A jolt followed by a scream woke me up.

"Oh, fuck!" Moore shrieked from the turret.

Liquid ran down my helmet and the side of my face, dribbling from my chin. I automatically looked up, then had to do a double-take to make sure my eyes weren't deceiving me.

Moore stood in the turret, frozen, with her pants at mid-thigh level. A Gatorade bottle squeezed horizontally between her thighs as she relieved herself.

Maddox and Whipple stared at me, looking shocked as they tried to hold back nervous smiles. Apparently we had hit a bump just as Moore relieved herself in the Gatorade bottle, and I was the recipient of an unsolicited golden shower—in Afghanistan of all places.

I had a split-second to decide how to react. Moore stood frozen in place, her face washed in a look of *Fuck, I can't believe what just happened.* Urine dripped from my chin, bead by bead.

I smiled. "Grape flavor," I said, and reached up and gently pulled the Gatorade bottle from between Moore's thighs. I opened the back gate, dumped the contents out and handed the bottle back to Moore, who still stood frozen with her pants down.

My companions' faces flushed with embarrassment, especially Moore's. Whipple held out a pack of baby wipes.

"So that's how it's done," I said, swabbing my face with the wipes. "I'm glad this was a rainstorm and not a mudslide."

The women tried hard to stifle their laughter, but were unsuccessful.

1643 HOURS / NOVEMBER 27, 2010

The rest of the trip to Shir-Ghazi went smoothly—no ambushes or shootouts with the enemy. Shir-Ghazi was a dump of a place in the middle of nowhere—which, by the way, could be said about almost all our bases in Afghanistan. Berms of dirt formed its perimeter. In some areas, hesco barriers stood guard between the occupants of the camp and the bloodthirsty enemy beyond. The topography of the camp was uneven; it sloped upward at about a 20-degree angle from the front gate to the back. Like all FOBs, Shir-Ghazi had two gates on opposite ends of the camp.

In contrast with the Marines stationed at Shir-Ghazi, the Georgian soldiers were somewhat unfriendly, maybe because they didn't speak much English, or maybe they didn't want to be there. Who could blame them? They took heavy losses on an almost daily basis. The Georgians lacked proper weaponry and equipment to combat the enemy. So, our military provided the them the same gear as the Marines used to fight the Taliban and their persecutors that infested and controlled the surrounding area. The Georgians fought hard and died hard. They killed and got killed. The Taliban were so brazen that at night they crawled up to less than a thousand yards of the camp and planted IEDs in the path of outgoing or incoming patrols.

We got our convoy situated and Lt. Maddox went to meet with the

Marine camp commandant. She came back after an hour and ordered the cargo unloaded. The Marines didn't waste a moment getting to work.

To get a better read on the place, I took myself on a solo sightseeing tour. The camp looked shoddily put together—no toilets and no showers, just two dozen or so tents. A big hole in the ground acted as a burn pit, for all the trash and human refuse. The pit burned 24/7—it looked like a crater from a massive explosion. A stack of thick black smoke billowed constantly from its foul-smelling depths. A makeshift field toilet sat next to the burn pit for easy shitbag disposal. The outdoor shower stalls were made of plywood. An overhead bucket served as the water reservoir, and a thick, dirty piece of plastic functioned as the shower curtain. The soldiers used bottled water to fill the ten-gallon reservoir bucket above. The ground provided a natural drainage system for the runoff, with mud up to your ankles. It's hard to imagine how anyone could feel clean after taking a shower there. Furthermore, the base had no hot water for showering, and in wintertime, the desert temperature dropped to low forties. The conditions were wretched. A constant stream of injured Georgian soldiers and destroyed or damaged vehicles flowed into the camp. Medevac helicopters picked up the injured like clockwork.

By dinnertime, the Marines had finished unloading the cargo. Maddox, Whipple, Moore, and I sat in the back of the MRAP eating our MRE dinner. Maddox sat across from me. We were bundled up, trying to keep warm. The only element missing was a small campfire. Moore covered the tactical lantern with a T-shirt to dampen its sharp glow. The subtle ambience and my three female companions reminded me of the night I had had dinner with my lover Sophie and two other friends, Sarah and Justine. There I sat, in the dimly lit, upscale Boa steakhouse on Sunset Boulevard in West Hollywood sipping a glass of Caymus Cabernet Sauvignon, miserable and at war with myself, listening to Sarah and Justine complain about the improperly butterflied steak—Boa, a place where decadence was on full display; a place where the tempting aroma of pricey aged flesh burning on the grill drifted from the kitchen and mixed with the assorted scents of perfumes emanating from the patrons.

And now here I sat in a dimly lit, frigid steel cage in the middle of a war zone, at peace with myself as I dined with three female warriors on the contents of an MRE bag that emanated a downright pugnacious aroma. Life's duality was on full display, partly in memory and partly right in front of me. Back in L.A., Sarah and Justine had chatted feverishly about how the yarmulkas had to be studded with actual cubic zirconia for their upcoming wedding. Here, Whipple and Moore discussed how to save mere dollars from their meager salaries for a financially-secure future. Back there, I'd had to maintain my image at any cost, especially in front of "friends" like Sarah who spread rumors as easily as she spread her legs, even though I was nearly bankrupt. Here, no one gave a shit about my image as long as I did what I was hired to do.

Whipple and Moore dined with such appetite that one would think they were dining at a Michelin Star restaurant. They ate with their hands and used their sleeves as napkins. Maddox was more refined; she took small bites and chewed the food slowly. The similarity between the two circumstances was eerie. Both Hollywood and Helmand are enemy-infested viper dens. The sensation of sitting in the company of three strong and independent women in a land where women are considered weak and get treated as property was splendid.

Thoughts of Sophie and our last wordless conversation emerged from forgotten memory. We'd had nothing to say after she found out I was deploying. I felt guilty for not missing her. But then again, I suffer from gamophobia, a commitment disorder.

Maddox and I listened to Whipple and Moore. We exchanged a glance and faint smiles that faded quickly. It wasn't hard for us to read the other's mind.

Hila.

0600 HOURS / NOVEMBER 30, 2010

We left Shir-Ghazi for Leatherneck in the early morning after having spent three days there, and none too soon. Everyone in the convoy felt uneasy. We knew IEDs waited for us just outside the gates. The convoy pulled out through the rear gate and crept forward methodically to identify and avoid IEDs. It took us nearly four hours to clear a distance of approximately ten or twelve miles, thankfully without any incident.

Maddox turned to me as we approached the village where we had met Hila a few days earlier. "We should check on Hila," she said as she got on the radio, "Stop the convoy at the spot we met the burqa."

I didn't expect to see Hila there. Another chance encounter was highly unlikely, if not impossible. The village appeared unusually quiet for the late afternoon, as if time had stopped. Generally, kids played outside or sat by their mud huts, but not today. The small village looked abandoned and ghostly. Even the flying birds had gone missing from the skies, and the dirt road was empty save for one old leather-skinned man sitting alone on the side of the path.

"Pull up to him," Maddox told Whipple, and gestured for me to join her.

I felt uneasy. The wintry bitter wind picked up, kicking up moondust all around. We walked up to the old man, a relic from years of unending hardship, war, and tortured existence.

"Ask the old man if he knows Hila," Maddox said to me.

Showing respect to the old man, I addressed him as "father." "Good afternoon, father, long life," I said in Pashto, putting my hand on my heart, a sign of respect and sincerity. "We are looking for a young woman. Hila. Do you know her?"

The old man didn't respond, so I asked again.

He looked up from his squatted position and slowly shook his head. A few long seconds passed, then he said, "The girl who spoke to the infidels a few days ago?"

"Yes, her name is Hila," I replied excitedly.

The old man lowered his head slowly, moving it from side to side. "Some children found her beheaded body," the old man said, pointing to the ditch next to him. "Here. Right here."

My heart shattered and sank deep in my chest as I translated for Maddox.

Her jaw tightened and her face washed with agony. "Ask if he knows who killed her."

I did.

"Who do you think?" the old man said in a fragile, wheezing voice. "Her husband is a Talib; either someone told him about the encounter or he saw it himself." The old man pointed to the site. "Here. Right here. They found her here. She will have no more tomorrows. His voice quivered. *"Hagha zama lemasy wu."*

"She was his granddaughter." I took a couple of steps over to the ditch.

Maddox stood next to me and we both looked into the ditch. Maddox looked at me. The tip of her nose turned red as she tried to hold back the tears gathering in her brown eyes. We shared a moment of personal ruination between us.

"This is the land of broken souls, waiting to die," Maddox whispered under her breath.

0545 HOURS / DECEMBER 19, 2010

At Leatherneck, the big chow hall was unusually quiet. I checked in and walked over to the counter to get my usual breakfast of two boiled eggs and oatmeal.

"Mark! Over here. Over here, Mark!" someone called.

I turned to see what the commotion was about and came face-to-face with Mark Wahlberg. We smiled at each other, but he was whisked away by his crew before I could say anything. He was there to boost the morale of the troops, and I have to admit that seeing him there buoyed my spirits, reconnecting me with home.

0835 HOURS / DECEMBER 25, 2010 / CHRISTMAS EVE

Camp Leatherneck brimmed with personnel from all over the southern region. Anyone and everyone who could get a pass to come to the base to celebrate the holiday had done so. A celebratory mood took over as crate after crate of care packages from family and charitable organizations poured into the base. Soldiers and contractors took their favorite items from the care packages sent by relatives and left the rest of the items for others; this is how the system worked, and everyone got something they needed.

As usual, on the next mission the other terps reported in sick to avoid going beyond the wire. The destination this time was FOB Dwyer—another place with a bad reputation for death and dying. The other terps wanted to partake in the festivities and the big Christmas meals, but dreaded working in Dwyer, smack in the middle of a vast area of Taliban-controlled villages. Most terps assigned there either quit or got reassigned. I volunteered for the mission.

This time, however, our cargo was a two-pack of high brass. Normally the higher-ups traveled by helicopter, but from time to time they hitched a ride to get some action and boost morale. That's where the logistic team came in. We served as chauffeurs of a sort.

At about 1014 hours we went through the roll-call-and-weapons-check routine. Everyone mounted up, and off we went. Again, I was assigned to the convoy commander truck, Lt. Briggs. It was a 6x6 MRAP that also carried our two VIP clients, Marine Lieutenant General Jaxon and Marine Full Colonel Kendall. The convoy was small, only ten trucks. We left rather early for our mission instead of at the usual 0200 hours. I assumed our cargo had a lot to do with the timing of our departure.

Soon we veered off the paved road and onto desert terrain. Lieutenant General Jaxon took off his helmet and set it next to him. In his mid-sixties, black, with a salt–and-pepper flattop haircut, Jaxon was built like a tank, and his demeanor personified a leader in every sense of the word.

"Where's your ribbon, son?" Jaxon asked me.

He spoke softly yet with a commanding tone of voice.

"Wish I could say I'm a Marine, sir," I replied. "I'm a terp."

"Hold up," Kendall said. White, mid-fifties, he looked more like a CPA than a soldier. A Brainiac. From the way he wore his uniform it was evident that he was a detail-oriented kind of a man.. "You're th—"

"Sanj." I interrupted the Colonel.

"Don't tell me you volunteered for this mission," Kendall said.

A smile and a slight nod was my response.

Jaxon smiled and gave me the A-okay sign.

2307 HOURS / DECEMBER 27, 2010

We spent the three hours trying to get an LVSR out of the bomb crater it had fallen into. The young Marine driver had dozed off and driven the heavy truck into the deep pit.

"Pull up to the crater," Briggs told Corporal Martinez, who was driving our MRAP.

"Sirs, buckle up, we're pulling out of formation," Briggs said. "Melfi, hang on tight," he told the gunner in the turret.

BOOM. The reverberation from the earth-shattering, eardrum-piercing explosion coming from under my truck shook my internal organs and wracked my brain. We'd hit an IED. I felt the force and pressure of the blast under my boots as its kinetic energy travelled through the protective armored skin of the truck, lifting the passenger side of the weighty MRAP. Time slowed down. Everyone held on tight. The truck teetered on the driver-side tires. Lt. General Jaxon grabbed Melfi from his belt and yanked him down from the turret to the floor in one quick, strong move. After a few long seconds of hovering on three wheels, the truck dropped back down, right-side up.

Kendall, Jaxon, and I exchanged startled looks.

"You okay, Melfi?" Briggs called out.

Melfi's face was pale white. "All good, sir," he said in a shaky voice. He knew he would have been crushed if the truck had flipped over. It was by the grace of God that we'd landed right-side up. Briggs decided to break the convoy up in two. A portion would continue to Dwyer with our VIPs, and the rest stay behind until other LVSRs could be dispatched to pull the massive machine out of the crater and tow away our disabled truck.

Since I was the only terp on the convoy, Briggs transferred me to a MATV to stay behind.

0351 HOURS / DECEMBER 29, 2010

We stayed in place for two days with no sign of rescue: all LVSRs were either out on missions or out of service. Everyone was on edge. Our four-vehicle convoy was a flock of sitting ducks, not to mention Briggs' blown-up truck and the LVSR in the ditch. We were vulnerable against RPG attacks or an on-foot onslaught by a merciless enemy. We knew we were being watched. Maybe the enemy thought we were laying a trap for them, and so they should; our side did employ this tactic to draw out the enemy.

"Hey Sanj," Cpl. Bostos said from the turret.

"Hit me," I said.

"Got more smokes?"

I pulled a pack of Marlboro Lights from my bag and gave it to him.

"Keep the pack, I have plenty more."

"Thanks, bro." Bostos smiled. "It's fuckin' freezing, man."

The night-time temperatures dipped into the low 30s. We used the food warmer packs from the MRE meals to give us a few minutes of warmth. Ordinarily, you wouldn't be able to keep one in your hand because of how hot it got. But this was no ordinary time. The weather was so cold that we wrapped our hands around the boiling packets and still didn't feel anything.

"Stay in your vic," a voice said on the radio. "A pack of Kuchi dogs is surrounding us."

Kuchi Afghan Shepherd dogs, fighting dogs, are oftentimes massive in size. The male Kuchi can weigh 170 pounds or more. They are bred for protecting nomads and their herd of sheep, goats, and camels from wolves and large predatory cats. They roamed in packs and did not hesitate to attack people.

The small porthole provided me with a tight shot of the landscape. The red lights reflecting from the dogs' eyes seemed to look straight at me. The hounds of hell were on the prowl, and evil wasn't far behind. Even from the safety of the armored trucks, the presence of the dogs was nerve-racking.

1013 HOURS / DECEMBER 31, 2010 / NEW YEAR'S EVE

The rescue convoy finally showed up with two LVSRs. Relieved, the Marines went to work and after multiple attempts pulled the downed LVSR from the crater.

0127 HOURS / JANUARY 01, 2011

We got back to Camp Leatherneck, exhausted—mostly due to the cold weather we'd endured. The remnants of the New Year celebrations still continued on the base. All I wanted was a shower.

0243 HOURS / JANUARY 10, 2011

Another small convoy left through the gates of Leatherneck accompanied by our counterpart, the Afghan National Army, or ANA. Our mission was twofold: deliver provisions to Kandahar Air Field, KAF, and in the process train the ANA in logistics. The other terps on my team had it easy. Outbound teams now requested me even when I didn't volunteer for a mission. So my terp mates stayed in the safety of the base, ate hot meals, played games, napped, and socialized while I exposed myself to great harm outside the wire in harsh winter conditions. At first, I was bothered by the underhanded behavior of the other terps to the point that I decided to take it up with Global Vigilance's site manager. My mind changed quickly. The battalion had placed great responsibility on my shoulders by entrusting me with their lives, and I had to reciprocate and protect them with mine. This sense of duty pushed me to the razor's edge; my commitment to the warriors kept me there.

A torrential downpour made the terrain like Nutella: thick and sticky, slowing our progress. The inside of the MATV felt like a freezer even though the heater was on full blast. It felt even colder for me since I was sitting under the turret and therefore received a constant pounding by the rain. I'd made a hole in a black trash bag and pulled it over myself to keep dry and sustain at least some body heat.

"Sarge," a male voice said on the staticky radio.

"Send it," Kent responded.

"ANA truck stuck in mud. Need terp and tow."

We pulled out of formation and moved up the column. Tensions ran high in the truck. The soft, muddy terrain acted as a double-edged sword: it could make an IED more sensitive, or it could make it a dud. Nevertheless, it was unnerving.

Kent looked at me and smiled. "Hey, bagman. Let's take a shower."

I ripped the trash bag off, jumped out into the pouring rain and joined Kent. We immediately got drenched. The weight of our sodden uniforms and flak vests doubled as we walked in ankle-deep mud to the downed truck. Every step required pulling our feet up and out of the mud.

Six Afghan soldiers were hooking chains from one Afghan truck to another.

"You need help?" I asked the Afghans in Dari.

"Thank you, we are good," replied one of the young Afghans with a big smile.

Kent and I stood watching over them. The truck was hitched after twenty or so minutes.

"Tell 'em not to move until everyone is off the deck," Kent told me to tell the Afghans.

I relayed the message, but maybe the Afghans had waterlogged ears. Their tow truck began moving while Kent and I were still on deck. A thunderous blast struck us from behind, knocking us face down into the mud. A strong taste of copper materialized in my mouth. The towed truck had rolled over an IED. Bewildered and disoriented, we managed to pull oursleves out of the muck. It took a minute before we realized we were okay. Kent cracked a smile at me. My jaw muscles were numb as if injected with lidocaine, but I managed to force a smile in return. Luckily no one got hurt.

1832 HOURS / JANUARY 15, 2011

For a few long days, we stayed in KAF, the largest U.S. base in Afghanistan's southern region, its boardwalk lined with shops and restaurants, including TGIF, Nathan's Hot Dogs, and a slew of other vendors. A few man-made lakes sat here and there, with one smack in the middle of everything. These were no ordinary lakes. They were dumpsites for all the human refuse and who knew what else. Plenty of posted signs warned people not to dive in the lakes. One read, "Brown Trout Fishing—Fridays ONLY." Flytraps hung everywhere. The "Brown Trout" lakes attracted the pesky fuckers. The bouquet of chemicals and rotting shit permeated the base. The Taliban targeted KAF regularly with rocket and mortar attacks, which made KAF's environment very volatile. If the rockets didn't kill you, the malicious fragrance from the lakes would.

My team and I were enjoying a nice meal in the chow hall when sirens blasted. Everyone ran out and took shelter in the bunker located next to the hall. The incoming mortar rounds hit uncomfortably close to our position, rattling the bats that shared the bunker with us enough to make them flee. After a short while the shelling stopped and the all-clear siren sounded off. Everyone went back to their abandoned meal in the chow hall as if nothing had happened.

6
DOG IN UNIFORM

FEBRUARY 14, 2011

My reputation for dependability grew as I volunteered to go on every mission, including the ones that no other terp wanted to go on, and this put me in a category all to myself. Often, while outside the wire on assignments at other bases, I volunteered to go on QRFs, or Quick Reaction/Response/Recovery Force missions. QRFs are units that respond rapidly to developing situations, typically to help recover or assist other allied units in dire circumstance. QRF missions are exceedingly dangerous; many times my team rushed into raging firefights with plenty of zeal to help our guys. So addicted to the adrenaline rush had I become, I looked forward to going on QRFs.

The Taliban hibernated during winter, sitting back until their world warmed up. We knew damn well that with the swelter of summer things would get hot in more ways than one. None of this mattered to me or stopped me from volunteering. Eventually, it got to the point where teams requested me specifically. I had earned the trust of everyone to the point that I was the only terp allowed to carry weapons and ammunition in and out of the armory before and after missions.

Unlike the other terps who never helped with the tedious chore of cleaning up, I stayed behind in the staging area and assisted after every mission until all the work was done. This did not go unnoticed by my superiors, or Global Vigilance, or the other terps. My rapport with most terps and my tentmates was friendly, especially with Shafi, who was the most relaxed and easygoing one.

My relationship with Ziar, however, simmered constantly beneath the surface. He was intimidated by my bond with the battalion and the higher-ups. After all, he had considered himself the alpha male prior to my arrival. But his slothful personality and toadiness ticked me off. He kissed the Marines' asses in front of them and talked smack behind their backs. On a few occasions, while sitting around the tent drinking tea, Ziar would divert the conversation to how stupid and ugly Iranians were. He also did his best to portray me as a bootlicker. He didn't know that I could be as nasty as a billygoat with sharp horns, ready to mix it up. The more he stirred the shit, the closer we got to a duel—and in a way, I welcomed the impending conflict. To me, this job required unbending commitment, and I was applying myself to the task absolutely, no matter what the cost.

In the meantime, the only other person I couldn't break the ice with was Lt. Laramy. She obstinately blocked my every attempt for the smallest conversation. Her eyes would never meet mine even when she addressed me. This provoked a sense of insecurity within me even though I felt more confident about myself than I ever had before.

I hardly spent any time in my tent during my downtime. Instead I roved between Leatherneck, Bastions I and II, and at times the adjoining Afghan base, Camp Shorabak, where I bought naan. On a couple of occasions, Afghan officers invited me over to Shorabak's chow hall for an Afghan meal of rice and potato or rice and lamb or chicken. The few vendors in Shorabak sold local treats that vendors on the coalition side didn't, such as watermelon seed, local pastries, cheap Chinese mobile phones, and a bunch of other useless crap. At some point Shorabak became off limits to everyone official business notwithstanding. Apparently, a male Marine advisor was gang-raped by some of the ANA soldiers as he took a shower there.

My routine was set: 0430—gym, 0630—shower, 0700—breakfast, and on into the day. Sleepy time was around 2130 hours. Sometimes I watched a movie on my little notebook computer, other times I listened to music I'd collected from the other terps or the Uzbek girls working in the barbershop, who had some great club music. On average, I walked ten miles a day going from one small bazaar and café to another on all three bases. I got to know most of the local Afghan shop owners and their employees, who entered the base every day to open their shops and price gouge any foreigner who looked their way. Most shop owners and their employees were decent folks. They always invited me for tea and pastries, and I gladly accepted. In return, I bought them what they asked for from the PX, since they were not allowed to roam the base or visit any of the facilities. The hipper vendors wanted to know about the world outside, and asked plenty of questions. None of the vendors knew my name since I never disclosed it, but I knew all their names. They simply referred to me as Mr. Irani.

The daily sounding off of "Op Minimize, Op Minimize, Op Minimize" from Camp Bastion loudspeakers served as a constant reminder of the ongoing events beyond the fragile safety of the base. Hearing the female voice announcing those terrible words was dreadful. Every time a British soldier fell in battle, the Brits shut down all internet and telephone access to prevent news of the death from reaching home before the military could notify next of kin.

The flip side of "Op Minimize" was "Op Minimize is Lifted," also repeated three times. This usually came a few days after the initial chilling announcement. By then the soldier's family had been notified.

The American version of "Op Minimize" was "Red River," but this call never affected Leatherneck because of the sheer size of the base. It applied to all other smaller FOBs and COBs. The "Op Minimize" announcement and the daily sound of the call to prayer depressed the hell out of me.

Physically, I got to be in my best shape ever. Exercising provided the mental fortitude for dealing with the prison-like lifestyle. I shoulder pressed 150 pounds, more than my weight. I kept a strict diet while on the base, except on Sundays when I allowed myself to enjoy a donut or two from the British coffee shop in Bastion. Nevertheless, I was often jarred on those short Bastion visits when I passed by the hospital and the medevac landing zone. Many times I had the misfortune of witnessing body bags getting unloaded from the helicopters. The hospital staff did their best to shield the grim scene from passersbys—but still.

Living on a base in a war zone resembles living in a prison except that, here, beyond the gates awaited merchants of death. Even at that, I detested dealing with boredom during my downtime between missions. It drastically increased my nicotine intake. I smoked two or three packs a day, knowing darn well that I wasn't doing myself any good. But the sensation of nicotine infiltrating my body made me feel stronger, leaner, meaner. It seemed asinine to think about the possible long-term effects of smoking. Like Kent had said when we first met, *"It's a good addiction."*

Aside from the constant threat of death by brutal means, life on the base was very simple. No longer did I require a pricey wardrobe. No one cared about labels. I wore one of my two uniforms when I went on missions. The footlocker I'd bought from the PX housed my socks, a dozen pairs of underwear, T-shirts, fleece, computer, passport, and a couple of tactical pants. Also, unlike LA where I had many fickle friends, here I had only a handful of loyal companions who would lay their lives down for me. Aside from my teammates, one of the higher-ups from the battalion, Colonel Webber, had become a conversational mate. We would breakfast, lunch, or dinner together and talk about historic events in the region. Colonel Webber was interested in my Iranian point of view, and I in his military perspective. Our mutual respect gave the friendship strength.

FEBRUARY 22, 2011

Out of boredom one cold, cloudy day, I walked over to the bazaar after lunch, where a row of maybe a dozen shops stood on the side of a dirt road. A couple of the shops were actual structures, but the rest were either shipping containers or had been jerry-rigged from scrap pieces of tin or whatever else the Afghans could get their hands on. A thick layer of moondust covered the glass displays in the shopfronts.

I met with the usual group of Afghans who owned and manned the shops, but on this day something different caught my attention. Amanudin, the young guy who wore tight jeans and western-style clothes and asked a barrage of questions about America, was now wearing traditional Afghan clothes and had fashioned a beard. He invited me over to his shop for tea.

I accepted. Hot tea sounded good after a heavy lunch and on a grey cold day. Other shop owners came over, and we exchanged greetings. A group of soldiers and civilians shopped and bargained with some of the shop owners.

Rubbing my chin, I jokingly asked Amanudin, "Your girlfriend's request?"

His response caught me off-guard. "No, Mr. Irani. These fucking infidels. They come here and think we are their slaves. Their women come and buy belly-dancing dress from us, they shake their body in front of us, tempting and corrupting us."

I knew that the dinky shops did sell belly dancing outfits and other risqué female couture—the shop owners made good money off the cheaply constructed, third-rate, suggestive outfits—but I didn't understand the change in Amanudin. Why now, why like this?

Another shop owner brought tea. We sat drinking, but Amanudin didn't let up on his rant. "*In kos madar zanika bayad tajawoz kard, tarkeh zad*," he said in Dari. "These motherfucking women must be raped and whipped."

The other men tried to calm him down, but he wouldn't have any of it.

"*Che khabar shodeh, baradar?*" I asked in Dari. "What's happened, brother?"

"This bitch American came here and bought many whore clothes from me," Amanudin raged. "Don't these infidels know Muslims suffer outside this base?"

I could see that something had completely shifted in Amanudin. He had crossed into a dimension of extremes, and returning from such a dark place required extreme measures. It was ill-advised for me to stick around. I drank my tea in a hurry, said goodbye to everyone, and left quickly without raising suspicion.

FEBRUARY 24, 2011

A few days after the Amanudin encounter I sat in the chow hall alone having dinner. A Marine appeared at my table's edge.

"Is this seat taken?" he asked in an official tone.

"It's yours to take, sir," I replied.

He sat down across from me. I smiled and sized him up, a soldiers' soldier, in his early sixties, lean and fit, with tanned skin that accentuated his blond-gray flattop haircut and piercing blue eyes. When we made eye contact, I nodded as if to say, *Bon appetit*.

"How's the chicken tonight?" he asked.

"Not as dry as usual."

I continued eating, from time to time making eye contact with my dinner companion.

"I know who you are," he said halfway into the meal.

Was he talking to me? Maybe he thought I was someone else.

"*Ta'ajob nakon, man midoonam to ki hasti,*" this time he said it in fluent Farsi. "Don't be surprised, I know who you are."

My eyes damn near popped out of their sockets. I wouldn't have been as surprised if the chicken at the end of my fork grew wings and flew away.

"*Shohratet pichideh atraf,*" he said as he took a bite of his chicken, "*Gordanet toro yeki az khodeshoon midooneh.*" Your reputation precedes you. Your battalion considers you as one of their own."

"I –"

"*Esme man Sargeord Strickland-e, va esme to Sanjar Rohām.*" He said. "My name is Major Strickland, and you are Sanjar Rohām."

"*Khosh vaghtam Sargeord,*" I said. "Nice to meet you, Major."

"*Shenidam kheili shakhse ghabele etemadi hasti.*" He coolly chewed his food. "*In haghighat dareh?*" "I hear you are a very trustworthy person. Is that true?"

I couldn't predict the direction of the conversation, so I tried to keep a poker face. I didn't know who this guy was or what he was up to. I kept silent and continued eating my meal.

"*Man midoonam in kheili ajibe, vali ma be to ehtiaj darim baraye kari,*" he said. "I know this is very strange, but we need you for a job."

"*Man che kari momkene baraye shoma anjam bedam, Sargeord?*" I asked. "What could I possibly do for you, Major?" I now assumed the Major's use of Farsi was to earn my trust.

"*Ma midoonim to male in sarzamin nisti.* We know you're not from this land." Then he added in English, "We know you don't have a dog in this fight."

I chewed my food slowly to allow myself time to think. "*Dorosteh, man az in sarzamin nistam,*" I replied. "It's true, I'm not from this land." I held Strickland's cold gaze. "But I do have a dog in this fight," I said in English. "He wears that uniform." I pointed to his Marine uniform.

Strickland's stone expression didn't change. "Some people will contact you shortly. They will brief you. You are not to discuss any of this with anyone, not your battalion, not even your employer. We clear?"

"Yes, sir," I replied.

Strickland didn't finish his meal. Instead, he picked up his tray and blended into the crowd of uniforms in the chow hall.

On a drizzly cold afternoon a couple of days after the Strickland encounter, I walked over to the battalion compound to say hello and shoot the shit with the guys for a bit. I didn't see any of them there. I stopped by my POC's tent, Lt. Laramy. She wasn't there. Inside, the tent was nice and warm compared to the cold, damp weather outside.

Gunnery Sergeant Kovak sat behind his desk doing paperwork.

"Hey Gunny, how goes it?" I peeled off my baseball cap.

He looked up. "How didja know I wanted to see you?"

"I didn't. I just stopped by to hang with the gang."

Lt. Laramy walked in. I said hello and she responded with her usual rigid nod.

Gunny Kovak got up from behind his desk and walked over to me with his hand on his holstered sidearm. "Ya gotta death wish, Sanj?" he demanded.

He was standing toe-to-toe with me before I could open my mouth.

"Are ya outa your fuckin' mind?" he snapped. "Ya keep volunteering to go on every Goddamn mission. Dontcha know this is a numbers game?"

I looked at Laramy from the corner of my eye, thinking she would step in and yank Gunny's leash. Not a twitch from her.

"Sorry, Gunny, I don't unders—"

Gunny's nose got pointier as he got worked up.

"I know about the last missions and the explosion."

"But Gunn—"

"I don't wanna see your ass-mug around here for the next two weeks. You understand?" He turned his back to me. "The other terps have to get their shit together and do what they got hired to do."

"But—"

"Haven't ya heard?" Gunny faced me. "Ya never take laxatives and sleeping pills together."

"What the hell is that supposed to mean?" I asked, dumbfounded.

"How the fuck do I know what it means?" Gunny scratched his balls. "Ya figure it out."

"Okay," I said, still bewildered.

"I've asked Lt. Laramy to give ya two weeks off and make the other terps earn their pay. *UNDERSTAND?*" He pressed down on his holstered sidearm.

I understood his concern. The battalion rotated the companies on missions to lessen their exposure to harm, and here I was, going out with every company, every time. The more time I spent outside the wire, the higher the chance of injury or death.

I looked over to Lt. Laramy. "Thanks for the vacation, Lieutenant," I said appreciatively.

She looked back at me, emotionless. "Don't venture too far. I could make a last-minute call," she said.

"Now get outta here!" Gunny shooed me away. "Don't let me catch yer ass in here."

Although unsuccessful with catching up with the crew, I left the compound feeling good about the two-week break; it would give me a chance for some alone time since no such thing existed on the missions. I set off to the café in Bastion to grab a coffee in celebration, maybe catch a soccer match on the television. On one hand, the strong sense of belonging, purpose, and direction I felt inside topped off my somewhat dwindled verve tank. On the flip side I felt uneasy because I wasn't going out with the teams to protect them. I had all but forgotten about my life back home. The bonds of camaraderie with the battalion fed my soul and made me feel liberated even though I was a prisoner in a war-torn country.

I took the back way to Bastion I, an infrequently used dirt road with barely any car or foot traffic. Halfway through my walk a drizzle began to fall but my mood was all sunny on the inside. With my fleece zipped up all the way, I pulled my baseball cap down, lit a cigarette, and picked up the pace. There I was, walking alone in the confines of the base and feeling great, whereas at home I was free, with plenty of people around me, and I usually felt like shit. It was another instant when I understood the true meaning of living in the moment.

As I drifted along with my thoughts, a silver Chevy Tahoe with blacked-out windows pulled up next to me and stopped. At first, I thought someone wanted to offer me a ride.

The passenger window rolled down.

"You the guy they call Sanj?" asked the passenger riding shotgun, a black male.

I pulled the cigarette away from my lips and nodded.

"Get in." He gestured to the back door with his head. "Put out that shit stick."

I opened the passenger side rear door and climbed in. The Chevy was brand-new and fully loaded. A white guy sat in the driver's seat.

The black guy turned around and faced me. "I'm Tony." He pointed to the driver. "That's Joe."

I tried to appraise the two. Tony's body covered the whole seat. His left triceps was visible from where I sat. It bulged from under his sleeve, revealing his massive build. Joe, on the other hand, was a smaller guy. Both displayed military haircuts. They reminded me of Los Angeles police officers.

"Nice to meet you both," I said.

"Major Strickland mentioned us to you already," Tony said. "We need someone like you to help us out."

"What can a terp do to help?" I asked. "I am limited in my capacity."

"Your capacity is what we're missing from our toolbox," Joe said.

I stayed silent, waiting for them to continue.

"We want you to be our eyes and ears inside the base," Tony said as he adjusted himself in his seat. "We want you to attend the bazaar, mingle with the other terps, go to the mosques and gather any information you ca—"

"We want you to be the fly on the wall when you're around the Afghans and others." Joe darted a look at me in the rear-view mirror. "It's essential that we keep everyone safe on the base. That includes you. 'Atmospherics Intel' is what we're after."

"Not sure what 'Atmospherics Intel' means," I said.

"It means eavesdropping on ongoing conversations around you to get the overall feel for what dominates the discussions people are having, especially local nationals. We need someone to bring us intel from inside and outside the wire." Tony turned almost all the way around in his seat. "You have what we're missing."

"You want me to attend the mosques on the base?" I asked sarcastically.

"Yeah, we need to know what goes on in there," Joe replied.

"But I'm not Muslim," I said.

"We know," Tony replied.

"But no one else does," Joe said.

The car drove along at the 5 mile-per-hour speed limit as we spoke. Tony wrote something on a piece of paper. "You can call us on this number. Just go to the camp commandant office and use the SIPR phones there." He handed me the paper. "I want you to call us before you go on your terp mission with the battalion and as soon as you get back."

SIPR, or Secret Internet Protocol Router, is a system used by the DOD and the State Department to transmit classified information.

"Small one-story building within eyesight of your employer's office, southeast of it." Joe looked at me in the rear-view mirror. "Surrounded by T-walls, that's our office."

"Come to the office only after dark," Tony said. "Make sure no one sees you coming or going."

"You'll brief us once a week or as needed." Joe pulled himself up in his seat. "Remember this road. The same location we picked you up from. We'll pick you up at 1100 hours for our weekly briefing."

I nodded.

"You start immediately," Tony said firmly. "Don't be aggressive in your intel gathering. Do it passively."

I tried to analyze my options.

"Now, where were you going when we picked you up?" Tony asked.

"I was going to grab a coffee at Bastion I," I replied.

"We can't be seen together. You'll have to walk to Bastion," Joe said.

In the end, I agreed to help. But I still didn't know who "Joe" and "Tony" really were or who they worked for.

The Tahoe stopped. They both turned around to face me.

"We'll look after you." They exchanged a glance with each other. "We know how you care about the battalion you work with," Joe said.

"Thank you for your service," Tony said.

We shook hands, I got out and the car drove off. I lit another cigarette and started walking. What had just happened? On one hand, I didn't know if I could trust these people since I had no idea who they were and what agency they belonged to. On the other hand, we were on the same team. I tried to imagine different scenarios and outcomes. Did they want to use me as a disposable pawn? What would happen if I got caught by the people I was tasked to spy on, by Global Vigilance? The forced proposition was both thrilling and daunting. Just a few short minutes ago I'd felt almost cheerful, but now the forecast was cloudy with a high chance of shit-storm.

I began attending the Afghan mosque and the mosque belonging to the Bahraini soldiers. The Bahraini soldiers were friendly and cordial. They gave small packages of dates sent from home to all the worshipers in attendance. I sat on the floor like everyone else but all the way in the back of the room. I didn't know what the prayers were so I mimicked others when it came time to stand, bow, or sit. I murmured an Arabic phrase under my breath which I knew from my years in Iran, and I always greeted and said goodbye to those in attendance in Arabic. I never heard or saw anything suspicious in either mosque. There were friendly parishioners and unfriendly ones, but nothing to take note of.

After my initial encounter with Tony and Joe, I visited the bazaar a few times specifically to check on Amanudin. He wasn't there the first couple of visits, but one day I saw him and the changes both in his appearance and speech were disconcerting. His friendly face had given way to one filled with antagonism and malice toward the infidels. I engaged him in a smalltalk to extract information from him. During one conversation, he made vague references to the fuel farm across the dirt road from the bazaar, where huge fuel reservoir tanks of hundreds of thousands of gallons of volatility were housed. The fuel stored on Leatherneck served most of Kandahar region. It was the lifeline for all our operations in the territory. Amanudin didn't say anything specific, but the distant, hollow look in his eyes told a particular story.

MARCH 04, 2011

I hung up the phone and headed to the rendezvous point on the dirt road. It took a good half-hour for me to get there. The mid-day sun warmed my face while the chilly wind penetrated my clothes.

The silver SUV pulled up and I hopped on board and exchanged greetings with Tony and Joe.

"We didn't think you'd be calling us so soon," Tony said.

"Neither did I, but there is something I think you need to know."

"What's that?" Joe asked.

I gave them the rundown of what I'd done since our first encounter, then described my unsettling conversation with Amanudin and chronicled his transformation.

"What's your gut feeling about this guy?" Tony asked.

"Look, I don't want to get anyone in trouble," I said. "I don't wanna ruin someone's livelihood, and I sure as hell don't wanna see any harm come to our guys."

"You think we should take a closer look at this Amanu guy?" Joe asked.

"Just to be on the safe side," I said.

The dynamic duo exchanged doubtful glances that read, *The rookie is overreacting*.

"Listen, I didn't ask for this. You guys approached me." I sat back.

"You've put great responsibility on my shoulders."

"I know, I appreciate you volun—" Tony said.

"This guy didn't volunteer," Joe said. "We put him there, let's put his mind at ease."

The car stopped. Joe and Tony exchanged glances again.

"Ok, here's what I want you to do," Tony said with a bit of hesitation in his voice. "Be at the bazaar tomorrow at 1200 hours. Walk over to the subject. Put your right hand on his shoulder, that's all."

"Don't worry about the rest, you won't be compromised," Joe said.

The dynamic duo seemed genuine. It gave me some comfort.

"I hope you guys don't get me fired from my job," I said as I opened the door, "You have no idea what it took to get here!" I jumped out of the car and closed the door.

I started walking aimlessly; I truly had no idea which direction to go. The idea of bodily harm, or even death, did not bother me as much as the idea of losing my job.

The SUV slowly pulled up next to me. I turned. Tony and Joe looked at me through the passenger side window. We held each other's gazes for a moment, then the SUV slowly drove off.

1145 HOURS / MARCH 05, 2011

I walked to the bazaar. The usual group of shop owners welcomed me. I kept my friendly tone with them all as I looked around the place. It was a cold, overcast day; the bazaar wasn't as busy as usual, only a few civilians and soldiers looking through the displays.

Amanudin waved his hands and invited me over. I walked over, we exchanged greetings. Amanudin seemed in a jovial mood. He offered me a seat and brought hot tea. I looked out to the dirt road and the parking area next to the bazaar. A dozen or so civilian vans with tinted out windows were parked there. I couldn't see if there were any occupants in them.

"Amanudin, you look great, brother," I said as I picked up a cup of tea from the tray. "I'm glad to see you in a good mood."

"Irani brother, I am in a great mood." Amanudin pointed to the sky. "Allah is with me; I feel him."

I felt wicked, villainous. I took a big sip of the scalding tea, which immediately burned my pallet. I put the cup down on the tray and stood up.

"I'm glad to see you happy, brother." I put my hand out to him.

Amanudin stood, smiled, and took my hand.

"Mr. Irani, everything in my store is yours." He pointed to the dusty items on the display table and glass display case. "Please, take anything, a gift from me to you."

Internally, I was conflicted. I felt brazen, righteous, and at the same time meek and dishonest. I felt bad for Amanudin. But deep down I knew this guy wouldn't hesitate to slit my throat if and when the time came.

"Thank you, brother; your friendship is your gift to me." I put my right hand on his shoulder.

Amanudin pulled me in and hugged me.

I broke the embrace, turned, and walked away.

A swarm of people with guns drawn poured out of the vans parked nearby and descended on the bazaar. Some were uniformed but most were civilian-clothed. Two K-9 units joined the fray. Everyone, including me and other shoppers, was rounded up. I saw Joe and Tony in the mix. The raiders separated shop owners from shoppers. The K-9s and a dozen or so personnel searched the shops. All shop owners got zip-tied and forced to sit on the dirt ground.

Joe, Tony, and a few plainclothes individuals came over and began questioning the shoppers. After checking IDs and taking down personal information, they let the shoppers loose. They kept me at the end of the line. They walked up as if they'd never seen me before, took my ID, questioned me, and released me.

As I walked away, I looked back at the bazaar. I felt like shit: duplicitous, conflicted, and overwhelmed with guilt. Maybe I'd overreacted. What if my actions destroyed the livelihood of these people and their families?

A few days passed with no word from Joe and Tony. The news of the bazaar incident had spread like wildfire. My tentmates and the other terps made up wild stories about the event and presented their bullshit as firsthand information. I joined in on the gossip so as to not arouse any suspicion toward myself. Hell, at times I dished out the thickest bullshit.

After all, I had been the only terp at the bazaar that day.

MARCH 08, 2011

I received word about my next terp mission, a big one, an exciting one: two weeks with the Air Force, Navy, Army, and the Marines. This news got me excited. I missed my teammates and the mission adrenaline rush. I had a bad case of cabin fever and itched to get out of the confines and safety of the base. Outside the wire felt right to me—at least there the bad guys wanted to kill you, while inside, you died of boredom.

That evening, as I sat alone in the busy chow hall eating my dinner, someone walked up and asked, "Is this seat taken?"

I looked up. It was Major Strickland.

"No, sir," I replied.

The Major sat down and began eating his ice cream.

"Be at the office at 2300 hours," he said in Farsi.

We sat quietly for a while, then the Major got up and walked away without finishing his ice cream.

It was about 2300 hours when I worked my way over to Joe and Tony's office in the darkness. Their goddamned office sat in plain view of my employer's office, where my site manager and a few others stood outside under the florescent lights talking. I crept between the concrete T-walls surrounding my destination and tiptoed up the plywood steps. The plywood one-story building had cc cameras mounted all around it. I pushed the buzzer, and the door buzzed open. I hurried in.

Tony stood in the entryway. We shook hands as he led the way down the hallway, the warped plywood floor squeaking under our feet. A few other people working in the side offices appraised me as we walked by. We entered a small room where a thick layer of dust covered the maps and satellite images hanging on the walls and the state-of-the-art computers.

"Hey, I'm glad you could make it." Joe stood up from behind his desk. "Grab a seat. No one saw you coming, right?"

I nodded.

The three of us sat in a circle.

"You want some coffee?" Tony asked.

I nodded as my anticipation grew.

Tony left the room and returned with three Styrofoam cups of coffee and a container of powdered milk. We each grabbed a cup. Then Joe leaned forward in his seat. "We wanna thank you for the heads up."

"Your intuition was right on the money," Tony added.

"What happened? Amanudin?" I asked.

"Yeah," Joe said, "he paid off and paid off big."

My ears perked up. I tilted my head as if to say "Go on."

"We took everyone into custody after the raid." Joe sipped his coffee.

"Yeah, we searched the shops but came up empty," Tony added. "We searched their vehicles—"

"These people come in every morning and have to leave the base by 1700 hours," Joe said. "They go through a comprehensive check before entering the base every morning."

"The Bahrainis and Brits are tasked with searching them and their vehicles," Tony added.

"Will one of you tell me what happened?" I asked.

"Amanudin snuck in fifteen kilos of explosives in the gas tank of his car," Joe said.

I scooted to the edge of my chair.

"Yeah, the fuckers have ingenuity," Tony said. "They built a three-layer gas tank and wrapped the explosives in coffee beans. Even the K-9s couldn't pick up the scent."

I jumped to my feet. Tony stood up with me.

"You saved many lives." Joe gave me a hard look. "Lives of loved ones."

Tony put his hand on my shoulder. I looked up at his towering stature. "Unfortunately, we can't advertise this success or flaunt your name." He said.

"That wouldn't be a welcomed accolade," I replied.

"The people who need to know, know," Joe said.

I took a few seconds to digest the moment.

"Your first assignment, and already a rock star," Joe said approvingly.

I felt vindicated in the court of my conscience.

We stood silent for a minute, drinking toxic-tasting coffee.

"Oh, I am going on a mission in the next few days," I said. "Not sure when I'll be back."

"Keep your eyes peeled and ears perked while you're out there," Joe said. "Report any unusual activity—no matter insider or otherwise. And one more thing: watch your six."

I nodded at Joe.

"It's a thankless job, brother," Tony said.

7
SERPENT AND SHADOWS

2010 HOURS / MARCH 10, 2011

Six hours to kill before leaving my tent for the staging area, I thought to myself. "Six hours to kill" struck me in a downbeat way. Why would I kill the best moments of my life when I had no idea what fate had in store for me six minutes from now, far less six hours?

I had attended the mission briefing earlier with Ziar, Sami, and Shafi. The convoy was going to be huge, with other units bringing their own terps. My team would be the rear security escort. Even Lt. Laramy was going on the mission with the convoy. A Marine from MARSOC, or Marine Corps Forces Special Operations Command, had been assigned to my truck, for this trip a 6x6 MRAP—a six-wheeler with a lot more room than a MATV or the 4x4 MRAP.

The butterflies in my stomach wouldn't settle as I packed my gear. My pack included the usual: some beef jerky packets and Cliff Bars raided from the chow hall; they were my main source of nutrition as I still suffered from the occasional bout of diarrhea. I'd formulated my own remedy: Take Imodium AD prior to departure to dehydrate my system and control the Aztec two-step. The much-dreaded waiting period before each mission was the hardest part. The anticipation and vacillation I felt before each decampment hadn't lessened despite my strong craving to get the hell out of the base. I knew that once I closed the truck gate, all my anxiety would dissipate.

With my gear packed and ready, I lay on my morgue-slab bed with my earphones on, listening to somber music from Reza Sadeghi, a young Iranian artist suffering from polio. "*All alone on the seashore stand I do, like the waves with your memories roar I do…*" Reza's lyrics burrowed deep within my core. I realized that I hadn't fallen in love in what seemed like eons. Like an empty, rudderless ship with no destination, I had been drifting through life destination-less.

Shafi, Sami, and Ziar talked out loud as they prepared. Word had gotten out about the size and scope of the mission, and my tent had become the "terp news headquarters" for the other terps who stopped by, trying to snoop. My tent mates didn't observe the first rule we learned during our training—Op Sec. Disclosing or discussing missions with anyone was prohibited. Most terps did not adhere to this rule but I'm a stickler when it comes to following instructions.

The four of us left the tent around 0100 hours. My three companions waited for the bus, but I decided to walk. My gear weighed about fifty pounds. Aside from my protective gear, it included my double-layer winter sleeping bag. I'd also made sure to pack enough socks, underwear, T-shirts, and snacks to last me the whole trip. The solitary walk helped settle my jittery nerves, giving me some private time since no such thing existed in this lifestyle.

At the staging area, I helped my team prepare the truck. At about 0230 everyone gathered for roll-call and weapons check. Personnel who weren't regulars on the missions got assigned to vehicles. I walked back with Kent, Smitts, and Gospol to the very last truck in the convoy, our rear-security position. When all trucks fired up their engines at 0300, the rumbling of the powerful motors would shake the ground beneath my feet. Soon this herd of steely beasts would roam and dominate the real estate beyond the gates, and I was going to be a part of it—an inconsequential player but still participating in this great game.

A tall, lean Marine stood at the open back gate as I organized the inside of the truck, securing MRE cases, water, ammunition canisters, and everyone's gear. He seemed to be mixed-race.

"Is this Sarge Kent's vic?" he asked.

"Yeah," I replied.

He threw his gear in and climbed on board. He didn't say much while he put his gear away. I noticed he'd brought three backpacks—small, medium, and large—which he positioned with great care. Gospol dropped down from the turret to take some ammo boxes. The two just nodded to each other. Kent and Smitts climbed in their seats in front.

"Are you Sarge Kent?" the Marine asked.

"Yeah. You the Spec Ops?" Kent asked.

"Yeah, I'm Sarge Clover," the Marine said.

"Make yourself at home," Kent said as he installed the radio handle. "Did you meet Sanj? he's my terp."

Clover looked over his shoulder but didn't acknowledge me. He had a cold stare.

Word came on the radio to mount up for departure. We jumped down and grabbed our flak vests from the ground next to the truck. Smitts was his usual playful self.

"Oh, you are with us, ma'am?" he asked from behind me. "I thought you'd be in the convoy commander's vic."

I turned around to see who he was talking to.

"That was the plan, but they had to change trucks at the last minute," Lt. Laramy said as she carried in her gear.

Everyone climbed on board. I got in last, and closed and latched the heavy gate behind me.

It took another twenty or so minutes for the convoy to move. The atmosphere in the back of the truck felt tense, mostly due to the presence of Laramy and Clover. Laramy sat directly across from me, typical of an MRAP, where the occupants sit on opposing sides facing each other, legs intertwined. My knees bumped into Laramy's now and then as we moved along. Neither Laramy nor Clover said a word.

The time was 0349 hours. Convoys from other branches joined in as we moved through the base. A number of Afghan-owned and-operated fuel tanker trucks joined in as well. The U.S. and the coalition had adopted the strategy of hiring Afghan nationals to generate new local economies to entice the indigenous population to join the Afghan government and not the Taliban. This policy worked to a great degree, but there were those who took money from us but joined the Taliban anyway, or, were already Taliban and used our policy against us.

The closer we got to the gate in Bastion, the longer the trail of trucks became. Dawn had broken by the time we cleared the gates and the serpentine.

At 0723 hours the whole convoy came to a stop after the last vehicle, my truck, reached the paved Highway 1. Locals driving by the gigantic, heavily-armed convoy came face-to-face with an overwhelming display of force.

"If anyone wants to relieve themselves, this is the time to do it." Kent said.

It had taken us nearly four hours to clear the base and get to Highway 1. I looked at Laramy; she sat motionless. Clover got up and worked his way over our intertwined legs. I exited the truck to join Kent and Clover, who were pissing on the passenger-side tires. Afterward, I stepped onto the gravel shoulder to get a better look at the convoy. The motorcade looked imposing by every standard. The front of the procession was not visible from my vantage point.

"How long do you think this is?" I asked Kent.

"Pretty damn long," he said, buttoning up his pants.

"It's almost ten miles long," Clover said. "One–hundred-seventy of our vics, nearly a thousand personnel, not including the local trucks and their guys."

Kent and I looked at Clover. He seemed to be a man of few words.

The sheer size of the convoy exempted most bases in the southern region from accommodating it fully. The only places capable of holding such fleet were LNK and KAF. However, the convoy would shrink as each participating group detached once they arrived at or near their designated destination. I assumed the size of this convoy was by design, to psychologically fracture the enemy's desire to go up against such might and to force them to the negotiation table.

The convoy got on its way, slowly rolling down Highway 1. Eventually, off the paved road we went, onto hard-packed desert terrain. Laramy's presence succeeded in killing any conversation, music, or smoking. Our usual lighthearted mood was silenced. I stole a glance at Laramy now and then. God had blessed her with an unaccountable natural charisma. When she took a sip of Gatorade and lowered the bottle from her mouth, her upper lip glistened in the afternoon sunlight pouring in through the small window behind my head. She must have noticed my gaze. She wiped her mouth with her sleeve, and with it the smile from my face.

Lack of conversation and the movement of the truck rocked me to sleep. Later, sensing something in front of me, I opened my eyes. Laramy stood in front of me. Maybe her legs had cramped up. I closed my eyes.

BAM! An unnatural, high-pitched screech left my throat as my balls got crushed. I felt my eyes popped out of their sockets.

My shriek had scared everyone. Smitts slammed on the breaks, Gospol dropped down from the turret, Kent looked back in surprise, and Clover recoiled. Laramy's knee was firmly lodged between my legs. The passenger side of the truck had hit a pothole as she stood up, throwing her on top of me and lodging her knee right where it did not belong. Laramy's face was a mere inch or two away from mine. I inhaled her warm breath. Not sure whether to smile or cry from the pain, I settled on a grimace.

Laramy put one hand on my shoulder and the other against my seat and slowly pushed off, leisurely extricating her implanted knee from my groin. She sat back in her seat. My male companions stared, waiting for a reaction from me. It was hard to decide: Should I give in to the pain or laugh at their distorted faces? I forced a smile, a painful one. Kent, Smitts, Gospol, and Clover smiled back uncomfortably. I threw a look at Laramy. Her ever–so-faint smile betrayed her sternness.

"Sorry," she said in a decisive voice.

"All systems are go, ma'am," I responded, with a thumbs-up.

The mood inside the truck became more relaxed after the nutcracker incident. Conversation flowed, mostly between Smitts, Kent, and me.

"Hey Sanjman," Smitts said, "What's your real story? What are you *really* doing in this shithole, I mean?"

"What do you mean, my real story?" I asked.

"Well, people are talking about you," Smitts said.

"Who's talking? What are they saying?"

"You're different from the other terps," Smitts said.

The rest of the crew listened intently.

"I think you're a spy, if you ask me!" Smitts said.

All ears perked up as Smitts uttered the word "spy." Smitts had caught me by surprise, so my response was a silent smirk.

Needless to say, Clover and Laramy watched me closely the rest of the way.

Surprisingly, the convoy moved along without incident. Its enormity and massive firepower must have deterred the enemy from engaging us. Around 2200 hours word came on the radio for the convoy to stop for the night. Many got out to stretch. The rumbling of engines shuddered the desert floor and reverberated through the cold desert air. The red taillights of the convoy zig-zagged across the desert floor. It resembled a giant iron serpent slithering through the darkness to the horizon, sewing the sky and the earth together as it disappeared in the far distance where the moon kissed the earth.

We stayed within the tire tracks since venturing off could have proven deadly. The desert night temperature had dipped to bitter coldness. I lit a cigarette and took a deep drag. Kent, Smitts, Clover, and Gospol joined me. Laramy stepped out, but she didn't smoke, so she stayed a few feet away from us. Smitts pulled out a case of MREs. Everyone grabbed their favorite—tuna, hamburger, cheese and crackers, meatballs, pasta.

At almost midnight the convoy commander's voice barked over the radio: "All gunners, eyes open. Change shifts with others in your vic every three hours. Everyone must get some shuteye."

The weather became so brutally cold that even the flak vests absorbed the frigid air. I pulled out my sleeping bag, and so did Laramy.

"Damn, I musta left my sack behind," Clover said, looking through his bag.

"Did you forget your weapon, too?" Laramy said firmly.

Here was a tough–as-nails Special Ops guy getting his balls busted by a female superior. I respected Laramy's discipline and willingness to deliver a verbal ass-whipping.

I separated my two-layer sleeping bag. "Here you go." I offered the warmer part to Clover. "You'll freeze."

Clover gave me a look that could only mean one thing: fuck off.

"You don't need to correct his mistake," Laramy said.

I ignored her. "Take it," I extended my bag to Clover. "You'll freeze."

"Give me the other layer." Clover pointed to the thinner sleeping bag in my other hand.

"You don't get to choose," I replied with a rigid face as I let go of the bag.

I could feel Laramy's blistering eyes on me. I pulled my sleeping bag over my head and tried to sleep. The cold, unfriendly wind whirled inside the truck, making it into an icebox. I wore my wool cap under my helmet and breathed inside the sack to create warmth.

The night seemed endless. The spiritless chill exacted unforgiving punishment on everyone. I pulled the sleeping bag away from my face. My eyes met with Laramy's sleepless eyes. I had the feeling she was waiting for me to capitulate to the freezing weather and ask Clover to return my sleeping bag. I withdrew into my bag, more determined to tough it out.

0601 HOURS / MARCH 13, 2011

The morning arrived ever so slowly. The convoy moved painfully slow, like a cold-blooded serpent trying to soak up the sun's heat. Along the way, some of the locally-hired tanker trucks broke down, making the trip even more challenging.

1607 HOURS / MARCH 15, 20011

On the afternoon of the fourth day, word came on the radio for the last five trucks in the convoy to take positions on a hilltop overlooking a village. We dropped off Lt. Laramy with another truck before peeling away from the procession and heading up the hill.

The five trucks formed a wide circle, about 20 yards from one another and facing outward. We were to stay on the hilltop until further notice. As usual, we got out to stretch and relieve ourselves. I looked at the village below, less than seven or eight hundred yards away. Children played outside, and villagers moved about.

The five of us lit cigarettes and formed a line next to the truck and relieved ourselves. Strong bonds are formed at a certain unexpected moment in life, even with strangers. This group piss was such a moment!

We hadn't finished pissing when bullets began to ricochet off the armored truck.

Ping, ping, ping.

"Fuck, sniper fire," Clover yelled. "Get in."

Pants in hand, we hurriedly jumped inside the truck. Gospol jumped into the turret and turned the big gun toward the village. Binoculars came out to scope out the village. No one could spot the sniper's position. Bullets kept coming, but the rate of fire slowed.

Our circumstance further limited our options to do anything outside the trucks. Everyone had to stay put in the safety of our armored saviors. We smoked, listened to music, talked, and napped. Those were our choices. The sun faded and with it, the random sniper fire. We made our MREs and chatted as we ate. Clover even made some MRE coffee for the two of us; the others didn't care for coffee. Sharing my sleeping bag with him as the frigid numbing weather persisted had completely changed his attitude toward me. As Clover and I talked over coffee and cigarette, I felt rumblings in my stomach followed by sharp pain. Fuck, diarrhea again.

"Hey, man, you okay?" Clover asked, holding a cup of coffee, a cigarette dangling from the corner of his lips.

"No, man, I'm not feeling okay," I said as I doubled over.

"What's wrong, bro, you need a medic?" Clover asked.

"No medic," I said, writhing.

Meanwhile, Kent and Smitts were engaged in a deep conversation about their wives.

"I gotta step out for a minute," I said.

"Don't be crazy, man, the sniper could still be out there," Clover said nonchalantly as he sipped his coffee. "He could be using a Russian Dragunov sniper rifle with night scope."

"Listen, man, I got the shits. I gotta step out." I grinned. "Just do me a favor. Don't let anyone see me with my pants down." I looked at him pleadingly. "Promise you'll pull my pants up if you find me dead in my own shit!"

I opened the back gate, jumped down, and frantically searched for a place in the darkness to give myself maximum coverage from the sniper. The cold, pitch-black night added more anxiety to my desperate predicament and sparked my imagination as I searched to find a safe shitting spot. Images of the tall Taliban detainee from months earlier popped up in my head. Creepy thoughts coiled in my brain while my guts contorted. I even tried to talk myself into going back inside the vehicle, but my puckered butt cheeks demanded otherwise.

Finally, I decided the best place to squat was behind the middle tire and the axle of the 6x6 truck. I'd heard about fear giving people superhuman strength, but never heard of it making one elastic. With my pants down, I somehow managed to wedge myself under the truck behind the middle tire, giving myself protection from every angle. I let loose. My panicky eyes shifted from side to side as my ears listened for any sound. Halfway into my ordeal, I heard a voice.

"Sanj? Is that you under there?" Kent asked.

"Yeah, who else?" I replied hurriedly, wanting to get rid of the spectator.

"How the fuck did you get yourself wedged in there?"

"Just go, let me shit in peace."

I climbed back in the truck after the toughest thirty minutes of my life.

0514 HOURS / MARCH 16, 2011

The smell of coffee woke me early the next day. Clover greeted me with a cup of MRE Joe. I should have known better than to drink coffee. As soon as it hit my stomach, I knew I was in trouble. The caffeine further provoked my bout with skitters. It must have shown on my face.

"Again?" Clover asked in disbelief.

"Just remember what I asked you for last night," I said, and jumped out of the truck.

This time I had nowhere to hide, neither from the sniper nor the occupants of the other trucks. I walked in front of my truck. It faced the village. The mine roller hooked to the front of the truck provided some frontal coverage, so I pulled my pants down to mid-thigh, squatted, and leaned back against the bumper for support. My arms rested on the bumper, supporting my weight in my awkward hovering position. Unfortunately, I failed to anticipate the position of my pants, which were in the direct line of fire of my morning piss. Too late, I let it flow from both ends. I finished my affair and pulled up my pants, which featured a big wet piss spot in the front and the seat. I entered the truck.

Clover, Kent, and Smitts looked at me. Gospol dropped down from the turret, smiled, and slowly went back up.

"Did you piss yourself?" Clover asked casually.

"Yeah, I did." I tried to keep my composure. "What of it?"

"Nothing, bro, I've pissed myself dozens of times," Clover said, offering me a cigarette.

I looked at Smitts and Kent. Smitts handed Kent a twenty-dollar bill. They had made a bet on me pissing my pants.

It was 1308 hours. The morning passed at an inhumanly slow pace, but not for the son-of-a-bitch sniper who kept firing away at us.

Ping, ping...

"This shit's gonna stop," Clover said as he reached for his backpacks. He grabbed a few grenades, extra magazines for his M4, his Sig M18 sidearm, and a radio. "I'm gonna off that ass-juice," he said as he prepared his gear. "Sarge Kent, dial me in on my frequency. I'll keep radio silence until necessary."

Clover shoved the extra magazines in the ammo holder on his flak vest and secured them with the Velcro straps. Without hesitation, he opened the back gate and disappeared.

"Where's he going?" I asked Kent. "He leaves without permission or backup?"

"Relax, Sanj. MARSOC guys don't fall under regular channels of command; he don't need permission from us. Clover was in the battle for Fallujah, he's a tough son-of-a-bitch," Kent said with reverence. "He's got balls of steel."

An hour passed, then two. I looked out the window. In the meantime, bullets bounced off our trucks. It felt like Chinese water torture, slow, deliberate, and unrelenting.

Finally, at around 1530 hours, Clover came on the radio.

"Target spotted. A hundred yards out," he whispered.

We listened intently.

"You got PID?" Kent asked.

"PID." The sound of static and Clover's breathing came over the radio. "The fuck-pack is shielding himself with children."

"Can you neutralize?" Kent asked.

"Negative. Too many civilians around."

The radio went silent again.

At around 1713 hours my concern for Clover's well-being grew. But my companions seemed at ease. The day was quickly giving way to darkness when I heard banging on the back gate. I looked out the window and there stood Clover. I sighed with relief.

MARCH 21, 2011

First day of spring, the Persian New Year, Nowruz, directly translated as "New Day." A time when the earth awakens from its winter slumber and life is renewed. A year had passed since I had responded to that ad in a Persian newspaper looking for Farsi, Dari, and Pashto speakers. Answering that tiny posting had led me on a path never imagined.

A year ago at this time Sophie had joined the family gathering at my parents to celebrate the New Year. Although Jewish, my family always celebrates this Zoroastrian tradition that predates the Muslim conquest of Persia and the forced conversation of its peoples to Islam. I closed my eyes for a minute to reminisce. My mother, Mini, and stepfather Jimmy had done a wonderful job decorating their place with colorful flowers, giving their home a festive mood. The sweet smell of hyacinth trailed the tangy scent of traditional Persian foods like *reshte polo*, noodle and rice, and *sab-zi-polo ba mahi sefid*, dill rice with white fish. To one side of the room, a table displayed a beautifully-arranged traditional New Year symbolic offering of apples denoting affection and love, anodes as a stimulant of love, wheatgrass symbolizing tenderness, prosperity, and the connection between human life and nature. Samanoo, a wheat puree symbolizing birth and fertility of plants. Crane or sumac and garlic clove signifying flavor and stimulus for happiness in life. Colored eggs embodying birth and creation.

The image of my mother bringing the food to the table displayed vividly in memory. My family gathering around the dining table. My two young nephews running to the table and attacking the food like any healthy boys with a big appetite would. The clinking sound of utensils against china, the music, and the ricocheting conversations across the table rang in my ears. I remembered a bumper sticker I read once: *"I went in search of my friends and all I found were enemies, that's when I realized family is all I needed."*

I opened my eyes and looked at my four young companions in the truck. They were my family now; they were all I needed.

2246 HOURS / MARCH 22, 2011

After a punishing week, orders came on the radio for us to move on to FOB Nolay.

We moved relatively fast since there were only five trucks, nearing Nolay just before midnight. Thick, dark clouds shielded the moonlight from illuminating the landscape, further accentuating the bad vibe. The cloud cover glowed red, reflecting large fires burning a short distance away. Maybe the Taliban had overrun Nolay and set it on fire.

We made it to the valley below Nolay. Unnerved by what was taking place outside, I wiped the bulletproof glass to get a clearer look. Big bonfires burned, ATVs zig-zagged between the flames, shadows danced around. The glow obscured the identity of the people, friend, or foe? I grabbed a cigarette from my pocket and lit up. This surreal spectacle was the welcoming procession at the gates of the underworld, greeting us to hell. The shadows swirled around the bonfires like demons celebrating a feast of tortured souls. An ATV passed us by. A guy sat on its handlebars as the driver stood on the footpegs; neither one wore a helmet.

"We make airdrops for Nolay," Clover said as he smoked and peered out the porthole. "Water, food, and other worthless shit." Clover took a long drag from his cigarette. "Our guys come down to the valley at night when it's safer. We take what we need and leave the rest for the villagers, a gesture of good faith and friendship, you can say."

"What are the bonfires for?" I asked.

"We burn the chutes," Clover said. "The Taliban are ingenious fuckers. Who knows what they can make from the chutes and use against us?" he smiled wickedly.

A heavy, dark mood took over me as if Evil were infiltrating my soul and I had no defense against it. The anguish of the moment etched an everlasting impression.

Nolay was perched on a hilltop. Trucks had to climb a 45-degree hillside to get to the dirt driveway leading to the base. Many times, heavy trucks couldn't make it uphill and had to be pulled up by LVSR's. The trick was to approach the slope at an angle instead of going up straight.

We made it up the hill to Nolay by early dawn. Not an easy task with the mine roller attached to the front of our truck, but Smitts was one hell of a driver.

What a decrepit place. The gray weather, not to mention the relics of two destroyed rusty tanks sitting to the left of the staging area we parked in, depressed the hell out of me. The tanks were either remnants from the Russians invasion almost thirty years earlier, or from our fight with the Taliban who had seized the tanks from Russians and now used them against us. A few yards away from the tanks sat the bullet-riddled carcass of a couple of destroyed eight-wheeler APCs, Armored Personnel Carriers, belonging to our side. Doubtful their passengers had made it out alive or in one piece. Up above, two big white blimps hovered over Nolay, monitoring the surroundings 24/7.

I was sitting on the LVSR flatbed nibbling on some beef jerky when Kent approached with another Marine.

"Hey, Sanj, they need your help," he said, pointing to the Marine.

I jumped down from the flatbed.

"Can you help us in the field hospital?" the Marine asked.

"Yes, sir," I replied.

We entered the field hospital tent and walked to the far end of it. Doctors and nurses scrambled frantically between two tables. Initially, all I saw was an Afghan couple. The woman had lifted her burqa, unveiling the tears flowing down her anguished face. The man stood silent, stone-faced.

"Please tell 'em we're doing everything we can to help 'em," the doctor said to me.

I took a few steps closer. On the tables lay two young boys, one about eleven or twelve, the other seven. I took a step closer. The older boy's body was missing from the abdomen down. His eyes gazed into the afterlife, his half-open mouth screamed the last cry trapped in his throat for eternity. His tightly-clenched fists indicated the pain he had endured as he gasped for air, taking his last breath.

I turned to the other table. My brain moved in slow motion in contrast with the frenzied activity around me. The younger boy was missing nearly the entire right side of his body as he barely hung on to life. His little body was severely scorched. There was no skin or meat left on some parts of his small frame, exposing his fragile blackened bone. The skin on his forehead had peeled off, curled, and burned to a crisp. The irises of his wide-open eyes had turned into a solid shiny black. It was as if I could reach into them. They blinked as tears slowly rolled down from the outside corner of his left eye.

I thought I would faint. I had never imagined coming face-to-face with such devastation. But instead, for whatever reason, I was detached, my reaction unemotional.

"Tell 'em we're doing everything we can to save him," a doctor told me to say.

"Doctar sahib wowayel che hara marasta che zamong pa was ki wee warsara ba ye okro."

The doctor told me to ask what had happened. The father said he had been working in the field with his sons. At lunchtime, the boys walked home to bring back food. Somewhere along the way, the older boy had stepped on an IED.

I translated the information. The IED could have been planted by the father himself. Such incidents were not uncommon. I looked at the little boy. He kept repeating something. Without asking the doctors or nurses for permission I got up next to the operating table and leaned over to hear his tiny, fading voice.

"Zma wror tsanga dai?" he asked. "How's my brother?"

The crew was working feverishly on the little boy.

"*Sta wror kha dai.*" I said. "Your brother is okay." I touched the boy's burnt face; his skin felt brittle. "*Hagha ghwari che ta ghawi aw shoja ose.*" He wants you to be strong and brave."

My complete disconnect from the moment surprised me. I looked over at Kent, standing in the corner. His eye sockets had turned red, framing his tear-filled blue eyes.

The doctors' efforts were futile. The little boy died. I walked over to the grieving parents and stood with them. Nothing I could say or do would bring back their boys. I remembered the first few lines of the Arabic requiem for the dead.

"*Bismellah Al-Rahman Al-Rahim,*

Al-Hamdulellah Rab Al-Alamin,

Al-Rahman Al-Rahim,

Malik-e Yum Aldin…" I recited. "In The Name of Allah The Compassionate and The Merciful, Praise be Allah, Lord of The Universe, The Most Merciful, Master of Judgment Day…"

The nurses covered the boys' bodies. I slowly walked over to Kent. The only dry eyes in the clinic belonged to me. I tapped Kent on the back, and we headed for the exit.

Another doctor approached us before we made it to the door. He asked if I could translate for him. I agreed and followed him into a makeshift exam area enclosed with dividers where a young Afghan soldier sat on the exam table.

"He just showed up here," the doctor said.

"What's wrong, brother?" I asked the young soldier in Pashto.

He dropped his head. "My back hurts," he replied in Dari, almost whispering.

The soldier's shaky voice and hunched posture symbolized shame.

"Did you lift something heavy?" I asked. "Tell me so we can help you."

The young soldier was behaving skittishly. "My back hurts very much," he repeated.

I translated for the doctor.

The doctor examined the soldier's spine. "Ask him if this hurts," he said as he pressed on the soldier's lower back.

Before I could ask the question, the soldier said, "Not my back"—he looked me in the eyes—"MY BACK."

I looked at the soldier enquiringly. "You mean your bottom hurts?" I asked.

The soldier nodded.

I told the doctor.

"Tell him to drop his pants and turn around," the doctor said.

The soldier reluctantly turned around and dropped his pants.

"Tell him to bend over the table," the doctor said.

The soldier heeded and ever so slowly bent over the table. I gasped at the sight. His anus was covered with warts. The doctor and I shared a bewildered look. The doctor slipped on some gloves and examined the area. The young soldier's body shook from shame and humiliation.

I walked around the table to face the soldier. Squatting down, I put my hand on his shoulder.

"*Parwa nist. Ma inja astim be to komak konim*," I said. "Don't fret. We're here to help you."

The poor kid broke down crying. I grabbed some paper towels from the table next to me and handed them to him.

I managed to calm the soldier down and get him to confide in me. He said he was from Mazar-i-Sharif, in the north, and had been transferred to the south. His barracksmates had designated him "*chai bache*" or "*tea boy*,"—a job that involved more than serving tea. After the tea is served the tea boy is sodomized by almost everyone present. A common occurrence. Many soldiers in the south were shipped from the northern part of Afghanistan. They were Tajiki or Uzbeki. Most did not speak Pashto. The coalition sent soldiers to the south on purpose. The idea was to limit Taliban infiltration into the Afghan military to lessen the chance of Afghan soldiers turning their weapons on the coalition forces.

"I'm not able to do much for him here; I'll submit a request to get him transferred to Kabul." The doctor looked at me. "They're better equipped to deal with this," he said.

1318 HOURS / MARCH 28, 2011

Our stay at Nolay lasted a few long days. Convoys were not allowed to use any of the facilities there—chow hall, shower tents, or toilets. Understandably so. Nolay couldn't accommodate more than its own personnel. The only thing Nolay provided for visiting convoys was a plywood outhouse near the staging area. The three-adjacent-stall outhouse had no doors or curtains for privacy. Three refuse collection barrels cut in half sat directly under each hole in the plywood. Some unlucky low-ranking soldier was assigned to burn the content of the barrels every few days with help from diesel fuel.

I entered the fly-infested "toilet" one afternoon holding a pair of clean military-issue tube socks. By now I'd learned not to be picky. The ghastly condition of the makeshift toilet didn't bother me. Sitting in the middle stall allowed for some privacy from the outsiders looking in. Smitts and Kent joined me after a few minutes, each sitting on either side of me. The height of the seat prevented my feet from reaching the floor. Smitts suffered from a similar issue. The only feet on the floor belonged to Kent. We engaged in small talk as we went along. The casualness of the scene put a smile on my face. We would have had the same conversation over lunch or dinner.

"You two need to get some platform boots to reach the floor," Kent said.

"Hey, Sanj, why aren't you squatting over the hole like the Afghans do?" Smitts joked.

I took out a cigarette pack from my chest pocket, lit three cigarettes, and passed one to each of my neighbors.

"Hey Sanj, can you spare some wipes?" Smitts asked.

"Just use your hands," Kent said.

"Yeah, use your sleeve," I added.

We hadn't taken a shower for almost two weeks. We used baby wipes to clean up and everyone had run out of them. Hence the tube socks. Baby wipes were a much sought-after commodity on missions.

"Anyone got a knife?" I asked.

"Why? You need to saw off your shit?" Smitts asked, laughing.

I took the socks from my pant pocket. "Don't you wanna wipe?" I held up the socks.

Kent took the socks, pulled out his knife and cut them into twelve pieces. He took four and handed me the rest. I split the eight between myself and Smitts.

"No wipe, no problem," I said.

I pulled up my pants, buttoned up, and stepped out. Hand sanitizer was the method for hand washing.

Outside, I ran into the doctor who had examined the young Afghan soldier and inquired about the soldier's status. The doctor said he'd gotten him transferred back north and referred him to a doctor up there for treatment.

0730 HOURS / APRIL 01, 2011

We pushed off from Nolay and headed to FOB Jackson, in Sangin, with a convoy of thirty or so vehicles. FOB Jackson/Sangin was an even deadlier place than Nolay. Taliban snipers and drug lords had exacted heavy tolls on the Marines in Jackson/Sangin. The FOB backed to a bazaar, Salaam Bazaar, on one side. The Marines called it Slum Bazaar. Thick slabs of farmland, trees and poppy fields enfolded the other three sides of the base. A river ran through the FOB, dividing it into two sections connected by a pair of dirt paths with bridges. One bridge was narrow and could only handle pedestrian crossings, and the other was wide and sturdy enough to handle our heavy trucks.

One side housed the Americans and the other the Afghan National Army, ANA, and the Afghan National Police, ANP. Poppy plants covered large patches of the landscape in Sangin; opium trafficking from this area provided a good portion of funds necessary for the Taliban's operations. Counterfeit money also had a hot market in this place. Word had it that the head of the Afghan National Police, on the other side of the river, had two tea boys living with him, and no one dared to challenge his authority on this issue. Even the American and coalition forces looked the other way.

The convoy descended from a hilltop and headed toward Slum Bazaar, a five-kilometer long, tightly packed commercial area that on this day,

Friday—the weekend—was jammed wall-to-wall with people, cars, motorcycles, donkeys, sheep, goats, and carts. We had to travel the full length of the bazaar to reach the FOB's front gate. This situation could have proved deadly, especially in Sangin. One suicide bomber on foot or in a car could wipe us out, along with any unfortunate bystanders.

We decided to stop outside the bazaar, to allow some time for the crowd of shoppers to thin out. We formed three columns. Our truck was the last in the third column. Our stoppage brought out an avalanche of villagers. The usual interaction between soldiers and locals played out. We played with the children, kicking their deflated plastic soccer ball around, and handing out stuff.

"I don't like this," Smitts said to Kent and Clover as we stood together, smoking.

"You don't like playing with the kids?" I asked.

"Nah," Kent said. "He means he doesn't like being exposed the way we are."

"Should I piss my pants now or later?" I asked, only somewhat joking.

"You don't know the history of this place, do you?" Smitts asked.

"We lost many good Marines here in Sangin," Kent said.

"Yeah, at the hands of a goddamned fifteen–year-old Tali sniper." Clover said indignantly. "The douchebag was a great shot, one shot to the neck. One bullet, one kill."

"We could be in his crosshairs, then," I said worriedly.

"He was iced by one of our snipers," Clover replied. "But there could be others in his place."

"We put the word out that there's a bounty on sniper's head," Kent said, smiling. "Someone from here ratted him out and got a brand new motorcycle in return."

"He was hiding between the branches high up on a tree," Clover added. "The snitch gave us his location, our boy returned the favor. One bullet to the neck. One shot, one kill." Clover smiled wickedly.

A couple of hours passed, but the bazaar did not quiet down and neither did my sense of alertness. Word came on the radio to mount up and get ready to push through.

Slowly, the convoy wormed its way through the lively bazaar, everyone on high alert, guns ready. The five kilometers took more than an hour to complete.

Hescos outlined FOB Jackson/Sangin on three sides, and a narrow dirt path led to the inside of the base. Beyond the vehicle bridge to the left of the path, hesco barriers surrounded a cluster of tents and actual, clean, mobile shower trailers the likes of which did not exist on LNK. The landing zone was located at the end of the dirt road at the far end of the base, with three or four transit tents next to it. The base didn't have much of a chow hall, just a tent that served only MREs. There was an MWR tent, a USO tent with free books ranging from Tom Clancy thrillers to cheesy romance novels by Rebecca Brandewyne, and a twenty-four-hour self-serve coffee maker. A small mud hut structure had been converted into a chapel. A drug lord's three-story concrete villa with a basement, situated on the American side, served as the headquarters for the Marines, intelligence, and other groups converging in Jackson. The villa was pockmarked with bullet holes. Parts of the parameter wall encircling the villa had collapsed altogether from mortar rounds. The villa even had a swimming pool, albeit devoid of water. A nice-sized concrete pad next to the pool served as an open-air gym area, with rusty weights, life-cycles, and other decomposing exercise equipment.

The Afghan side consisted of a few one-story brick, mortar, and plaster buildings, one of which was occupied by American military contractors and advisors. A big, solid iron gate separated the Afghan's courtyard from the bazaar. A large patch of land planted in dozens and dozens of pomegranate trees sat beside the Afghan section, and I enjoyed the fruits on multiple occasions.

1327 HOURS / APRIL 03, 2011

We didn't have a place to sleep in Jackson, so we nodded off inside the trucks or on cots next to them. I didn't have much to do. My teammates mainly kept busy with jobs that did not require my involvement. I spent most of my time sitting by the river that separated the two bases, smoking and watching the Afghan soldiers fish. The river served as a form of meditation, its peacefulness juxtaposed against the tribulation just a short distance away. Aside from its soothing quality, the river provided a sort of entertainment as well. On the Afghan side, a makeshift plywood outhouse had been installed upriver right on the water's edge so that its deposits fell directly into the current. Afghan soldiers washed their clothes a few feet downstream from the latrine. A few more feet downriver they washed their dishes, and a few more feet down they brushed their teeth, washed their faces, swam, bathed, and even fished. I received a couple of invitations to lunch or dinner from the Afghan side, but I respectfully declined after witnessing how they washed their dishes and pots. The last thing I needed was some type of viral infection or parasite.

The cold air and lack of a warm sleeping bag made nights agonizing, but I toughed it out and pretended all was fine.

The alarm sounded on the fourth day of our stay at the base and everyone scrambled to their stations, weapons ready. Kent, Smitts, Gospol, and Clover grabbed their long guns and headed to the south end of the base. I followed.

The watchtowers had their heavy weapons pointed to the field behind the base. Marines, contractors, and other armed civilians lined the hesco barriers. I squeezed myself between my team members. All binoculars pointed in the same direction.

"Check this out, bro." Smitts handed me his binoculars.

I looked through the field glasses. A donkey laden with heavy cargo was approaching the base on its own. The poor beast of burden walked slowly and unsteadily as it traversed the uneven terrain. At times it looked like it would collapse from the weight of its cargo.

"About a thousand yards out," Clover said.

Word quickly got around. The donkey could be carrying explosives. The Taliban had attempted similar attacks on the base before. We could've easily blown the donkey to smithereens, but instead, an EOD or Explosive Ordinance Disposal team was dispatched to intercept the donkey before it got any closer to the base. This is the difference between us and the Taliban: We value life, all life, even a donkey's.

Two EOD vehicles approached the donkey in the middle of the field.

The donkey stopped. One of the vehicles deployed a robotic arm with a camera attached to it to view the content of the donkey's cargo. There was a chance that the explosives could be detonated remotely, another common tactic employed by the Taliban. I felt secure, flanked by the trained killing machines who showed great compassion even for a donkey, but I prayed for the occupants of the EOD trucks in the field.

It took a very long time to examine the content of the donkey's cargo. Finally, the rear gate to one of the trucks opened. One of the EOD guys stepped out and geared up in a bomb/blast suit. Apparently the poor donkey carried bad news on his back.

Not a whisper could be heard. I looked up. The white balloons hovering above the base were certainly monitoring the action and surveying the area for secondary threats.

Wearing the heavy bomb suit, the EOD specialist slowly approached the donkey, lifted the burlap cover, and went to work on whatever had been hidden underneath. My heart pumped faster, adrenaline rushed through my veins, and I perspired even though the weather was cool. A junkie I'd become, addicted to adrenaline.

After a long, slow, deliberate process, the specialist gave the all-clear sign. Excitement filled the base. We watched as the two trucks provided cover for the EOD personnel as he walked the donkey back to Jackson.

The base erupted in cheers as the EOD crew returned safely. The explosives were rushed away to a restricted area of the base to be analyzed and recorded. Everyone else gathered around the hero of the hour as he held the donkey's harness. The base commander, Lt. Colonel Bisset, shook hands and congratulated the individual for a job well done. And it *was* a job well done. It's baffling how anyone could be daring enough to do such work. The EOD people must have ice running through their veins and balls made of titanium.

Marines patted the donkey and fed him apples from their chow hall rations.

"What're we gonna call the new prisoner?" someone yelled, referring to the donkey.

"Call him Saddam," someone said.

"No, call him Osama," another replied.

The base commandant held up his arms to quiet everyone.

"What should we call him?" he asked the EOD guy.

Scratching his head, the man replied, "Hm, let's call him Tony the Famous Detainee."

Everyone hollered, cheered, and high-fived each other. In the land where every day is The Day of The Dead, saving even a donkey's life is reason enough for celebration.

0928 HOURS / APRIL 05, 2011

Five days had passed since our arrival in Sangin. One morning Clover joined me as I sat by the river with coffee in one hand and a cigarette in the other—my usual companions in the crisp air.

"Hey Sanj, you up for a gig?" Clover asked.

"A gig? You askin' me to join a band?" I smiled.

"Yeah, music could be played, if you know what I mean."

"What's up? Whose ass do I gotta kick?" I asked, still smiling.

Clover lit a cigarette. "We have intel on a drug lord. He's gonna be at a mechanic shop at the other end of Slum Bazaar in a bit." Clover took a long drag. "We're gonna hit him."

The man's eyes had a different look to them, a predatory gleam.

"You want me to go with you?" I asked.

"I trust you. That's why I'm asking you to go along."

Kent and Smitts joined us.

"Hey, I'm asking Sanj to take a stroll with me in the bazaar later today," Clover said to the other two.

"What?" Kent looked surprised. "By whose orders?"

"No one ordered it. I just asked him if he'd go with me," Clover replied.

"Are you crazy?" Smitts turned to Kent. "He's crazy. This man is crazy."

"Know that you can say no," Clover said to me.

"I know." I took a sip of coffee. "I'll go."

"One more thing before you commit," Clover said.

"What's that, do I gotta dance too?"

Clover looked me straight in the eyes. "We'll be walking the entire length of Slum Bazaar and back. You still game?"

Kent and Smitts' waited for my response.

"Good to go," I said.

It was about 1030 hours when we left FOB Jackson. Our group was comprised of a dozen Marines, four DEA and FBI agents, and a few Afghan soldiers. We walked out the gates and onto the dirt path leading to Slum Bazaar. The cadaver of a suicide bomber's car from a few weeks earlier sat on the side of the road.

"You missed the barbecue," a Marine said to me.

I looked at the remains and ran my hand along its side as I slowly walked by. The images of twisted and charred cars that we see on the news in America are distant and detached. Seeing, touching, and smelling the sharp odor emanating from a suicide bomber's car is a chilling experience. It leaves a perpetual ghoulish impression in one's essence.

We reached the bazaar after a deliberately slow, methodical walk. The team separated into two columns, one on each side of the narrow street, with tightly crammed shops on both sides. Other narrow streets fed into the main strip, making it easy for the Taliban to ambush or snipe us.

The bazaar was bursting with merchants, shoppers, bicycles, motorcycles, cars, herds of goats and sheep, and donkey-drawn carts. Our teams walked with ten to fifteen feet between each person. I was the most vulnerable member because I had no weapon. The Taliban could have easily spotted me as the *tarjoman* or interpreter, making me a ripe target. All they had to do was come up on me from behind and slash my throat or shank me a few times and then disappear into the crowd. I monitored my surroundings, and picked up random conversations drowned out by calls from vendors shouting prices to lure buyers. The arteries on the sides of my neck bulged and throbbed as blood rushed to my head. Even my sense of smell magnified, detecting the aroma of freshly baked naan and kabab wafting among the shops, the scent of freshly slaughtered meat, and an array of aromatic fruits, apples, pomegranates, and vegetables—basil, leek, coriander, watercress, and scallion—as they drifted in the air. The pungent smell of trash piles, sheep, goats, and their dung added extra texture to an already aromatic environment.

The point person, one of the DEA agents, gave the halt signal. I looked at Clover in front of me. With his nod, he asked my status, and I nodded back, "I'm alright."

Two Afghan men walked past me, stopped, and slowly walked back. My abdomen tightened, pressure built inside my head, and my ears began to burn as if held next to a flame. I parted my feet so as to have a more solid stance, my butt cheeks tightened as my asshole puckered, and my balls retreated. I clenched my fists, ready to strike.

The men got within a couple of feet of me. "*Pa Khodai qasam dai za pohegam che de da Kafaro sara tsa okram*," one said to the other in Pashto. "Swear to God, I know what to do with this infidel."

"*Za ba da hagha sterga obasam aw ter pkho landi ba ye kram che pakhbala sterga ye waweeny*," the other man said. "I will cut one of his eyes out and step on it in front of him as he watches with his other eye."

"I slice the meat off his body and feed it to him," said the first man.

All sounds and smells faded into the background as I zeroed in on their conversation. Pressure built in my head, in my eyes.

"*Leri shai koniano. Taso dwara ba wawzhanam*," I blurted in Pashto. "*Leri shai, mor ghoto*." Get lost, faggots, before I kill you both. Go, motherfuckers."

The men looked at me in rage and disbelief.

"*Leri shai koniano, leri shai*," I repeated as I shooed them away. "*Mor ghoto*."

Calling men "faggots" in Afghanistan is a tremendous insult. In this hyper-male society, any verbal epithet to men is an assault to their manhood, usually resulting in physical altercation.

One of the men spat in front of me and then they hurried away into the crowd.

Neither Clover nor anyone else from my group inquired about the exchange and I wasn't about to dramatize the story even by retelling it. Such encounters and interactions with the locals was to be expected, especially on a busy day in a tightly-packed bazaar.

We walked all the way to the mechanic shop, as per the intel. The shop was closed, no sign of anyone. Either the intel was bad or the drug lord had been tipped off. In any case, we walked back to Jackson without incident. The sight-seeing tour took over five hours. By the time we got back, I didn't have an ounce of energy left in me. My legs were fatigued, my flak jacket and helmet felt like a fuckton of bricks.

"Hey, Sanj. Thanks for steppin' out with me," Clover said, offering me cigarette.

"Someone has to protect you." I took the cigarette and held up my lighter for Clover to light his own smoke.

APRIL 07, 2011

Tony the Famous Detainee probably received more love and attention than a good portion of the local population did. The Marines made a small corral for him, and Tony in return helped with some of the less-exciting chores around the base. He carried heavy loads from the one side to the other and back. A few months later, I read in the *Stars and Stripes* newspaper that Tony the Famous Detainee had been transferred to a farm in Arizona to live the rest of his days in peace. Apparently, the Marines had observed some Afghan soldiers paying romantic visits to Tony late at night. Unbeknown to the Afghans, their every move was being monitored by the night vision cameras on the big white balloons hovering above.

APRIL 09, 2011

It was time to go home. After a few weeks of roughing it and showering with baby wipes, we prepared to leave for Leatherneck. Everyone looked haggard, but morale never wavered.

We left Jackson at 0200. The convoy had shrunk to twenty-three Marine trucks, empty after delivering their provisions, which meant we could travel faster through the rough terrain.

By now the missions had become somewhat routine. We went out, we got ambushed, we got blown up, and we came back. The unspoken possibility that any mission could be our last didn't bother anyone; we knew that safety was never an enduring state of events.

We left FOB Jackson/Sangin and headed down the Slum Bazaar strip. The bazaar felt ghostly. Dim lights flickered here and there, but all the shops were shuttered. I couldn't stop thinking of what hid behind the closed doors and lowered tin shutters: bomb makers, planners, butchers, and for sure, decent folks.

The convoy rolled slowly by the cemetery just outside the village. The howling of hounds echoed through the air, serenading the souls of the departed.

Everyone kept to themselves. Gospol adjusted his sling seat. Smitts turned on his little boom-box, and mellow Latin music drifted over us. Kent worked on the BFT, or Blue Forces Tracker, a GPS that displays the routes and placement of IEDs discovered but not neutralized. Clover rearranged his backpacks. I felt at ease, content, a feeling I hadn't felt in Los Angeles with my oldest friends. My troubles at home had lost their importance. Being in a war zone brought clarity and gave direction to my life. Now I lived in the moment and nothing else mattered.

I thought of my family. They seemed a lifetime ago. The grinding, conflicting emotions that I had felt within me before coming to the land of the Afghans had all but subsided. Fear of dying had vanished inside me. My thoughts consumed me, but not in a bad way. I remembered Janis Joplin's song *Me and Bobby McGee*, and the line *"Freedom's just another word for nothin' left to lose."* I sat imprisoned in the confines of an armored vehicle, in the middle of hostile lands, yet I felt freer than ever, completely disjoined from my family, friends, and past. My only loyalty was to the people in the convoy. To attempt to describe the organically-developed kinship among complete strangers in a war zone is to betray its bonds of comradery.

My watch showed 0542 hours. The convoy moved along the barren terrain as the sun came up. Smitts' music played over the self-imposed silence that dominated the atmosphere inside the truck. Occasionally someone would light a cigarette, or grab a drink or a pop-tart. Our collective energies had merged, making conversation unnecessary. Random glances between us meant, "I'm just checkin' on you." Clover broke open a case of MREs, and without uttering a word passed them along to us all. We ate in silence and listened to the slow music.

At about 1300 hours we drove along a narrow path next to a village to the right of the convoy. A mud wall thirty feet away separated the village from the road. To the left sat an open field fronting a majestic mountain range some ten or so kilometers in the distance.

Somewhere up front, a vehicle broke down and the convoy stopped in its tracks.

The radio erupted. "Keep eyes on the wall," the convoy commander said.

We had stopped in a perfect ambush spot. Gunners in the turret trained their weapons in all directions, especially on the mud wall. Word came over the radio for my truck to move up to the disabled truck to provide cover and assistance. We slowly pulled out from the tracks, crawled up to the immobilized truck and stopped.

"Can I step out for a quick shake of the lizard?" I asked.

"I gotta take a leak too," Kent said.

We stood between my truck and the disabled truck as a way of protecting ourselves. I faced the big middle tire of the MRAP. Kent stood a few feet away, next to the front tire.

No sooner had I started pissing than—

Tatatatatatatatata – Tatatatatatatata

A barrage of gunfire rained down on us from behind the mud wall. I instinctively dropped to my knees. The ambush had succeeded in scaring my piss away. I crawled next to Kent, who had taken cover behind the big tire of the disabled truck. The two Marines working on the truck managed to climb back into their vehicle. Kent and I were the only ones left out in the open. All turrets turned toward the village wall and unloaded their deluge of death on the enemy. Not much was visible from my squatting position as return fire ricocheted off the armored trucks. I could only hope that neither Kent nor I would get hit by one of the bouncing projectiles.

Just then, Taliban fighters opened fire from the front and the rear of the convoy. We were boxed in from three directions. Kent got his carbine ready. Using the truck as cover, he popped up.

Tatatatatata. He fired away and ducked. Stood again. *Tatatatatata.*

Ducked again.

The Taliban began firing mortar rounds on our position from somewhere in the village. It was impossible to know how far back they had set up their launchers, or if they were using the villagers as a human shield.

The sound of battle elevated, which only meant that more Taliban fighters had joined the fray. The mortar rounds landed closer and closer as the enemy bracketed our position and walked in their fire. The force of the explosions and of the guns on top of our trucks kicked up moondust all around us. I stayed low in my squat, lit a cigarette, and leaned back against the tire.

Kent emptied his magazine on the village, released the empty magazine and reloaded his weapon in an instant. I couldn't tell if I was scared or not. Somehow, I felt at ease as I smoked away. A big smile formed on my face.

Kent dropped down next to me. "The fuck you laughin' at?"

I looked at him with a big grin. "Nothing, I just realized I'm stuck here with no weapon." I took a drag from my cigarette. "Nothing to shoot the enemy with, except my big gun. Maybe I can piss on them," I said, grabbing my crotch.

We laughed.

"Light me up," Kent said.

I lit a cigarette for him and held it up between my fingertips, my elbow resting on my knee. Kent ducked and I held the cigarette to his lips. He took a hit, stood up, and fired away. We cackled the whole time as the ambush intensified.

I had no concept of time. At some point, two Apache helicopters appeared in the sky above us. The convoy commander must have called in the big guns for support. The Apaches circled above a few times, then one bird dove down and opened fire, its deadly M230 chain gun bringing down whatever portion of the mud wall our heavy rounds hadn't already flattened. The sound of rounds exiting the chambers brought news of death and destruction to the enemy. The distinctive smell of gunpowder from the Apache drifted to the ground. After a quick strike the Apache pulled up and the second bird replaced it, diving in a coordinated courtship between two angels of death. This dance continued for a good ten or fifteen minutes.

Finally the guns fell silent and the Apaches pulled away. The ringing in my ears deafened me to anything else. Slowly, I rose to my feet and looked at the mud wall. Nothing was left of it. My desire to know how many Taliban had met their maker overwhelmed me to the point that I caught myself celebrating the demise of others. For some inexplicable reason, I liked my dehumanized self.

Complete silence fell upon the land that, until a few short moments ago, had squalled with the sound of death. The members of the convoy exchanged glances, voiceless dialogues. We knew we'd been given the chance to live another day. Every life-or-death experience further tightened our bonds of kinship.

8
DAISY CHAIN AND LADYBUG

I went on back-to-back-to-back missions for the rest of April, May, and June. I'd often return from one mission and leave on another a few hours later. My body was taxed to its limits and beyond, but my adrenaline addiction fueled me. In a seemingly demented way, I craved getting ambushed; so did the companies I accompanied. Jousting with the enemy always presented its dangers and was never looked upon as a game, but the sensation of the moment counterweighed the risks. Gunny Kovak kept a keen eye on my activities and shook his head every time he saw me in the staging area getting ready to head out again. At one point Lt. Laramy told me she'd give me enough rope to jump, but not enough to hang myself. That was the most acknowledgment I had received from her in all this time. I gained the respect of my tentmates and many other terps, except Ziar. He waited for me to buckle, to crap out.

APRIL 2011

April is poppy harvest season in Afghanistan, and most Taliban fighters temporarily trade their AKs for sickles, but would return to the battlefield by June. In April, the Taliban announced the launch of Operation Badr (Operation Full Moon or Harvest Moon), a series of conventional and unconventional attacks across the country, including the northern region.

The battalion held a bbq/talent show in its compound. We had no missions scheduled and everyone was in attendance, including the top brass. Two LVSRs parked next to each other formed a stage. Anyone who dared could go up and showcase his or her talent. A couple of Marines tried their hand at stand-up comedy routines. They got booed off the stage. Others went up and played the guitar or performed hula dances in cut-out paper skirts. Hot dogs and burgers flew off the grill before they were fully cooked. This was one big family outing, except that here, we stayed in.

MAY 2011

I sat in the chow hall by myself on 2nd of May enjoying a bowl of jello and ice cream while watching the news on the flat-screen TV. The volume was always muted, so I read the scrolling headlines beneath the voiceless anchor.

> **"NEWS ALERT: OSAMA BIN LADEN KILLED BY US NAVY SEALS IN ABBOTTABAD, PAKISTAN."**

It was an unforgettable moment. The always quiet chow hall erupted in celebration. Soldiers cheered, high-fived, smiled, and applauded. A heave of electricity shot through the big space. The news re-energized my fatigued body and depleted soul as if I'd gotten an intercontinental ballistic nuclear missile shoved up my ass. Finally, the butcher of the innocent had gotten his long-overdue retribution.

JUNE 28, 2011

Nine members of the Haqqani network, an Al-Qaida affiliate, killed at least 9 people in an attack on Hotel Inter-Continental Kabul, which was frequented by Westerners and VIPs. The Pakistani intelligence agency or ISI was thought to have had a hand in the attack.

The Taliban in the Kandahar region had a couple of new toys, two anti-aircraft guns mounted inside vans. They'd already attacked a few of our convoys with deadly results. The weapons were hard to hunt down since they were concealed inside van models popular in Afghanistan. Joe and Tony showed me some of the grisly pictures of our destroyed trucks. The rounds from the guns penetrated the armor as if going through silk, shredding to pieces every occupant inside the truck. One van was tracked down and destroyed by our side but the other evaded detection, lurking somewhere in the rough country. Fearful of this, most terps refused to go outside the wire, and who could blame them?

A group of us terps sat together in the chow hall. The others gorged as usual while I ate a bowl of fruit and jello. Hot weather always kills my appetite.

Lt. Laramy and Lt. Maddox stopped by.

"I need someone for a last minute mission," Laramy said. "Small convoy, maybe seven or eight trucks, a quick run to FOB Edi."

None of my lunch companions made a move. It was to be expected, and to be fair, I had my apprehensions also.

"I'm the convoy commander. We leave tonight," Lt. Maddox said.

No one uttered a word or made a move.

"You cruising in an MRAP?" I asked Maddox jokingly.

"Four-by-four." Maddox smiled.

"When should I be at the staging area?" I asked.

Laramy jumped in. "You don't need to be a hero."

I looked her straight on without responding.

"Be at the staging area at midnight." Maddox smiled in approval.

There was something unfinished between Maddox and me. Hila's demise had been a moment of personal devastation for us. Maybe this mission would bring closure to the concealed feelings of guilt we shared.

Laramy looked at the other terps. No one made a move. She exchanged a glance with Maddox then looked at me again. She seemed unsettled. I wondered if she actually cared about me.

The staging area lacked its usual electric feel. Everyone was quiet and focused.

Cnl. Webber walked up. "Hey, Sanj, thanks for volunteering. I know you're doing more than you have to."

"To say I'm not scared would be a lie." I smiled feebly.

Webber nodded. "We have assets monitoring the area as we speak. We'll get 'em."

After roll call and weapons check, everyone went back to their trucks.

My companions were Lt. Maddox, Cpl. Whipple and Sgt. Moore, same as our first time out together.

Our cargo must have been something sensitive and urgent because the convoy moved rapidly through the base. I was given a scanner to listen in on the locals' mobile phone chatter to identify possible threats as we journeyed.

As the convoy veered off Highway 1, the level of alertness kept everyone silent. Moore rotated the turret to surveil the surroundings. Whipple kept pace with the rest of the convoy and drove the heavy truck as if it were a compact sport car. Maddox worked on the BFT, and I had the headset adjusted tightly on my ears as I scanned different radio frequencies listening to any conversation the device picked up. Maddox and I exchanged glances now and then without uttering a word. We each knew exactly what was going through the other's mind.

Driving non-stop, we reached Edi in just under 24 hours. The adrenaline was running so high that no one showed the slightest sign of fatigue. Our stay in Edi lasted just long enough to drop off the cargo, refuel, and head back.

At 0330 hours we were about a half hour away from Leatherneck. Then the radio sounded off. "The threat is eliminated. Repeat. The threat is eliminated." The radio went silent for a brief moment. "We own the night."

The convoy picked up speed as if a weight had been lifted off the trucks. Tension drained from the atmosphere faster than a belch expelled from a drunken sailer.

The mission took less than four days and surprisingly, without any skirmish with the enemy. Back at the compound, Moore and I made a few trips to the armory to return the fifty-cal and ammo canisters. I returned the scanning gear assigned to me and helped Whipple clean up inside the truck. Whipple and Moore thanked me for helping them. With my day bag over my vest and helmet in hand, I headed for the gate. As I passed Lt. Laramy's tent, she and Lt. Maddox walked out.

"Hey, Sanj, wait up. Thanks for going on this mission with me." Maddox's face displayed gratitude.

"We both needed this trip together, Lieutenant," I replied, knowing full well what Maddox meant.

Lt. Laramy looked puzzled, trying to figure out the exchange between Maddox and me.

To my mind the mission had affirmed what Maddox and I sought from one another but had never acknowledged. The shared journey had succeeded in bringing us closer even though we didn't speak or bring up Hila the whole time.

JULY 12, 2011

Azeem Wali Karzai, the brother of the Afghan President Hamid Karzai, was assassinated by his long-time head of security. Rumor had it that Azeem was working for the CIA while controlling a large opium-smuggling network.

On this day, two British soldiers, both male, went missing. All available search and rescue assets from the southern region were summarily employed to find them. Their bodies were discovered later, most likely killed at the hands of the Taliban. Word had it they had been raped multiple times before their brutal demise.

News of an attempt to kill a female terp by several Afghan soldiers as she left the showers at night in FOB Marjah spread throughout the camp. It was alleged that the soldiers tried to strangle her from behind using piano wire, a favorite tool of the Taliban. They missed her neck and the wire got wedged between her lips, slicing her cheeks open to her ears.

JULY 15, 2011

Lt. Laramy issued another two-week reprieve for me. She and Gunny Kovak kept careful watch over me, fully aware of the fact that all the companies wanted me on missions. I welcomed the time off, as I was feeling signs of physical and mental fatigue.

Much of my time off was spent hanging out at the café in Bastions or the new Italian espresso bar and pizzeria at the newly-opened Bastion 0. Aside from exercising religiously, I kept a good diet, including a heavy dose of nicotine. I purchased a box of Cuban cigars from Bastion 0 and shared them with Colonel Webber, from the battalion, any chance we had to connect. Our favorite place to hang out was the Danish coffee shop at Camp Viking, which was a part of Bastion II.

Camp Viking belonged to the Danish. The Danes had a small cozy coffee shop that resembled a grandma's kitchen. The elderly Danish women running the place had that aura about them, baking homemade cakes and cookies daily and selling them for next to nothing. A sand-filled volleyball court sat to the side of the coffee shop's outdoor patio. Watching the female Danish soldiers play volleyball on the sand provided a much-welcomed break from the testosterone-charged atmosphere of too many guys in too cramped a space for far too long. Colonel Webber and I would sit on the patio, drinking non-alcoholic beer—which by the way got me drunk—and smoking cigars.

I also continued my surveillance work for Joe and Tony. I visited the mosques, the bazaars, and kept tabs on the other terps. The lonely dirt road, the silver tinted-window Tahoe, the slow drive around the base, and the drop-off at the same depressing spot was a recurring theme. We met once a week, but I didn't have anything to report. The bazaar incident had put all the shop owners and workers on alert. The vendors kept tightlipped, but they were still friendly toward me and always invited me over for tea and pastries. Nonetheless, I kept a keen eye on them; they could easily become vindictive and try to get even. I think Joe and Tony enjoyed hearing my stories from beyond the wire, since they couldn't leave the base. I'd like to think they lived vicariously through me.

The July nights were hot and clammy. A large group of male and female terps came over to my tent for a terps' shindig. They brought with them a variety of Afghan pastries, and made tea. A festive mood filled the air as the crowd gathered and sat all over in front of my tent. They played Persian pop music, which was very popular amongst the Afghans. The party was a nice change from the normally tense atmosphere. Conversation topics ranged from family to exaggerated mission stories.

I sat on a campfire stool and talked with Manouchehr, a polite, lanky, clean-cut guy in his mid-thirties. Manouch, as I called him, didn't belong there; he was like a harp in a heavy metal band. His polite manners were too gentile for dealing with the military, the environment, and the enemy.

"Mr. Irani, God bless you for going on all the dangerous missions," he said. "My own people don't want to go to the places you go."

"Thanks, Manouch, I appreciate your acknowledgment."

As he leaned over to pick up something from the ground, a gold medallion necklace fell out of his shirt. It was the Bahai symbol, a nine-pointed star with the name of their prophet Baha, which means "Splendor" or "Glory," etched on it in Farsi. I knew what the symbol meant because I had Bahai friends back in L.A.

"I wouldn't wear that thing out here if I were you Manouch," I said as he hurriedly shoved the medallion back under his shirt.

"You know what it means?"

"Yeah, I do. You know that most Muslims don't take kindly to that symbol and the religion it represents, especially out here."

Color faded from Manoch's face. "Promise you won't tell anyone, please."

"Your secret is safe with me," I replied.

Manouch became quiet. He looked worried.

"On my father's grave, I swear—not a word, Manouch," I said.

He smiled uncomfortably.

"You're in safe company," I said.

If only Manouch could see my dog tags, which clearly stated my Jewish creed.

At midnight and the party was still continuing full force. The clammy air buzzed with music, conversation, and laughter. Terps came and terps went. Some of our neighboring soldier tent-dwellers joined the gathering, although one rule in Leatherneck was that females and males were not allowed to enter each other's tents.

I went into my tent to grab a pack of cigarettes from my bunk. Ziar was sitting there with a half-dozen other terps, looking at a *Round Mounds* magazine and commented on the hefty female ass-dunes adorning its pages. When I glanced over at him Ziar was salivating, his lustful eyes devouring the images of big mounds of flesh in thongs.

I walked over to my bunk and grabbed the cigarettes from my backpack.

"Thank God for the infidel and *Yehud* women," Ziar slobbered. "Maybe they got some Irani bitches in here too!"

Yehud means "Jewish" in Dari. Had Ziar discovered my heritage? Whatever the case, if Ziar had wanted to get a rise out of me, he'd succeeded.

"I see you're facing your newly discovered Mecca," I said as I walked by.

"Hey. Fucker. What did you say?" Ziar asked.

I stopped, turned around, and faced the group. "Now I know where you bow when you say your daily prayers."

"What did you say?" Ziar leaped up from his chair threw his shoulders back to look bigger. "I'm a good Mosalmon." He pointed his stumpy finger at me. "What are you, you don't even say *nomaz* (pray)."

I squared my shoulders. The outside noise invaded the anxious atmosphere inside the tent.

"I pray for God to protecting me," Ziar said angrily. "God doesn't protecting you."

I cracked a smile at his fucked-up English. "Yeah, you say your prayers between infidels' legs." I took a step forward. "Maybe God gives you an Irani pussy in your dreams. Fucker."

"Fuck you!" Ziar said with a slight lift in his heels, "Fuck you. Fuck you, Irani."

The other terps grabbed him.

Unbeknownst to me, Shafi had walked in and stood behind me. When he put his hand on my shoulder, I turned around ready to punch and be punched.

"Come, Mr. Irani," Shafi said in Dari with his relaxed attitude. "I have your back." He led me out of the tent. "His mind is ill."

News of the incident with Ziar spread to other terps. It even reached Colonel Webber, Lieutenant Laramy, and the rest of the battalion, not to mention my employer's new site manager, who made inquiries about the incident. As far as I was concerned the whole episode had been harmless.

A few days after the terp party, Manouch sat down with me at the chow hall and flashed me his dog tags. He had taken my advice.

JULY 17, 2011

My 45th birthday. I had never liked this day and didn't tell anyone about it. Instead, I watched a movie on my laptop in bed with my earphones on. My tentmates were busy doing their usual routine: cards, music, and tea. The confined area of my bunk bed shielded me from everyone's view. Then I heard a loud voice and pulled one earphone out.

"Ok, everyone, gather 'round," Gunny Kovak said.

I pulled my boots on, left my private nest, and joined the others.

"I have names for the next mission," Gunny said. "Show up for briefing tomorrow at 0900 hours if your name is called."

"Ziar. Sanj. Be there on time," Gunny said, and then turned around and left.

JULY 18, 2011

Lethargically, I listened to the information disseminated at the briefing. The next mission was going to be short, no more than a week. I looked up from my notepad just in time to lock eyes with Laramy. Neither of us backed away from the stare-down. I found Laramy fascinating, though not in a sexual way. Her self-confidence and strength of character were admirable, and in such stark contrast to the plight of the Afghan women.

After the briefing, I hung out with Kent, Smitts, and Clover for a while. Clover was going with us on this mission, though he would not ride in our truck as rear security. He'd been assigned to another vehicle.

Figuring we'd be done ahead of schedule, I packed lightly for the mission. Ziar attended to his backpack as well. I noticed that the normally noisy tent lacked energy. It was unusually quiet. Maybe I was projecting my mood outwardly. I walked outside and sat on the empty ammo canister, leaned back against the concrete T-wall and lit a cigarette. Butterflies fluttered in my gut, as the pre-mission angst hadn't lessened after all this time. Lethargy countered the anxiety, zapping me of every ounce of energy.

I smoked a few cigarettes back-to-back.

0100 HOURS / JULY 19, 2011

When I arrived at the staging area, Kent, Smitts, and Gospol were busy getting the truck ready. I walked to the armory with Gospol to sign out the big 50-caliber gun—a heavy piece of deterrent. Gospol signed for the gun and picked up the actual body while I grabbed the barrel. Terps were strictly forbidden from entering the armory, but I was allowed in. My team spirit and reputation had earned me the right, even though I didn't expect any preferential treatment from the battalion. My objective was to be a contributing member, and my actions illustrated my honest attempt. The Marines reciprocated with elevated regard.

Ziar was chitchatting with Laramy as I walked out the armory. They saw me exit the place carrying ammo canisters. Ziar pointed to the armory and then to me. I could read his lips asking Laramy why I was allowed to enter the forbidden place, and unaccompanied. Laramy followed me with her unyielding gaze.

Everyone gathered for roll-call. Ziar was assigned to the third truck from the front. He didn't look very happy about being so close to the front, since the first few trucks and the very last one were prime Taliban targets.

At approximately 0237 hours engines rumbled and exhausts roared. I closed the back gate of the 4x4 MRAP and my anxiety vaporized immediately. My lethargy, however, didn't. This would be a short mission, I reminded myself. Then again, I knew not to count the days, just complete the task.

The convoy consisted of twenty-two Marine trucks and twenty Afghan fuel tanker trucks carrying JP-8 fuel (JP-8 is modified jet fuel used by the U.S. military). When we stopped at another staging area near the fuel farm to incorporate the local trucks into our convoy I was ordered to gather the Afghan drivers and brief them on the mission. This was a part of my duties any time we had Afghan nationals, military or civilian, accompanying us on missions.

I directed the Afghan trucks to fall-in in proper arrangement. The column formation of the convoy was staggered: every two or three Marine trucks were followed by a few Afghan trucks to provide coverage and security for the *haji* tin cans on wheels. When I finished directing the formation,

Smitts pulled up and I hopped in.

Our mission included the delivery of fuel and provisions to FOB Musa Qala, followed by COB Signes, and finally FOB Shamshir. The subdued mood inside the truck prompted me to take my helmet off, lie down across the seats and close my eyes. The same empty feelings of worthlessness I had felt prior to my deployment devoured me. My demons had caught up with me, again. I thought about what I would do once my contract ended. Did I have it in me to sign up for another tour; would I sign up for another round? If not, what would I do back home? Would I ever again see the people I was with now? Laramy?

These questions sucked the energy out of me like leeches draining every ounce of vigor from my fatigued body and soul. A kerosene lamp can't burn brightly or last long without getting topped off. Impulsively, my physical and mental dexterities had burned so very brightly for nearly ten months without dulling or needing replenishment. But now, my corporeal and cognitive luster were dimming. The ceaseless, intangible stresses of living in a war zone had slowly settled inside me. My thoughts would not unhand me. Still, eventually, I fell into a deep sleep.

0729 HOURS / JULY 20, 2011

"Hey, Sanj, wake up," Gospol shook me. "You slept the whole way, man; wake up."

I opened my eyes. Gospol sat across from me, his boyish, smiling face exhibiting sparse patches of stubble growth.

"Bro, you slept the whole way to Musa Qala," Smitts said. "We didn't wanna wake you u— "

"You looked so cute, Sanj," Kent said as they all smiled.

"Yeah, we wanted to cuddle with you," Smitts said with puckered lips.

The convoy stopped at Musa Qala River's edge. Much to my disappointment, my sleep hadn't diminished my dejected mood. I had dreamt about a girl I'd met during my five days in Odessa several years back. Like flame to kerosene, we had been drawn to one another. For the first time in my life, I'd pictured myself living the rest of my days with someone, but I'd cut and ran—another occasion in my life ruined by my acute case of gamophobia.

Sucking on a water bottle, I gazed out the porthole. The river's edge hummed with activity. A couple of farmers with tractors charged people to haul them across the river. Donkey-drawn carriages carried water and other cargo from the river to the village. Kids played on the shore.

Loud *thump* as something hit the side of the truck. Before we knew what was happening, a barrage of rocks pelted the trucks.

The radio sounded off with an urgent voice: "Kids throwing rocks. Gunners get low."

I looked to see where the rocks were coming from.

"Yo, motherfucker, back off, get the fuck away!" Gospol yelled at the kids before he dropped down from the turret. "Hey Sanj, how do you say 'get lost' in Pashto?"

"*Worak sha*," I said.

"How do you say 'motherfucker?'" Gospol asked.

"Man, you don't wanna say that," I said. "These fuckers will go crazy if you say shit about their mother."

The tip of the convoy moved slowly into the river, following the tractors' path since the locals knew where the large drops in the river bed were. Those potholes could have easily swallowed any vehicle from the convoy. In some places the current moved swiftly enough to wash away even the heaviest LVSR, not to mention the tin haji trucks.

The teenage boys and kids didn't tire of throwing rocks at us. Some of the rocks found their way inside the truck through the turret. One of the bigger rocks struck Gospol's left hand.

"Motherfucker," Gospol said, clutching his hand.

"Let me see."

Gospol's hand had already bruised and swelled up.

"Don't think you broke anything." I grabbed the first aid kit hanging on the side wall. "Gotta get the medic to check it out when we get across." I wrapped his hand with gauze.

Our truck took the brunt of the barrage, since we were the last vehicle and had to wait until everyone else had cleared the river shore before we could proceed. Meanwhile, orders came to use the Green Dazzler. Much to his credit, Gospol didn't let his injured hand slow him down: He took out his dazzler and "bedazzled" the little and not-so-little shit fuckers. The dazzler always rattled the locals because they knew what followed—live rounds.

At midday our truck rolled slowly into the river after hours of getting pelted with rocks. Smitts maneuvered the weighty armored vehicle coolly as we drove across a fifty-yard section of the river rapids that had to be at least four feet deep.

Finally, we pulled into FOB Musa Qala and stopped on an incline behind the rest of the convoy. We joined the others for roll call. The villa in the Musa Qala compound stood strong as it bathed the bright midday sun.

Under any other circumstance, FOB Musa Qala would have been a pleasant weekend retreat. Perched on a hillside overlooking the river, Musa Qala had belonged to a drug- and warlord. The place was built like a citadel: a white multi-story concrete villa fenced in by thick walls. Remnants of fruit trees told the story of a once-thriving compound. The enduring bullet-riddled facade of the villa confirmed the integrity of the structure and the quality of its workmanship. On the other hand, parts of the solid perimeter wall had collapsed, either from explosives or mortar rounds, somewhat like the wall at FOB Jackson in Sangin.

After roll call, I wandered around in search of a toilet. I was walking up the path toward the main structure when I heard my name.

"Rohām. Rohām!"

I looked around. I couldn't believe my eyes: it was Pakistani Murad Khan. I hadn't seen him since the night at LNK when we got assigned to different teams.

"Khan Sahib, *tsanga yie?*" I said in Pashto. "Master Khan, how are you?"

We shook hands and hugged.

"Rohām *worur, chiri di? Khpel-zon tsanga da?*" Khan said with genuine joy. "Brother Rohām, where've you been? How are you?"

I told Khan I had to relieve myself.

He pointed to a row of "piss pipe"—a 5-inch PVC pipe rammed into the ground at a 45-degree angle and used exclusively by male residents of the camp.

After that, Khan took me on a tour of Musa Qala. The villa had been named "The White House" by the soldiers living there. We climbed up a damp stairwell to the rooftop. The solid stone steps had fractured, with chunks missing. The paint on the walls had faded and chipped away. But the panoramic views from the rooftop were exotically dramatic. We walked over to the edge of the roof, which had no safety railing or anything resembling such. I looked at the striking hills in the distance and the village we'd just come from on the other side of the river. The villa was built on a slope, and looking down, I realized we were at least two hundred feet from the ground. A cool, delicate breeze carried the smell of kabob.

"We can't stay up here for too long," Khan said with his hands over his head. "Snipers from the village will shoot us."

"You're serious or joking?" I asked.

"I am serious, man." Khan took a hit from his cigarette. "Fuuuuck, it's too dangerous up here," and he raised his eyebrows and arms again.

"Why the fuck you tell me this now?" I chuckled. "You wanna get us killed?"

"Let's get the fuck out of here," Khan said.

The smell of kabob permeated the semi-dark stairwell. Khan said the aroma came from the small bazaar outside the camp. He and his team bought kabobs from there once or twice a week. I asked if I could buy some once we got back to ground level.

Khan led me to a young Afghan soldier. "Tell him what you want and pay him. He'll bring you back the food."

"How much is it?" I asked.

"Five dollars for one course. You get one can of soda with it."

I reached into my pocket. Took out two one-hundred-dollar bills and handed them to the soldier. Dollars are readily accepted in the land and are in high demand by locals and merchants.

"*Baradar, chel adad kabob az bazaar bekhar,*" I told the soldier. "Buy forty kabobs from the bazaar."

He looked shocked.

"*Yeki baraye khodet.*" I smiled. "One for yourself."

The young Afghan soldier smiled in appreciation and took off for the bazaar.

Khan and I swapped stories as we lounged on the dirt in front of his ground-floor corner room at the White House. He shared the room with a few army soldiers from the PsyOps, or Psychological Operations, team he'd been assigned to.

"Rohām, you are a Professor," Khan said.

"Professor? How so?"

"Remember that day in Leatherneck you told me to give it time, even the K9s will start looking good." Khan couldn't contain himself; he began laughing until his eyes teared.

His laughter was contagious.

"You are a professor!" he repeated.

The food came. I gave one meal to the young soldier.

"My treat, Khan." I held out the container. "I can't offer you pussy, but I can offer you kabob."

I carried the other thirty-eight meals down to the staging area, separated out five meals for me, my teammates, and Clover, and called the others to come grab some kabob. Everyone gathered to eat. My team members arrived to be greeted with a warm meal.

Everyone ravenously devoured the kabobs, which consisted mostly of lamb fat with a couple of small pieces of meat, along with naan and rice. They used their hands; no utensils with this meal.

The convoy commander walked over, rubbing his stomach. "Hey Sanj, thanks for the kabob. It hit the spot. We all appreciate your generosity."

"Glad you enjoyed it, lieutenant," I said with a smile. "Let's hope we don't get the shits from it!"

"Yeah, right? That wouldn't be fun, now, would it?" he smiled as he walked away.

Ziar sat eating with a few Marines. Even he had benefited from my generosity. We exchanged a few glances. He looked pissed. I smiled. I was under his skin now, and I liked it. Yeah, you cheap goat-fucker, enjoy Irani generosity.

JULY 21, 2011

The convoy was getting ready to pull out of Musa Qala. Our next stop was COB Signes, about fourteen kilometers out, followed by FOB Shamshir about fifty clicks away. Members of the convoy came up and thanked me for yesterday's meal. I felt a profound sense of gratification. Most of these Marines were simple farm kids. What I had done felt inconsequential to me, but not to them. Their reaction made me realize how shallow and jaded the Los Angelinos I knew were. I would have never received such gratitude among my so-called friends and colleagues, where simple joys had given way to entitled, demanding, and sanctimonious attitudes.

Kent and I organized the column formation, incorporating the local trucks into the convoy. Inside our truck, the mood had changed from lethargy to jovial. Smitts played some club music on his makeshift MP3 sound system. Kent worked on the BFT system. Gospol had all but moved out of the truck and sat inside the gun turret.

I wondered why my mood had changed so drastically. I kept coming back to the meal and the reaction of the Marines. Their sincerity was priceless. It appealed to my less self-consumed side.

Little did I know that this lesson would change me forever.

0928 HOURS / JULY 21, 2011

The drive from Musa Qala to Signes went without a hitch. We drove on flat desert terrain with mountain ranges on the horizon to the right of the convoy. The plain lacked vegetation; khaki hues dominated the wide-open landscape. I looked out the front windshield and got a glimpse of COB Signes. The place sat in the open, smack in the middle of nowhere.

We pulled inside the nominal camp. Everyone dismounted and got to work unloading provisions and fuel. I looked around the runty COB. The place was half a football field in length at best. Some parts of the COB had hesco barriers, while in other parts two rows of concertina wire provided the only impediment between the inhabitants of the COB and the savages beyond. There were maybe a dozen tents in the whole place. One was the command tent—the others, I had no idea what they were. About twenty or so MRAPs and MATVs were parked near the tents, and on the opposite side, two M777 Cannons sat about 15 yards apart from each other.

Some of the Marines in the COB slept in small individual camping-style tents. They'd dug holes two or three feet deep in the ground, placed the tents in the holes, and slept half-submerged in a sort of a grave. They did this to protect themselves against sniper fire and shrapnel from enemy mortar rounds. All in all, the living conditions were inimical, wretched, and extremely dangerous. It took more than guts to live in such a hellhole.

I stood near my truck, smoking and looking with disbelief at the crummy place. The base depressed the hell out of me, but not the Marines manning it. They worked with purpose and confidence. The contrast between the condition of the place and the mood of the soldiers couldn't be more evident.

Out of nowhere, an earth-shattering bang shook the ground. I instinctively dove under my truck for cover, and so did a bunch of local drivers and others from my team. Another loud bang kicked up moondust. Frantically, I looked around from under the truck. The residents of the COB were walking around casually. Slowly, I crawled out. Clover walked over.

"Scared you?" he asked with a big grin.

"Fuck, I think I crapped my pants." I checked myself. "What happened?"

Clover pointed to the M777. "Some fuckers just got smoked."

"Those were the cannons?" I asked.

"Yeah, drones send the coordinates and we smoke the rodents," Clover said casually.

After about three hours at the COB, the convoy pushed off and headed to FOB Shamshir.

It was just a bit after 1600 hours when we arrived at our next destination. FOB Shamshir was sandwiched between a village nestled on a hillside and tall cornfields. It was another Taliban-infested, aroused, and inflamed region. The white flags flying on top of some of the mud huts did not mean "cease fire" or "surrender"; they meant the Taliban ruled over this village.

The usual dirt-berm and hescos encircled the parameter of the base. Camouflaged and sandbag-fortified watchtowers protected the FOB's boundaries. Shamshir witnessed almost non-stop action.

Once inside, we got assigned to two so-called "tents" situated next to each other, though they were nothing more than two rows of hescos about 20 feet apart with a tin roof connecting them, heavy green plastic tarps as doors, rocky uneven dirt floors, and a few broken cots strewn about. Everyone claimed a small space on the floor.

Kent, Smitts, Clover, and I sat by a fire pit near the chow hall eating our MRE dinners. After, I broke out some Cuban cigars. We were joined by the camp commandant, Lt. Braun, a tall, handsome man in his early thirties. I offered him a cigar. He gladly accepted and joined us in conversation.

Random machine gun fire provided the background music as we talked. As I listened, I thought about our guys outside the wire in the thick of battle and prayed we wouldn't lose any souls that night. Lt. Braun told us how the battle raged on almost 24/7 in the region. The casual demeanor of the moment felt bizarre, like two universes separated by a worthless pile of dirt. Set foot on one side of the pile and any step could be your last. Set foot on the other side of the pile, and you could be enjoying a nice Cuban cigar. Compartmentalizing the situation was the only way to deal with the fucked-up duality of daily life in such an environment.

"The craftiness of these people is impressive," Lt. Braun said.

"Yeah," Clover said, "over thirty years of war has taught them to do more with less."

"We've seen how the local drivers fix their haji jingle trucks with next to no spare parts." Smitts puffed on his cigar. "These guys are fuckin' remarkable."

"Talk about remarkable," Braun said, "You wanna know how they mitigate a multi-million-dollar technology?"

"Our technology?" Kent asked.

"Yeah, our night-vision technology," Braun said. "We conduct foot patrols and night missions; these Taliban are a different breed…"

Everyone listened intently.

"…They dip heavy blankets in the icy water in irrigation channels and wrap themselves in the freezing blankets, and huddle in the bush. Our n-v goggles don't pick up their heat signature; they ambush our foot patrol as we walk by."

Braun's words astonished us.

"You gotta be shittin' me?" Smitts said.

"Wish I were. We've taken heavy losses," Braun said.

A look of contemplative sorrow emerged on Braun's face. I'm sure he'd lost friends and subordinates. How does one deal with such a heavy burden and continue living a normal life? The group fell silent. I glanced over at Clover. He caught me observing him. We locked eyes, then he disengaged and stared into the fire. I looked back at the group. Everyone sucked a little harder on their cigar. Only they and their creator knew what was going through their minds. Certainly, it wasn't pleasant.

At 2200, the few fluorescent lights we'd brought inside the shoddy accommodations cast a yellow tint on everyone's complexions. Other Marines conversed about cars, dogs, hunting, girls… Our other tentmates, the rats, joined in on the festivities. They had smelled food and were out in force. They crawled over us as we spoke. No one seemed to mind the presence of the inquisitive critters as they searched for a morsel to grab and run off with.

"Hey, Dick Dick, come over here," Kent said to one of the Marines.

Dick Dick was no more than twenty-two years old, a farm boy through and through. His real name was Richard Dick, so the battalion had named him Dick Dick. I think his parents had played a bad joke on the poor kid. Dick Dick wore old-man style boxer underwear and his Marine boots. He came over.

"Hey, show Sanj the helicopter," Kent said.

"Yeah, Dicky man, show Sanj your talent," Smitts added.

Not knowing what was about to happen, I waited.

Dick Dick grinned. He put his hands on his waist and gyrated his hips. Under his grandpa boxers his pecker spun around like a helicopter rotor. His grin widened as he did a 360. The other Marines cheered, clapped, and whistled as Dick Dick displayed his talent.

Sanjar Rohām

1207 HOURS / JULY 23, 2011

The midday sun shined brightly. With assigned tasks completed, provisions and fuel unloaded, all we had to do was sit and wait.

The local Afghan drivers had congregated under a canopy shade in a corner. I walked over to check on them. I always made sure to take good care of the Afghans and befriend those I deemed sharp and opportunistic. It was a good approach to cultivate sources, build relationships, and earn trust, not that I would ever trust them fully.

The drivers lounged on the dirt in the shade, listening to music on their cell phones and talking amongst each other. One of them, Sattar-Khan, called me over. I had a good rapport with him since he had gone on multiple missions with us. In his mid-thirties, Sattar-Khan was physically strong, shrewd, and a hustler. He thought he had skunked me because I played nice and naive with him. But his hustle didn't amount to much—a carton of cigarettes, a couple of screwdrivers, *Maxim* magazines, and some useless knickknacks from the PX. Sattar-Khan sported a semi-Fu Manchu mustache but didn't have much facial hair. He was one of the drivers I had targeted and nurtured as a source.

As I squatted down next to him he reached into his pantaloon pocket and pulled out a few pieces of Pakistani candy wrapped in silver, gold, and red foil. He offered the candy. I took a piece, unwrapped it, and popped it in my mouth. The tiny, overly sweet, rose-water flavored candy tasted perfumy. I could taste it in my sinuses.

"*Joor asti agha Irani?*" Sattar-Khan said in Dari, his smile both dubious and cunning. "You good, Mr. Irani?"

"*Zendeh bashi Sattar Sahib, zire saye shoma,*" I replied. "Long life Master Sattar, under your protection."

Sattar pointed covertly. "See that asshole over there, Abdullah Shirzai? He is taking pictures of the camp with his phone."

I stayed in my squatted position and observed Abdullah for a moment or two as he stealthily took pictures of the layout of the base.

"I give you this information for free," Sattar said.

"What is offered for free is usually the most costly," I replied.

Sattar and I exchanged a hard stare. I reached in my pocket, took out a $20 bill and sneaked it into his hand. In this land, loyalties are bought and sold rather cheaply.

I got up slowly and sauntered away, greeting and shaking hands with some of the other drivers. Then I walked directly to Lt. Braun's office and notified him what had happened. Braun called over one of his terps and grabbed Sgt. Kent, Smitts, Clover, and a dozen other Marines. I stayed back to avoid drawing any attention from the drivers. They had to think I was on their side.

The Marines corralled all the drivers and confiscated their mobile phones. The drivers raised their voices and objected strongly, but Lt. Braun and his crew went through the phones searching for intel. The suspect's phone contained some extra pictures of the base, aside from the shitload of pornographic material that all the mobile phones had in common. Lt. Braun had one of his Marines delete the pictures of the camp from the suspect's phone. The driver's information and mugshot were taken and he was fingerprinted. His iris' were scanned for recognition using biometric technologies, and entered into the databank of suspects.

Lt. Braun gave all the cell phones to Sgt. Kent. They would be returned to their owners before we depart from the camp. When we got back to Leatherneck, I would pass the info on to Joe and Tony.

The afternoon was hot and lazy. Some of the Marines from the convoy slept, some exercised in the tent housing the gym, others watched movies on their laptops. Gospol hung out with a few other Marines his age. A few Marines stretched a tarp between two rows of trucks to provide shade from the scorching sun. Kent, Smitts, and Clover played cards with a few other soldiers under the tarp. I stood over them watching. Ziar walked over.

"Hey, why don't you play?" Ziar asked in a condescending tone.

"Don't know how."

"You guys should let the Irani play," Ziar said. "Don't worry, he don't know how to play, just like he don't know how to talk Pashto."

I no longer had the patience for this dingleberry. "And you don't know how to keep your hole shut."

The card playing stopped. The men eyed Ziar and me, waiting for something to erupt.

"What did you say?" Ziar's eyes widened. "Say you're sorry."

"Okay. You're sorry," I said.

I'd always known the hostility between Ziar and me would spill over at some point. I just didn't want it to happen while we were out on a mission.

"You show me respect," Ziar said, pointing his stumpy index finger at me. "Do it now." He came close and chest-bumped me.

I took a step back. I didn't want his breath touching me.

The group watched in silence.

Ziar took another step forward and got right in my face again. "You wanna hit me? It looks like you wanna hit me. Maybe you wanna cry!"

By now we were standing toe-to-toe and nose-to-nose. Having every intention to avoid a brawl, I dropped my head to evade his septic breath. "I don't hit girls, and I sure as hell don't touch shit. But I'll kick your bitch nanny-goat ass with pleasure." I said.

From the corner of my eye I noticed Kent, Smitts, and Clover ready to step in.

Ziar smiled nervously and took a couple of steps back. "You are lucky. It's time for my afternoon *nomaz*."

But now I didn't want to back down. I took a few steps forward to close the gap. "Go say your prayer. It could be your last!"

Ziar quickly turned and ran off like a circumcised dog, his butt tucked in, his tail between his legs.

Smitts stood up and put his arm around my neck. "Sexy you are when you get angry," he said. "You really don't know how to play cards?"

I sat down. Kent patted me on the back and Clover gave me a look of "right on brother."

"I'm impressed, an eyerani city-boy knows what a nanny is," said one of the card-playing Marines in his relaxed southern drawl. "My mama always says, never trouble trouble unless trouble troubles you."

0712 HOURS / JULY 25, 2011

The convoy geared up for departure. The early morning air felt hot and thick. I brushed my teeth and used some baby-wipes to shower—the usual cleansing of armpits, crotch, balls, ass-crack, face, and neck. Not necessarily in that order. This routine was a common hygiene practice during missions.

Lt. Braun walked up. "Hey, I didn't want you to leave without saying thanks for the intel and the cigar."

I pulled out a handful of cigars from my backpack and offered them to him. "Enjoy the cigars, lieutenant. Thank you for your hospitality."

"Oh, no, that's too many." Braun waved his hand.

"Please, take them, share them with the others." I pushed the cigars into his hand. "Thanks for all you and the rest of the Marines do here." My throat tightened. "Please stay safe. God bless."

Braun noticed my emotions. When I held my hand out for a shake, he grabbed it, took a step forward and gave me a brotherly hug.

The convoy cleared the serpentine and headed into open territory just before 0900. The formation of a few Marine trucks interrupted by a few local tankers crept slowly through the enemy stronghold. The reputation and the name of the area we were nearing had everyone on high alert. We were about to enter a "Kill Box"—a zone where ambushes and attacks are eminently guaranteed. No convoy ever passed through this area unscathed. The Taliban's presence was strong there and they inflicted substantial losses on anyone who dared to pass. I had heard the chatter among the local drivers prior to our departure from Shamshir. They were concerned about, if not downright petrified of, going through this area.

"Hey Sergeant Kent, motorcycle behind us," Gospol yelled from the turret.

"You have PID?" Kent asked.

"No, sir," Gospol said with excitement, "More motorcycles."

Kent radioed the rest of the convoy.

Motorcycles were buzzing around us like a horde of flies before Kent put the radio down. I looked out the back window and the side portholes. The white turbans on the riders' heads announced Taliban. They were out in force and out for blood, with AK47s and RPGs (rocket-propelled grenades) visibly slung over the shoulders of both riders and passengers.

Their numbers grew rapidly.

"Do not engage until and unless fired upon," the convoy commander said over the radio.

This was the rule governing the coalition forces. You had to be fired on before you could return fire. Our guys were not even allowed to return fire if an enemy fired at them and then dropped his weapon. This is what happens when lawyers get involved in war fighting. Still, the situation reminded me of cowboys and Indians of the Wild West. But with deadlier weaponry.

Ping. Ping. Ping.

The Taliban opened fire on the convoy as they zigzagged over the desert floor. These fuckers were damn good riders. They fired their weapons with one hand while skillfully controlling their motorcycles on the uneven rocky desert floor with the other. Some bikes had two riders on them; one fired while the other maneuvered.

"Permission to fire at will," the radio blared with the commander's voice.

I lined up the ammo canisters to hand to Gospol as needed.

The Taliban had us boxed in from behind, the left, and the right. Their AK rounds had no effect on our trucks, but the haji tin cans on wheels were a different story. The convoy picked up speed as rounds were exchanged.

I handed Gospol an ammo canister. He loaded the 50-caliber and continued firing. The local drivers in the convoy panicked and broke formation, which only confused the already bewildering situation. Now our gunners had to be careful not to hit the local drivers as they got in the gunners' line of fire.

We were nearing a village. The road ahead bottlenecked, but the stampede of haji trucks showed no sign of slowing. It was every man for himself. I couldn't blame them. Surely, I would do the same under similar circumstances.

The white-turbaned biker gang didn't relent. I looked out every side to see if any Tali bikers were biting the dust, but everything moved at a dizzying pace, making it difficult to see clearly. The Marine trucks had to pick up speed just to continue protecting the bullet-riddled haji trucks.

Suddenly we came to a halt. In their attempt to escape the barrage of lead, a few of the local trucks had smashed into each other, blocking our narrow getaway path. Some of the Marine vehicles were boxed in by the haji trucks, hindering their ability to return enemy fire.

Our truck was the last to arrive at the gridlock. Kent prepared his weapon as he directed Smitts to pull to one side.

"Sanj," he shouted, "get ready to hit the deck."

I snapped on my helmet chin strap. Adrenaline pumped through my veins at a nauseating rate. "Good to go," I replied.

Kent shouted orders to Gospol to cover us, then opened the door and jumped out. I opened the back gate and followed, immediately running to the side of the truck away from the enemy vantage point. Some of the local drivers had abandoned their vehicles; they ran around frantically and directionless, like poisoned, dying rats. Chaos ruled. A few Marines hit the deck to help bring order and security. Clover ran over as bullets clattered all around. The sound of lead bouncing off the armored hide of our trucks reverberated harmonically.

"Tell those fuckers to get in their trucks!" Kent shouted, pointing to the abandoned trucks. "Tell 'em to get in or we leave 'em behind!"

I ran over to a group of petrified drivers. *"Tar lasse!"* I said in Pashto as I got mobbed by the drivers. Then, in Dari: *"Bala sha!"* "Get in!" I pushed the drivers toward their abandoned trucks.

Clover and a couple of Marines were shielding me with their bodies. Their selfless gesture motivated me to do more, exposing myself to danger to get them out of harm's way, ASAP.

Kent ran over to Ziar's truck and banged on the door. Ziar cracked the door open. His and Kent's hand gestures told me all I needed to know: Ziar refused to leave the safety of his truck to help us, to help me, with the drivers. Kent waved his arms at Ziar to get out. Ziar closed the door.

An old Afghan driver tugged at my arm in the madness of the moment.

I pushed him off. *"Bala sha!"* I said. "Get in."

My harsh response did not deter the old man. He tugged again.

"*Speen girya, ghwari che wawzhal shey!*" I yelled in Pashto. "You wanna die, old man?"

"*Sahib, Pashton gap nemizanam,*" he said in Dari. "Master, I don't speak Pashto."

"You wanna die, father?" This time I asked in Dari.

"Master, I'm shot," he said as his knees buckled.

The old man clutched my arms to keep from falling. I grabbed his elbows to steady him, then took a second look at the old man, moving his baggy clothes around to find the wound or the bleeding.

"*Koja?*" I said, searching his body. "Where?"

The old man signaled me to look at his neck. He pulled his scarf down and pointed with his index and middle finger. I thought my eyes were deceiving me: two bullets had entered the old man's skinny neck, one on either side of his windpipe, and both had exited from the back of his neck without hitting any arteries. Not a drop of blood. I could see through the holes. Lucky motherfucker.

"Don't worry. Get back to your truck!" I ordered the old man.

He didn't move. I looked into his tired eyes, which gazed back at me as if begging me not to force him to go. I grabbed his hand and pulled him toward his truck.

Clover kept an eye on me this whole time. He followed.

"Please master, don't open the door," the old man begged when we got to his truck.

"You have to get in," I said forcefully as I opened the driver's side door. "We have to go!"

Clover stood with his back to me. I looked up inside the truck and gasped at the grotesque sight. The twenty-some-year-old driver had been shot in the face. The bullet had entered through the young man's cheekbone and exited from the crown of his head, blowing the back of his skull completely off. Gray matter, blood, and bone fragments were splattered all over the interior of the truck. A river of thick blood oozed down what was once a face, drenching his clothes.

Clover glanced back. "Oh fuck," he shouted, turning back to face the enemy. "Close the fuckin' door, let's go."

I slammed the door shut and pulled the old man with me as I ran back to my previous position. Clover came along to provide cover. I grabbed another driver and ordered him to take the old man to his truck.

The situation calmed a bit, but the bullets persisted. The number of turbaned bikers diminished until they slowly melted away into the landscape as if a disappearing mirage. A number of downed Taliban bikes a short distance away indicated either dead or injured enemy combatants left behind by their comrades. The brethren would return to collect the bodies once we left the scene.

Kent joined me. "Fucking Ziar, man," he said, agitated. "He's a fuckin' pussy."

"No worries, we got this covered." I tried to calm him down.

Kent nudged me with his elbow. "Yeah, you can always piss on them with your pee-shooter," he said with a boyish smile. Amidst the death and despair surrounding us, we'd both managed to crack a smile.

Then I felt another tug of the arm and looked to my right. Another local driver stood next to me.

"Get in your truck. I don't wanna die for you," I shouted in Pashto.

The driver looked apologetic, his posture semi-bowed.

"Master, look under your feet." He pointed at the ground.

I looked down. I was standing firmly on top of a remote-control IED detonation command wire. One push of a button by even a child hidden nearby could have set off the IED on demand, sending us to God's abode. I followed the wire with my eyes. Kent was standing on the same command wire.

The driver pointed to a small mound of dirt ten or twelve yards away.

"*Bam*," he said. "Bomb."

I felt my pupils dilate.

"*Mehrbani, Sa—*," he said. "Please, Mast—"

I ignored the driver and yanked Kent's arm. He looked at me. I looked down, and his head followed in the same direction.

"Fuck, that's a command wire," he cried. "Get the fuck back in the truck!"

We scurried away, and after what seemed to be an eternity, got everyone loaded up and got the convoy moving. We slowly cleared the bottleneck and the Kill Box.

The convoy moved sluggishly on through the warm late afternoon. Exhaustion set in as adrenaline faded. I thought about the old man with the bullet wounds in his neck. About the young man who had been shot in the face, his head blown off. I struggled to imagine the fear he had felt as he tried to flee, and wondered what went through his mind as he took his last breath. He probably hadn't gotten a chance to think of anything. His lifeless body was sitting in the bullet-riddled haji tin can on wheels being towed by one of our trucks. I pondered what would go through my mind when it was time for me to take my last breath. None of what I was going through mattered to anyone back in the States. They weren't experiencing it firsthand. They saw only a watered-down, sterile version of what news outlets showed them, a sanitized and nicely-packaged version with sound effects.

Spending time in a war-torn land repeatedly reminded me of how worthless life is. People got killed here almost every minute of every day—children, men, women, young and old were being slaughtered by their own people, and no one seemed to care. I lit a cigarette and sat back.

After putting some distance between us and the Kill Box, we made a pit stop. The local drivers gathered around and informed me that they were leaving. A mutiny of sorts, I guess. We were in the vicinity of their village, they wanted to go home to their families. Who could blame them? The truck containing the dead young Afghan was unhitched from our truck and attached to one of the Afghan trucks. We gave the locals a few cases of water and MREs. All the local drivers left except for two: Sattar and his skinny buddy, Wahidi.

Dusk descended upon us as we moved ever so slowly through the desert. Even our trucks felt sluggish after the earlier action. They had taken a beating.

Smitts got the music going. Gospol had fallen asleep in the turret. The poor kid must have been physically exhausted. I took off my helmet, lit a cigarette and put my legs on the opposing bench. Smitts and Kent lit up also.

Smitts looked back at me. "Damn Sanj, I saw your ass in action. Balls, bro." He held up his hand as if cupping oranges. "BALLS."

I was so spent, even blinking required effort, but I managed to crack a smile.

"You fuckin' kicked it today." Kent turned to look back. "You sure you're a terp? You're a Marine if you ask me."

I treasured their words. They had accepted me with open arms. I knew this was a once–in-a-lifetime experience. Torn between two cultures, I had never felt this kind of kinship, neither with the Iranian nor with the American community. I had floated from group to group, each the exact opposite of the other, never associating with only one circle of friends. And now I had finally found where I belonged, under austere conditions and deadly circumstances. All my life I had rushed through the happy and the sad moments without faithfully savoring or contemplating them. Always hastening to get to the next imaginary destination where bliss dwelt. Or so I had thought. The aloof and noncommittal shroud that I'd created to shield my true self from the hurt and harm of the world had covertly infiltrated and subjugated my soul, transforming me into a stranger to myself. And now I had arrived at the time of surrender, a moment of accepting my true self for who I really was and not running away from myself. Now I was in no rush to get to the next destination, even though the circumstance was not so desirable.

Darkness enveloped the land as we slowly pushed on. Mountains stood menacingly close to the left of the convoy. The jagged, rocky face of a precipice ventured very close to the narrow path we were on. I'm sure I could have touched it if I had a window to roll down! Sattar and Wahidi rode in front of us by about 20 yards.

Most of the convoy had cleared the narrow path when out of nowhere, two flames appeared on the steep mountainside.

"Sarge," Gospol yelled. "On our 22, on our 22."

I sat up just in time to see two Molotov cocktails arc down from thirty or forty feet above us. One of the bottles hit the roof of the Sattar's truck; the other struck its tanker section. Both cocktails exploded in flames, engulfing the truck.

Sattar jumped out and ran toward us for protection.

"Gos, get down!" Kent told Gospol. "Keep your weapon on the mountainside."

The convoy halted.

Gospol put his night-vision on and scanned the mountain.

"Come up here, Sanj," Kent said as he cracked his door open.

I crawled over our gear to the driver's area.

"Tell him to get in his buddy's truck," Kent said with his weapon trained on the door. "Tell him to walk alongside the truck; we'll cover him."

"*Andiwal lari bala sho*," I told Sattar, "*Kate ma bia, mohafezat mikonim azat.*"

Sattar walked alongside.

"Gos," Smitts said as he concentrated on the road, "get down as we pass the burning truck, in case it blows."

Gospol slouched low in the turret. "It's like the mountain swallowed the fucker," he said.

We slowly passed by the burning truck.

0602 HOURS / JULY 26, 2011

Daylight broke. I don't know how Smitts could stay up all this time. His stamina was extraordinary. I looked to see what we had to eat for breakfast. We were running low on both food and water. We hadn't packed many provisions since this was supposed to be a short run.

I passed out MRE packs to everyone. We ate as the convoy shuffled along.

"We should be in Leatherneck by tonight," Smitts said.

"I just wanna take a shower and call my wife," Kent said.

"Yeah, take a shower and rub one off," Smitts laughed.

The midday sun was brutal. The thermometer inside the truck read 118° Fahrenheit. The weight of the helmet and body armor added to the misery. Gospol rotated the turret to check the surroundings, and the convoy came to a stop.

"Check this out, Sanj." Kent pointed to the BFT screen. "Come up here."

I crawled over empty boxes and gear. "What is it?"

"You see the blue circles?" Kent pointed at the BFT screen. "Those are us. The powder blue circle is this truck. See the red diamonds? Those are enemy and IED locations."

The BFT screen was peppered with red diamonds. We were smack in the middle of a minefield, the ground surrounding us littered with the deadly traps. And those were just the ones we knew of.

"Sarge Kent, pull up," the commander said on the radio.

Tension was high as we slowly pulled out of formation and gingerly moved up to the front.

An old man sat by a cluster of destroyed, abandoned mud huts here in the middle of nowhere. He leaned against what was left of a three-foot-high mud wall.

"Take your terp and ask the old man if there's another route around," the commander ordered.

"You heard the man, Sanj," Kent said. "Let's go."

We got out. I watched every step as we edged toward the old man. The sun was so hot and bright that one couldn't even see one's own shadow.

Much to my surprise, Ziar got out from his truck and walked toward the old man.

"Maybe he wants to make up for his fuckup," Kent said.

"Some people are consummate shit-piles," I replied in my most jaded manner. "He's one of them. His mother didn't birth him, she shit him."

I surveyed the surroundings for another village. None to be seen. The old man sat in the middle of the sterile desert, alone. He had on a white turban. Yet his wizened face and white beard made him look like a kindly grandfather.

"What do you think?" Kent asked as we got closer.

"I wouldn't trust my own shadow out here," I replied. "He's a mine-herder looking after his flock."

We reached the old man at the same time Ziar did. I eyed the old man suspiciously. Streaks of orange color ran through his long silver beard: remnants of henna, a popular dye in the Muslim religion, used often by men. The old man's sunbaked skin made him look ancient. His white eyelashes were unusually long. His leathery eyelids framed hollow eyes, which told me he had exchanged his soul for pure evil and hatred. His right elbow rested on his knee and his forehead rested in his hand. The tip of his right index finger was bent at an almost 90-degree angle. Most likely it had been broken and never fixed. His staff leaned on his left shoulder.

"Ask him which path hides IEDs," Kent said.

Ziar jumped in before I could open my mouth. "*Pa kum lar maynona pot ye?*" he asked.

"*Maynona?*" the old man replied with an ominous smile as he reached for his balls and began fondling them. "*Deltah dashteh de, tsok deltah maynona pot ki?*"

"Mines? This is the desert, who would hide mines here?" I translated for Kent.

Clearly, the old man was unaware of our knowledge of the IEDs.

"Three roads." The old man fondled his balls. "Take any, don't fret."

The mere fact that he was playing with his balls in our presence said volumes about him.

"He says we can take any path," Ziar said. "He said they are clean."

"The old man is lying," I said.

Kent and Ziar looked at me.

"I wouldn't trust this cocksucker." I pointed to the old man with my head. "Look at him, he's playing with his balls; you know what that means? It's a gesture of disrespect. He's basically telling us 'To hell with you.'"

"You don't know shit," Ziar said. "This is my country. You know nothing."

I squatted to be at eye level with the old man. "*Nikah, deltah tsanga raghali ye, de sahra pa manz tse kawi? Deltah nezhdi keli nashtah!*" I held the old man's hard stare as I pointed to the surroundings and translating for Kent. "Grandfather, how did you get here, what are you doing in the middle of the desert? There are no villages nearby!"

The old man's eyes were deep as I gazed inside them. One was filled with deceit and the other with acrimony.

"I rode here with some travelers," he said in Pashto. "They went in a different direction. They left me here."

I looked up at Kent as I translated.

"You can't translate," Ziar said aggressively. "That's not what he said."

I jumped to my feet. Ziar met me eye to eye and bumped his flak vest against mine.

I pushed back.

"Hey." Kent got in the middle. "Cut it out. This is no time for this shit."

"Don't listen to him, man," Ziar said to Kent. "He is Irani shit. Old man said the roads is all clean."

"Sarge, I'm telling you what he said," I said fervently.

Ziar pointed at me. "He is full of shit. He doesn't know what he fucking saying."

During all this, I had one eye on the old man. He was fully enjoying the tension.

"Ask the old man which path?" Kent told Ziar.

Ziar asked the old man.

The old man pointed to the right. "My travel companions took that path."

Ziar translated for Kent. Kent told Ziar to get back to his truck, then walked me over to Clover's truck and knocked on the back gate.

Clover opened the gate.

"Hey, Sarge, let Sanj ride with you until we clear this area," he told Clover.

"*What?*" I looked at Kent, dumbfounded.

"Just stay in this truck," Kent said with care in his voice. "I won't compromise your safety."

"Co—"

"Hop in, Sanj, we gotta go," Clover said.

I reluctantly climbed into Clover's truck, which was the point or navigator vehicle.

"I'm gonna take the nav position until we clear this area," Kent told Clover.

"Roger," Clover replied.

After Kent's truck moved up front, the convoy started to move again at a snail's pace. Clover and I leaned forward to watch the pathway ahead through the front windshield. I took one last look at the old fucker as we passed him. He was still playing with his balls. A bad omen.

Up ahead, Gospol was throwing markers down from the turret, indicating possible IED placements.

My eyes watched fixedly. Clover sat back in his seat.

At just after 1300 hours there was a deafening explosion, and moondust poured in through the turret. Almost instantaneously, a severe taste of copper materialized in my mouth. Intense ringing filled my ears. Visibility in the truck was zero as moondust lingered in the air.

The radio went into a frenzy; everything sounded like loud static. Finally the dust settled just enough for me to see Kent's truck engulfed in flames. I took off my glasses, wiped them, and put them back on. I couldn't see Kent or Gospol. Smitts' body hung halfway out the door, engulfed in flames, devoured.

I looked at Clover. He saw what I saw.

"We gotta get 'em out!" I yelled without being able to hear my own voice.

I reached for the back gate. Clover grabbed me. His mouth moved but I couldn't hear a damn thing.

"What?" I yelled.

"You can't go out there!" Clover yelled back.

"We can't just sit here and watch." I could barely hear myself.

"You can't go out there." Clover grabbed and squeezed my arms. "There could be snipers waiting out there for us to get out."

"I don't give a fuck who's waiting."

"Listen to me." Clover squeezed my arms tightly. "This is probably a daisy chain trap."

"The fuck is a daisy chain trap?"

"They lay IEDs in a diamond pattern," Clover said as he looked at Kent's truck. "We could get blown away if we make a move in any direction."

The flames licked the sides of the truck like a hungry demon gluttonously eating its prey. All I could do was hope and pray for my friends to miraculously walk out.

Tears began rolling down my face. The driver and front passenger looked at me. Disbelief and fear displayed vividly on their faces even though they were completely covered in moondust. That could have been them in the burning truck.

I sat on my knees and watched through the windshield as the truck blazed. Black smoke drifted forcefully into the air as the big tires burned. The heat from the flames reached all the way inside our truck. I looked at Smitts' charring body, unable to distinguish if the moment was real or not.

Almost six hours passed. I capitulated to exhaustion and fell asleep after watching the truck burn for so long. My slumber was deep, dark, and dreamless.

A gentle stroke on the side of my face pulled me out of the void. I strained to open my eyes, but my tears had solidified the moondust on my eyelashes into concrete like substance. I forced my eyes open. Fine grains of moondust fell from my lashes as I blinked. Moondust had claimed me fully as its resting place.

I looked down at the palm of my right hand as it rested on my right knee. Moondust accentuated the lifeline in my ghostly-white palm. A bright red ladybug slowly crawled from the back of my hand into the palm and sat there. The whiteness of my palm intensified the ladybug's red shell even more. Grains of moondust fell from my eyes onto the ladybug as I blinked. The ladybug walked up my index finger, gently, slowly. Was this a dream? It walked back into my palm and sat there.

I looked up. The flames had died out. A few Marines with minesweepers were walking the perimeter of my old truck.

I looked back down at the ladybug, then opened the gate and stuck my hand out. The red beetle flew away.

My companions were covered fully in moondust. We all resembled clay statues.

"You passed out, man," Clover said.

"How long was I out?"

"Almost five hours."

I looked at the burned-out truck.

"A bird is coming to take the remains," Clover said somberly.

The words hit hard. The trickle of emotions I was feeling turned into a flood of uncontrollable tears. I wanted to cry out loud, but my voice had abandoned me.

Night fell, and no bird came. The convoy was running dangerously low on water and other provisions. Clover offered me half a Pop-Tart, but I had no appetite. He insisted I drink some water at least.

The driver looked back at me. "We're Marines. It's okay if we don't eat or drink. You're a civilian. You take priority over us—please eat, drink."

Clover looked at the driver. "Sanj is one of us." He looked at me. "He's kin."

I went in and out of consciousness the whole night. In the early morning two helicopters showed up. A few smoke signals marked the landing zone. The birds landed, kicking up a squall of moondust. We watched through the front window as the dust settled.

A few Marines carrying black body bags walked over to the remains of the burned-out truck and removed the remains of our fallen. What was left of each filled a space no bigger than a square foot. The Marines gave great care and respect to their fallen brethren. They painstakingly went through the wreckage so as not to leave the smallest fragment behind. The process took almost three hours. Finally, they carried the body bags over to one of the helicopters. The birds took off.

"The heroes have left," the convoy commander said solemnly on the radio.

We drove slowly past what had once been a beast of a truck. The massive force of the explosion had ripped off the driver's side door and thrown it nearly twenty yards out. The mangled piece of steel now sat alone in the forsaken land, its burnt shell becoming a lasting part of the desolate Afghan landscape.

Later, it was determined that the IED had contained 140 pounds of explosives. No vehicle could have withstood such a blast.

JULY 29, 2011

The trip back was also harrowing. We lost three more trucks to IEDs. Blown-up tire, driveshaft, and axle. Luckily, the IEDs were small and didn't result in any additional casualties.

0157 HOURS / JULY 30, 2011

We made it back to Leatherneck sometime in the middle of the night. I stayed with Clover's crew and cleaned out the truck. I grabbed a part of the gun from the turret and carried it with the gunner to the armory. Like a zombie, I went through the motions. Complete desolation robbed my mind of any thought or feeling.

After we finished the cleanup I left the compound. I can't remember walking back to my tent. I was bodiless, filled with quiet sadness. My legs did the walking without any command from my brain. My eyes were open, but I couldn't see anything.

The only person awake in my tent when I got there was Ziar. He was putting his gear away. I wanted to walk over to his corner and kill the motherfucker, but my body failed me in the attempt. I grabbed my shower kit and walked to the shower tent. My socks and underwear had to be peeled off and thrown away since I hadn't changed them in eight days or more, and hadn't showered in eleven. The stench coming off my body was revolting.

I walked barefoot to one of the shower stalls. Three or four Sri Lankan or Nepalese guys showered together in one stall. They were fucking each other. It didn't matter to me what they were doing, but they ran out of the stall and out of the tent, damn near naked. The plastic floor of the shower felt slimy and slippery under my feet. Normally I wouldn't dare walk barefoot in the showers. Normally.

9
SIX PLUS ONE

AUGUST 04, 2011

Leatherneck didn't feel the same anymore. My small corner of the tent became my solitary confinement. I hardly ate, and when I did I went to the chow hall late at night when no one else was there. I stopped exercising and gave up shaving. I shed about twenty-five pounds as the result of the last mission and my self-imposed fast. That paled in contrast to my emotional loss. On a couple of occasions I tried to muster a drop of emotional energy to meet with my site manager and the battalion to debrief them, but I just didn't have what it took to do it. I had taken leave of my senses and closed my heart to the world. My time was spent absent in spirit.

My mind was fractured, draining every bit of logic and common sense, and replacing with self-condemnation. The thought of briefing the battalion or my site manager added misery to my wounded mental state.

In the meantime, my weakness gave Ziar the perfect opportunity to cover his ass. Unbeknownst to me, he was providing his version of events to the battalion and the new site manager.

2000 HOURS / AUGUST 12, 2011

The heavy, muggy nighttime air increased the misery of the moment as I attended the Ramp Ceremony, a wrenching rite where the flag-draped coffins of fallen soldiers are placed on a C-130 for their final journey home. The battalion stood in two rows, one on either side of the open ramp. No one noticed me as I stood some distance away from the end of one column. None of the other terps had shown up to pay their respects.

Three military ambulances pulled up. The ceremonial cadre unloaded the coffins to the forlorn sound of "Taps." A priest walked in front of the procession reading from the Bible. Marines saluted as the caskets marched by. Some cried as they watched their own carried before them. It took great effort to drown my voice in my chest as I cried. My heart ached. Dick Dick, Colonel Webber, Lieutenant Laramy, Lieutenant Maddox, Gunny Kovak and others stood somber. It was obvious that their sobs were internal. They'd lost brethren.

Clover stood alone, away from the battalion. We exchanged wounded looks.

The Marine casket bearers placed the coffins on the plane with great care and respect and gave one last salute. Marines have a motto when they lower the casket of their fallen into their final resting place: *The Last to Let You Down*. Across the tarmac about thirty yards from where I stood, another Ramp Ceremony was taking place for a fallen Afghan soldier. A simple wooden Afghan flag-draped coffin was getting pushed into the cargo hole of a small plane. No fanfare, no "Taps," no teary eyes. The poor Afghan had no requiem. "*Iinaa alayh wa iinaa alayh rajeun*," I whispered in Arabic. "I am His and to Him I Shall Return."

AUGUST 26, 2011

I sat on the empty ammo canister outside my tent, smoking, as Ziar, Shafi, and Sami brought their gear and suitcases outside. They were going to be picked up and taken to the airport; they were done with their contracts.

From the night we got back to LNK after the fateful mission until this day, I had made sure to steer clear of Ziar. Coming face-to-face with him would have led to ominous consequences. On a few occasions, however, we did run into each other. This was bound to happen; we lived in the same tent, after all. Ziar's perpetual smug expression was detestable. I'm certain he sensed the malice I nurtured toward him within me.

"Mr. Irani, take good care of yourself." Shafi put his hand out.

I shook Shafi's hand. "Safe travels," I said, forcing a smile.

Sami wished me luck as we shook hands. I still had a hard time understanding his accent.

Ziar looked at me. "*Douzakh stasou pah entezari*," he said with an impish smile. "Hell is waiting for you."

My response to Ziar was a vengeful glare.

The noisy tent transformed into a quiet zone. Other terps no longer came by; their buddies had left. A couple of Pakistanis, both with the Surname Khan, replaced my previous teammates. Rahim Khan, the older of the two, was a quiet man and kept to himself. Ashraf Khan, the younger, never stayed in the tent and always played possum to avoid going on missions. We didn't hang together, but were friendly with each other.

News of my last mission had spread among the other terps. Every one of them added his or her own bullshit to the story: *"Irani and Ziar got into a fistfight in front of the Taliban,"* or *"The Irani didn't want to ride in convoy."* They morphed their gossip into a mind-boggling tale. When they tried to approach me, my attitude repelled them. I had neither the desire nor the intention to recall the experience.

AUGUST 28, 2011

The deadly elixir of guilt, anger, and self-loathing brewing inside me shifted my internal tectonic plates and ransacked my world. The battalion had all but stopped using me. My mental state was incapable of questioning why. I simply figured they were giving me time to myself to deal with the aftermath of the deadly mission.

I had no reason to observe a burdensome daily personal hygiene routine, so I skipped regular showering. Instead of using the toilet tent I resorted to using the porta potty next to my tent. Sitting on the toilet seat without an ass gasket had always been a no-no, but not anymore. Sweat poured out from every pore on my body as I sat on the rough seat in the sandy-beige plastic steam box that had absorbed the heat from the scorching summer sun. Flies flew in and out of the feces-filled reservoir from between my thighs. The stench of fermenting shit furthered my half-comatose state of being. In my haze I read the graffiti on the sandy-beige plastic wall: *We eat from a bag, sleep in a bag, shit in a bag, let's pray we don't go home in a bag!* I stepped out of the fly chow-hall, my Marine-issue sweat-soaked green T-shirt stuck to my body.

Sucking on a cancer stick, I sat alone on the empty ammo canister by my tent. Devoid of feelings, I felt alive in my memories only.

Older Khan approached. "They want to see you at the site manager office," he said in his thick Pakistani accent.

"They want to see me now?"

"Yes, they told me to tell you go right away."

"Okay. Thanks."

I finished smoking my cigarette, threw a tactical shirt over my sweaty T-shirt, grabbed my baseball cap, and headed to the site manager's office.

The afternoon sun was so hot that I had to squint even with sunglasses on. The scorching hot wind had forced everyone inside. I sat on a wooden bench outside the office and lit a cigarette. The heat made it hard to inhale the smoke. Joe and Tony's office building was visible from my vantage point, but their car wasn't there and the building looked deserted.

Random events popped in and out of my mind, choppy and disorderly. My vision had reversed and saw only what transpired internally. I remembered the night when I'd first met Sergeant Kent, when he'd signed and picked me and the other two terps from the site manager's office. Fact and fiction had become indistinguishable. Reality had no meaning.

"You are suspended until further notice," a voice said.

I looked up. Jason, the new site manager, stood before me. He looked down at me, his expression scornful.

"There's talk of a commission looking into your case," he said.

My mind hadn't fully detached from my thoughts. I looked at him, confused. "Suspended?" I adjusted my glasses as if that would help me comprehend better. "Commission?"

"Yeah, you won't be going on any more missions until the commission investigates you and your performance. You got three Marines killed." He said with zero compassion.

I reached for another cigarette. "Investigate what?"

"Ziar reported your inability to translate correctly. He said you suggested the wrong path."

"Are you kidding?" Blood shot to my head. "And no one bothered to ask *me* what happened?"

"Ziar Hassanzai came to the office the day after you got back." Jason stuck his index finger in my face. "You didn't."

I looked at Jason. He'd clearly already made up his mind, and nothing could change it.

"I got the call from Colonel Webber." Jason picked his nose with his pinky. "We knew about the deaths before you guys made it back to base."

"And Colonel Webber said I was responsible?"

"How the hell would he know? Ziar told me."

I sat back on the wooden bench. Ziar was a cunning, slimy fuck. He'd gotten the last laugh.

"Go," Jason said. "You'll hear from someone soon." He started to walk away, then turned back. "And take a fuckin' shower. You smell like shit."

The camouflage canopy above the patio area shook violently and the hot, twirling wind rammed fine grains of moondust into my ears and nostrils. I felt the grains in the back of my throat as I breathed. The usually bustling camp became a ghost town as everyone took shelter. I contemplated walking to my team's compound to tell anyone who would listen what had happened, but just the thought of going there gave me heart palpitations. The heartbreaking memories of that fateful day consumed my soul like maggots devouring a decomposing cadaver. I stood at the edge of despair.

SEPTEMBER 03, 2011

The unceasing monologue trapped inside my head was slowly corroding my focus. I figured that hitting the gym again would at least release some tension and refocus me to some degree. What I needed was a routine.

I began using the gym again, showering, and then grabbing breakfast at one of the cafés in Bastion 0 or Bastion I. For dinner I went to the Brits' chow hall in Bastion I. Slowly, I gained back some of my strength and previous physique. My daily walk by the hospital triggered flashbacks as I witnessed casualties getting rushed in. The "Op Minimize" announcement on the loudspeaker constantly rekindled visions of the twisted, burning truck.

I developed a simple friendship with the elder Khan. His thick Pakistani accent made it almost impossible to understand what he said, so I just nodded whenever I couldn't make sense of the conversation. Khan said his prayers consistently. I sat on my usual ammo canister outside the tent and watched him as he did the ritual washing of hands and feet prior to prayer.

Khan's paunchy figure made him look like a teddy bear. His nose had no bridge. It started from his forehead and came straight down. He kept his salt-and-pepper hair short, military-style. Like a little kid with poopy diapers, he shuffled his feet when he walked. He didn't look like the sharpest tool in the shed, but his sincere goodness couldn't be discounted. Some days, Khan followed me over to Bastion like a puppy following his master. I didn't mind. He didn't ask questions, and he didn't judge. I knew he cared about me, maybe because I was the only person who gave him respect and attention.

SEPTEMBER 07, 2011

I had no idea how long the investigation would take. As terps, we were kept in the dark about any military or administrative issues. Global Vigilance did not ship me home. I was still an asset to them, and they would make money off me as long as I was in the theater.

The afternoon sun burned the back of my neck as I walked aimlessly from Bastion II into Bastion I. The distinct sound of car tires on gravel got my attention. Without looking, I stepped away from the road for the car to pass. But it didn't; it moved along with me. I turned my head without lifting it. What I saw put a smile on my face: a silver Tahoe.

"Need a ride?" Tony asked.

I smiled wider.

"Get in."

I climbed into the car and shook hands with Joe and Tony. We hadn't seen each other since my return from my last tragic mission. We drove around slowly.

"What happened out there?" Joe asked in a friendly tone.

"Depends on whose version you want to hear," I replied coldly.

Tony gave me a hard stare. "Yours."

I rehashed the events of the fateful day, stopping a few times to hold back my emotions. For so long I had kept to myself and not shared my experience. Joe and Tony's sincerity felt real, and I had to get this off my chest before I sank deeper in incurable anguish.

They listened without interrupting.

"You have a track record with us." Joe looked at Tony. "We believe you, brother."

"I appreciate your faith in me," I said.

Joe pulled the car over on the same lonely dirt road, away from prying eyes.

"Keep in touch," Tony said. "We'll keep an eye on you."

"Will do." I shook hands with the duo. "Thanks for the ride," I said with a faint smile, and exited the car.

They drove off.

I lit a cigarette.

SEPTEMBER 11, 2011

The tenth anniversary of September 11th, 2001 cast a somber mood on the base. A warm dust-flurry blew moondust everywhere. I sat alone on a bench outside Bastion I café and Pizza Hut, smoking. Most everyone else went inside. I had the whole place to myself. A silhouette in the sandstorm approached.

"Hey, Sanj," he said.

I knew that voice anywhere: Clover.

"I thought I'd find you here," he said as he got closer.

"I'm that easy to track?"

He sat next to me and joined me for a cigarette. "Just came to say goodbye."

"Where are you going?" I asked, surprised and disturbed. I didn't have many friends as it stood, and didn't want to lose another one.

He pushed some dirt around with his boots as he took a couple of long drags from his cigarette. "I'm just another round in the chamber," he said. "They point the weapon and pull the trigger. I go where I'm directed." When he looked at me, his faint smile was fatigued. "It's okay to get attached, as long as you learn to let go. As Marines, we live in a world of worst-case scenarios. We live in the moment. You can't let emotions get in the way."

I listened to him like a student listening to his sage.

"People back home will never know what you've seen," he said, "They have no idea. It's messy and bloody. People die—good people, bad people." He dropped his head, and anguish overtook his face as he tried to conceal the sorrow that had drowned his soul. "This war won't end any time soon. I've lost many kin and I've gained a few." He took a deep drag. "Glad to have met you, brother."

We didn't make eye contact. I felt that he had to get something off his chest.

"In a world where peddlers try to sell you a bloodthirsty god without," he said, "You gotta find the merciful God within."

The wisdom hidden in Clover's simple words plunged my thoughts into depths I'd never dared to venture before. We sat in silence, sharing a moment of contemplation and reflection. Then Clover stood up. "Semper Fi, brotha," he said.

I got up. We shook hands, and just like that, Clover walked away.

SEPTEMBER 12, 2011

I heard the elder Khan's shuffling footsteps inside the tent. He walked hurriedly.

"Marines outside want to see you." He gestured with urgency. "Come, come."

I walked outside. Three Marines stood there.

"Are you Rohām?" one asked.

"Yes, sir."

"Present yourself at the camp headquarters at 1400 hours tomorrow."

"May I ask the reason, sir?"

"Give your name at the guard gate. They will direct you to the proper building. Please be prompt." They walked over to their gator, jumped in and drove off.

SEPTEMBER 13, 2011

The guard looked at the roster and waved me through, directing me to follow a stone pathway to a one-story plywood building.

When I entered, I saw Colonel Webber sitting in a corner. He got up, walked over, and we shook hands.

"Hey Sanj, how're you holding up?"

"I'm maintaining."

"I know." Webber shook his head. "I had to write the letters to the families."

My eyes welled up, but this was no place for tears. I dropped my head to conceal my eyes and swallowed my tears as best I could.

"For what it's worth…" Webber tapped my shoulder a few times. "I know you'd give your life for those guys. Just know you have a friend in me."

"Sir, the room is ready," a Marine called out.

Moments later I was standing before a three-member Marine panel. Other Marines, including Colonel Webber and Lieutenant Laramy, were in the room, along with a few civilians and Jason.

"Please take a seat," a panel member said.

I did.

"Mr. Rohām—am I pronouncing your name correctly?"

"Yes Sir, you are."

"I am Lieutenant Colonel Bridge—" He pointed to his left—"This is Lieutenant Colonel Callahan—" he pointed to his right—"This is Lieutenant Colonel Kunin."

Colonel Bridge was in his early 50s with cropped blond hair and distinct features. Colonel Callahan had to be around the same age, also with cropped hair, his uniform a size or two too small for his physique. Colonel Kunin, probably the youngest, in his 40s, was a mean-looking, hawk-eyed soldier.

I nodded respectfully to each.

"Now, please do not be alarmed with the formality of this hearing.

This inquiry is conducted for internal purposes," Colonel Bridge said.

"Yes, Sir," I said as I glanced over at Colonel Webber.

He gave me a reassuring look. Lieutenant Laramy was sitting next to him, stone-faced, showing not an ounce of emotion.

"Mr. Rohām," Cnl. Callahan said, "Please give us a detailed chronological rundown on your mission. Start from the very beginning, from Leatherneck."

I recounted the mission, including the altercation with Ziar, as best I could. The room was silent as I spoke, pausing at times to hold back my tears.

"How did you come to be here in Afghanistan, Mr. Rohām?" Cnl. Callahan asked when I'd finished telling my story. .

"Through Global Vigilance, Sir."

"Did you volunteer for this job?"

"Yes, Sir."

"What made you volunteer?" Cnl. Callahan asked. "I mean, you are not from this country, why would anyone endanger their life?"

"I can't speak for others, Sir; I can only speak for myself."

"Okay, what is your reason?"

"I needed a purpose, like everyone else in this room."

"With all due respect, Mr. Rohām, everyone else in this room is in uniform or wore the uniform at some point," Cnl. Kunin said as he glanced around. "They've dedicated their lives to the service of their country."

"With all due respect, Sir, it's my country, too."

"How would you describe your relationship with Sergeant Kent, Corporal Smitts, and PFC Gospol?" Cnl. Kunin asked.

"They were brothers."

"Brothers?" Cnl. Kunin said somewhat sarcastically. "You were accepted as such?"

"I think I earned it, along with their trust."

"Trust is a significant word." Cnl. Kunin raised one eyebrow. "Would you say Sergeant Kent trusted you? The others trusted you?"

"Yes, Sir."

"With their lives?" Cnl. Kunin asked.

I paused. There were three dead Marines.

"You were translating for Sergeant Kent and an old Afghan male?" Cnl. Bridge asked.

"Yes, Sir."

"Did you suspect the old man to be Taliban?"

"Yes, I did." Images of the old man emerged from my recollection. "I said so to Sergeant Kent at the time."

"You still believe that?"

"A hundred percent, Sir."

Colonel Bridge looked at me head-on. "Accusations have been leveled against you. Did you misinterpret what the old man said?"

"Accusations are not truths, Sir."

"Fair enough, Mr. Rohām," Cnl. Bridge said.

"How did you prepare for this job, in a classroom?" Cnl. Callahan asked. "You studied Pashto Stateside, is that right?"

"Yes, Sir. I passed the official US government exams."

"Your relationship with your Pashto instructor, Dr. Rasouli, was contentious in nature. Why?" Cnl. Kunin asked.

"He didn't want me there," I said.

"Why?" Cnl. Kunin fired back.

"He said I was physically weak for the job."

"Why did you go back to class?"

"Because I don't like anyone telling me what I can or can't do."

"How many times did you take the language exam?" Cnl. Kunin pressed harder. "Our records show that it took you three attempts. Why?"

"Everyone in this room has failed at something but didn't give up until they prevailed. Why?" I asked.

Cnl. Kunin shot me a hard stare and waited for me to answer.

"My first two attempts were cut short by the same Pakistani proctor, Mustafa, who spoke terrible English and didn't know any Dari. The exams are normally fifteen minutes long. My first two exams lasted four minutes at best. I failed. My third attempt with an Afghan proctor, Rokhsana, lasted almost ninety minutes. She was fluent in all three languages. I passed. Do your records show that?"

Cnl. Bridge nodded.

"Would you say you speak Pashto better than a native speaker?" Cnl. Callahan asked.

"Sir, the native speaker you speak of is responsible for providing misinformation." I looked around the room. "I don't see him being questioned here."

My challenge went unanswered. I didn't expect an answer.

"Why did Sergeant Kent choose to ignore your interpretation if he trusted you and you were brothers?" Cnl. Kunin asked.

"I can't speak for Sergeant Kent or his reason, Sir."

"Do you take any ownership of the events leading up to the demise of your team members?" Cnl. Bridge asked.

"I do, Sir." My eyes welled up. I felt vulnerable, like a kid in a circular room searching for a corner in which to hide. "I should have insisted more."

A long, uncomfortable pause. Not a sound in the room.

Colonel Bridge finished writing something down. He looked up. "Thank you for your appearance here today, Mr. Rohām." He gathered his papers. "Your statement will be included in the final report. Is there anything else you wish to add?"

I shook my head. A few tears fell before I could wipe them.

Colonel Bridge stood. "On behalf of myself, the panel, and those present here today, I thank you for your service and your candor. This panel is adjourned."

The group exited the room in an orderly fashion. I stayed in my chair.

SEPTEMBER 15, 2011

I reestablished my communications with Joe and Tony and threw myself back into work for them. At least I would be doing something. Kick-starting my senses and being useful again was vital. I began visiting the bazaar, attending the mosques, mixing it up with the other terps.

SEPTEMBER 23, 2011

Mid-day, same old dusty road, same old me walking alone. The Tahoe pulled up; I climbed in and greeted Joe and Tony.

"How're you holding up, pal?" Joe asked.

"Sustaining."

"You understand, we can't get involved," Tony said. "We can't let anyone know about us collaborating."

"I understand. I didn't expect you to."

"Just know we're here for you," Joe said.

"Push comes to shove, we'll get involved," Tony said.

Their words were heartening. I had no doubt they would intervine if need be.

Our meeting didn't last long, I didn't have anything to report. The Tahoe stopped. We shook hands. I exited the car on the same old tired dusty road. The Tahoe drove off, slowly kicking up moondust in its trail. I stood there, forlorn.

SEPTEMBER 30, 2011

Gradually, my decision to immerse myself into my old routine halted the mental decay that had been infiltrating my soul. I added a five-mile jog to my exercise routine before going to the gym. This was meant to somehow counterbalance my nicotine addiction. I left my tent at 0400 hours, jogged to Bastion 0, and along the chain-link fence separating Leatherneck from Shorabak.

A few early-rising Afghan soldiers jogged along with me on the other side of the fence. We challenged each other to run faster, to see who could make it to the end of the fence before we ventured off in separate directions. The young soldiers were no more than nineteen or twenty years of age, and of course they kicked my ass every time in our daily race. They had no idea who I was and what was going on in my life. I was anonymous to them, and anonymity was what I desired. They greeted me with their smiling faces every day. In a way, their smiles helped set the tone for the rest of my day. I looked forward to our daily conversationless encounter.

OCTOBER 03, 2011

Colonel Webber pulled some strings and got me placed with a team of DEA agents in charge of training the Afghan National Interdiction Unit, or NIU. The NIU team members were fluent in both Dari and Pashto, handpicked and trained by our Special Forces before being sent to the DEA for further training in drug enforcement tactics. The DEA guys treated me well and put me in charge of a six-member NIU team, all the members of which were under the age of twenty-five. Don't let their youth fool you, these kids could eat their American counterparts for breakfast and not even belch.

Qulam, the leader of the team, formed a close bond with me. Just a hair taller than me and weighing 130 pounds at best, he was an inquisitive, alert young man. All six members followed me wherever I went and surrounded me like bodyguards. We wore Marine uniforms with no name ribbons. Many times I was approached by soldiers and even Leatherneck Military Police inquiring about who I was, why I had six heavily-armed Afghans surrounding me constantly, and how was it that I got away without a name tag. My response was always the same: a wicked smirk.

The NIU team knew me as Reza; I didn't disclose my real identity to them. I went to the DEA compound at 0800 hours every day and translated between the DEA agents and the NIU six. The DEA guys had a relaxed but professional approach toward their Afghan trainees. They went out of their way to establish great rapport with the young Afghans, and in return, the Afghans performed brilliantly, surpassing expectations. Their appreciation, admiration, and loyalty toward their trainers couldn't have been more evident. They extended the same courtesies to me, for which I was humbled. The seven of us formed a tight bond. I have no doubt in my mind that any of the Six would lay his life down for me. Helping train the gang of six provided me with focus and direction once again.

One day at the chow hall I got some mashed potato with bits of bacon in it. The six always took what I got because they weren't familiar with most of the foods being served. Halfway into the meal, I realized they were eating bacon. Anything pork-related is strictly forbidden in the Muslim religion, and, of course, the Jewish faith.

"Ah…there is pork in the mashed potato," I quietly said to the gang as they ate.

They exchanged looks with one another. No one said a word.

Then Qualm said, "This is very tasty, Mr. Reza."

I looked at the other five. They were also clearly enjoying the taste of bacon.

"It's not a sin to eat bacon during war," I said. "God won't punish any of us."

"Mr. Reza is right," Mir-Agha, one of the NIU six, said after a short pause. "It's not a sin."

At six feet tall, Mir-Agha carried a 1969 PKM 7.62mm Soviet-designed machine gun, a weighty piece of deterrent, and the biggest gun on the team. Still, Mir-Agha was more of a poet than a fighter. He also carried a small notepad and a pen in his pocket and wrote romantic poems during our downtime, and read them to us. The boy had talent, I must admit.

Six set of eyes looked at me for confirmation.

"Eat, brothers," I said. "If it's a sin, it will be on me because I didn't tell you there's bacon in the food."

"If it is sin, then we will stand with you for the punishment," Saeed, another team member, said.

The group shared uncertain looks with one another, looking for affirmation, then turned to me for my blessing. A gentle nod of the head did the trick. They nodded back, smiled, and continued enjoying the bacon-filled mashed potatoes.

OCTOBER 12, 2011

A milestone. My one-year anniversary in Afghanistan. I celebrated the occasion out by the volleyball court at the Danish camp, alone, getting drunk on non-alcoholic beer and smoking a cigar.

OCTOBER 20, 2011

The online news broadcast was dominated by the death of Libya's dictator, Muammar Gaddafi. I watched a clip on one of the computers at the MWR in which an American anchor from MSNBC interviewed a Libyan politician belonging to the interim government.

"Will there be democracy in Libya now that the dictator is dead?" the anchor asked.

"Yes. Democracy according to Islamic law. *Inshallah.*" The politician replied.

The news anchor glowed with excitement and elation.

What a fucking imbecile, I thought. This idiot pole-stroker doesn't know there is no such thing as "Islamic Democracy," and yet he is celebrating it!

OCTOBER 23, 2011

The Six sat on the bare, cold, plywood floor taking a test prepared by their DEA trainers with me as the proctor. Butler, one of the agents, walked into the room.

"How's it going with the guys?" he asked me.

"They haven't asked any questions so far, if that's any indication of their knowledge." I smiled.

"Hey, I just got orders to take the team on a fieldtrip downrange," Butler said. "This'll be a good test for them. We gotta leave ASAP."

"Am I going?" I asked.

"Without you I'm mute." Butler smiled.

"Destination?" I asked.

"Afghan outpost, that's all I can tell you."

It was obvious that the information was on a need-to-know basis, and I had no need to know.

At around 1900 hours two other agents drove us to the LZ.

"Do you know where we're going, Mr. Reza?" Qulam asked on behalf of the team.

"Afghan outpost Qulam. That's all I know."

The bird took to the sky in the frigid night. Right before touching down at our destination, the pilot delivered some terrible news: Butler's mother had passed away and the military wanted to send him back home.

Butler's demeanor changed drastically. His usual upright posture sagged. "I gotta get back to LNK," he said in a subdued voice, wiping a few tears from his face.

"My deepest condolences, brother." I put my hand on his shoulder.

We touched down outside a square-shaped compound of mud huts with double iron gates. The team asked what had happened. With Butler's permission, I told them. The Six consoled Butler with their gestures.

"A favor, will you?" Butler asked me. "Stay here with the team and provide a report on their performance?"

"Sure. Whatever it takes," I replied.

We got off the helicopter, and right away I noticed soldiers forming a protective circle around the LZ with weapons ready.

A tall, mustached Afghan soldier surrounded by a group of heavily-armed warriors met us at the open ramp.

"I am the Major in charge," he said in Dari, and smiled wickedly. "Welcome to my garden."

The Major was probably around my age. He looked strong and was in great physical shape. The deep lines on his face told the story of a dignified but hard-lived life. He wore his beret perfectly. His disciplined stance exuded confidence.

Chatter broke out between Qulam and the others.

"You know the Major?" Qulam asked me in a hushed tone.

I shook my head.

"He is the head of the most feared Commando Unit in the Afghan military. He is known as Taymur *Mar Khor*. The Taliban are petrified of him. He is merciless."

I introduced myself to the Major as "the *Tarjoman*" and withheld my pseudo-name.

"I am Major Taymor Nuristani." He reciprocated with an unyielding look and a firm handshake.

Butler told me to explain his circumstances to the Major as we stood in the strong rotor wash of the waiting helicopter.

The major shook his head in sympathy. "Please translate, Tarjoman Sahib," he told me. "My men and I mourn alongside our brother–in-arms. Heaven gained a saint, we lost a blessing."

I translated for Butler, and the two men shook hands. Then Butler got back on the helicopter, leaving the seven of us in the major's care.

"Where are you from, Tarjoman Sahib?" the major asked as we walked to the compound surrounded by the Afghan soldiers. "Not from this land, for sure."

"Iran," I said.

Nuristani smiled. He ordered his men to get a place ready for us to shack up as we walked in through the compound gates which closed rapidly behind us.

I monitored our surroundings. This was no ordinary outpost and these men were no ordinary soldiers. They were Commandos, our version of Special Forces.

"Join me in my office, Tarjoman Sahib," The Major said.

The Commandos took my team and I followed the major.

Nuristani's office was a modest dirt-floored room with one wood-framed window facing the courtyard of the mud-hut compound. The light from the two kerosene lamps in the room didn't reach the ceiling and only lit the lower half of the small chamber. A cot with a couple of neatly folded blankets was in one corner. A metal bowl containing the Major's shaving razor and an old tooth brush sat on a small end table next to the cot. A battered wooden desk and chair sat in the other side of the compact space.

Nuristani pulled out a folding chair and placed it in front of his desk. "Please." He pointed to me as he went around and sat behind his desk. "Do you know where Nuristan is?"

"To the north-east, if I remember correctly."

"Do you know what Nuristan means?"

"Land of the Enlightened."

"So you know. I am glad." The Major smiled. "And did you know that Nuristanis and Persians have a lot in common?"

Nuristani was a learned man: he had said "Persians," not "Iranians."

"No, Jagran Sahib, I don't know." I replied. "Jagran" means "Major" in both Dari and Pashto.

"Both our people love to drink wine," the Major said, and smiled. "Do you drink wine, Tarjoman Sahib?"

In Afghanistan, "wine" refers to any alcoholic beverage.

"Only with friends!" I said, and smiled back. My response was a roundabout tribute to the Major.

The Major understood very well what I meant. He pulled out a bottle of Johnny Walker from his desk drawer along with two tea cups. "My people were called *Kafir* before we were forced to accept Islam, much like your people. We danced, drank, and celebrated life freely," he said as he poured. "And now, we are forced to kill." Nuristani put one cup in front of me.

I didn't touch the cup and waited for him to pick his up first.

"*Taymor Mar Khor* is the name I've earned from my people," the Major said with irony as he picked up his cup.

Mar Khor means "Snake Eater."

"Better to drink with a faithful Snake Eater than a traitorous friend," I said in Dari, picking up the cup.

"May the world go back to being kafirs." Nuristani raised his cup.

"*Be Kherad*," I saluted the Major in Dari. "To Wisdom."

Nuristani nodded in approval. We downed the drinks.

It was late afternoon the next day, everyone gathered in the compound's courtyard. A certain anxious energy permeated the atmosphere. The Commandos talked excitedly among themselves. Theirs was a tightknit brotherhood. Major Nuristani strode out of his room and his Commandos fell into formation. My team and I stood to one side. A couple of the Commandos dragged two barefoot prisoners to the middle of the courtyard. The detainees could hardly walk or stand; their hands were bound behind them and burlap sacks had been pulled over their head.

The Commandos kicked the prisoners in the backs of their knees, forcing them to the ground.

Nuristani walked up and signaled for the sacks to be removed. His soldiers obeyed.

The prisoners' feet were raw, with deep untreated lacerations on them.

"Soon you will meet your master in hell," Nuristani said with utmost certainty as he gestured his soldiers forward with a stiff nod.

Four Commandos grabbed the prisoners and forced them onto their backs. Two other Commandos tied the prisoners' feet to a tree branch and held them up. The seven of us watched in horror and astonishment as the Commandos took turns flogging every inch of the captives' bodies. The prisoners screamed, cried in pain, and begged for mercy, but the Commandos seemed to enjoy the caning. Blood splattered from the prisoners' feet with every ill-intentioned strike. Streaks of blood appeared almost instantaneously on the prisoners' thin, filthy, baggy clothes with every strike of the nimble but strong tree branch.

The assault wasn't limited to whipping. Boots to the gut and the ribs provided a short recess for the feet. The battering lasted until every Commando had had his turn. Witnessing the flogging was torturous beyond description.

"Lock them up. Give them food and water," Nuristani ordered.

The Commandos followed the orders and dragged the semiconscious men away.

Nuristani walked over to my astounded group frozen in place.

"We searched for these hyenas of hell for a long time," he said, hatred clearly displayed on his face.

"Taliban?" I asked. "Why not turn them over to the Americans?"

"Americans?" Nuristani smiled mockingly. "Americans give them doctors and lawyers. I give them misery."

By the time our fourth day arrived my team was getting anxious. We were supposed to conduct some kind of operation, but instead we sat idle. Even the Commandos had hunkered down. I decided to bring up the issue with Nuristani that night.

"Nuristani Sahib, my team was sent here for a reason, but we've not been briefed on any upcoming mission," I said, sipping the room-temperature Johnny Walker.

"Don't think I am not aware of this, Tarjoman Sahib," Nuristani said. "I have contacted your superiors to send a helicopter to take you back."

This came as a surprise. "May I ask the reason?"

"The two prisoners we have, do you know what they've done?" Nuristani asked.

"I don't."

"There was a little boy, Gulzar; he was eight or nine years of age. He was a determined boy with heart of a lion. Gulzar came by the front gate day after day, begging me for a job. He said he would work for leftover food; he wanted to help his family." Nuristani downed his drink and poured another. "I refused, but the boy persisted. He began working here. He showed up at exactly eight o'clock every morning, collecting the garbage, cleaning our rooms, and washing the dishes. One day he didn't show up." Nuristani went silent for a moment. "A week later his father came to the gate carrying a sack. It contained Gulzar's hacked body."

Maybe this was the same story Shafi had told me the first night I met him. "Your prisoners are the animals who did this?"

Nuristani nodded. "I allowed the human in me to come out. That boy would be alive today if I hadn't given him a job."

So Nuristani suffered from the same guilt I still agonized from over Hila's death. At least he had a chance to get even!

"This is why you call this place your garden?" I asked. *Gulzar* means "garden" in Dari.

Nuristani nodded.

"And is this connected to us getting shipped back?" I asked.

"We pick up Taliban chatter. They are planning a large attack on the camp to get their tribesmen back. You and your team must leave."

I wasn't about to argue with Nuristani. His Commandos were battle-hardened soldiers with no remorse and a score to settle. This was not a fight for my team to be a part of. And this was a land where settling vendettas was considered a moral duty passed on for generations. It was best to sit this one out.

The next morning as the helicopter landed a group of Commandos encircled the LZ and another group opened the front gate. Nuristani led the cadre that chaperoned us to our lifeline out of there.

Qulam and the rest of the team paid their respect to the Major and his Commandos as they boarded the helicopter.

"To Wisdom, Tarjoman Sahib." Nuristani smiled as we shook hands.

"May it protect you and your men, *Jagran* Nuristani," I said.

OCTOBER 30, 2011

According to unconfirmed circulating news, Nuristani and his Commandos had doused the two prisoners in gasoline and set them ablaze in the middle of the compound courtyard: Nuristani's Gulzar!

NOVEMBER 10, 2011

The NIU team received orders to ship out. The news wasn't well received by me or the Six, for we had developed a strong fellowship. The DEA guys had recognized my level of commitment to the success of the Six early on and figured I could be a mentor to them. They had allowed me great latitude in my two-pronged approach toward the Six. On one hand, I'd ignited a sense of nationalism in the group, and on the other, a sense of loyalty to America for so fiercely backing them in their struggle. I'd become their older brother and felt great responsibility toward them, and they relied heavily on my tutelage. These young men were children of war and knew nothing but war. What waited for them outside the base in their own native country was unwelcoming at best, and I didn't want the slightest harm to come to any of them. Their battles ahead were not going to be easy nor end anytime soon. I knew that not every one of them would make it out unscathed.

I shook hands, hugged, and kissed each one on the cheek as we said farewell.

"Don't forget us," Mir-Agha said, saddened.

"You will all be in my prayers, always," I said.

"This is not fair," Qulam said. "You alone carry the burden of six heavy hearts, while the six of us carry the weight of only one heavy heart."

"It's a cherished burden of honor, Qulam," I said.

Our goodbyes took an hour. I left the DEA compound in a sunken mood.

10
BEARDED WIFE

NOVEMBER 13, 2011

A Marine stood in front of my tent talking to young Khan.

"Hey, Rohām." Khan pointed me out to the Marine.

I walked over.

"You Rohām?" the Marine asked.

"Yes, sir, I am."

"I have orders to take you to the staging yard."

I hopped on to the gator parked a few yards away, and off we went. I hadn't been to the battalion's staging area since we returned from my last mission. Intense fear of entrapment and suffocation overtook me as we entered the yard. The gator stopped in front of Lt. Laramy's tent office.

"In there." The Marine signaled me to go.

Lt. Laramy sat behind her desk working on the computer. After a minute she stopped and walked over to me.

I stretched out my hand as a gesture of respect.

Laramy looked at me with a cold gaze. "Your hand is dirty."

I looked at my hand. It was stained from having held onto the rail in the gator.

"But my heart is clean," I replied.

Laramy glanced me over and let my hand linger without taking it. "You're being assigned to a new team." She straightened out her posture.

Getting back to work sounded great, getting assigned to a new team…

"Your first mission is coming up shortly," Laramy said. "This time you won't be chauffeured around in the safety of armored trucks."

The hair on the back of my neck stood up.

A civilian-clothed man entered the tent. He couldn't have been more than thirty-two or thirty-three years old, and stood just a hair under six-feet tall. His leanness was apparent beneath his T-shirt. His steely eyes meant business. His brown uncut hair was combed back. The five o'clock shadow on his face didn't disguise his chiseled jawline.

"This is the guy?" he asked. "The terp under investigation?"

"Yes. This is him," Laramy replied.

I stood still, not knowing how to react.

"You are assigned to me now, you understand?"

"Yes, sir."

"I hear that you speak Pashto," he said snidely, and watched for a reaction.

I didn't utter a word.

"I lead a team of ghosts," he said, crossing his arms across his chest. "We do the heavy lifting. Masters of mayhem and gods of chaos we are, getting ready to attend a soiree in hell."

"We're going to a party and I haven't got a tuxedo," I said.

"Hah. Wait till you see what the reception party to hell looks like." He scratched his beard. "We're cruisin' for bruisin.'" He took pleasure in saying those words. "Maybe that's why you were assigned to me."

Sweat droplets slid down the blade of my back and into my underwear.

The man sized me with a dissecting gaze. I felt like I was halfway through a swan dive into a pool of shit with my mouth open.

The man walked toward the exit.

"By the way…" He stopped with his back to me. "I'm called Bruiser." He strolled out.

That same night, I grabbed a bite at the chow hall and thought about my encounter with Laramy and Bruiser. It had zapped my energy to the point that it prevented me from walking to Bastion as I usually did. I looked around for an empty bench to sit on. A cluster of terps sat together. They lacked the slightest decorum as they pointed me out to one another.

Older Khan shared a bench with two Sri Lankan workers, so I joined them. Normally, the Sri Lankans—whose job was to empty the porta potties and other human refuse—sat by themselves. The trio greeted me with a welcoming smile as I sat down. I smiled back and nodded. The four of us quietly ate our dinner.

"May I join you?" a voice said.

I looked up. Surprisingly, it was Colonel Webber.

"Please, have a seat," I said.

Webber said hello to the others. The brass usually sat together at the far end of the seating area. No matter, it was good to see him.

"I wanted to check in on you," Webber said earnestly. "I heard about the new team."

I gave him a hard look. "I get a feeling this is a one-way ticket."

"These are elite operators. You're in great company." Webber returned the look.

I threw a jab back. "Snake Eaters!"

In military lingo Special Forces are called "Snake Eaters" because they eat snakes as a part of their survival training.

"I don't blame you for feeling this way, Webber said. "There's a lot you don't know and will never know; that's the nature of shadow operations. These guys are apex predators; they don't exist. I'm telling you more than I should. You wouldn't be assigned to them if you weren't the best. You're a force multiplier."

I kept silent and held his gaze.

"Of all our forces here in Afghanistan what percentage do you think go outside the wire?" Webber asked.

My response was a hardened stare.

"Only ten to twelve percent go outside the wire to do the dirty work—and knowing your track record, I'd say you're in the top 3 percent."

This was news to me. I had no idea about the percentages.

"Do you believe in God?" Webber asked.

I just stared at him.

"He wanted you here, now," Webber said with conviction. "This is the path he chose for you."

The night air was cold as I walked back to my tent. Older Khan sat on a cot outside the tent.

"Brother. *Kina. Ma ta kina,*" he said in his thick accent, gesturing me to sit next to him.

I sat down and lit a cigarette.

"Guy came. Give for you." He handed me a piece of folded paper.

I unfolded it: a note from Bruiser telling me to get my gear ready by 2100 hours to move to my new home, his compound.

A rush of anxious energy bolted through my body. I finished my cigarette and got ready to light another one.

Khan shook his head as if to say "No." His tamed soul showed genuine concern.

I lit it anyway. "Life is like nicotine, Khan Sahib; you know it's gonna kill you, but you enjoy it."

I finished the second cigarette and went inside the tent that had been my home since almost my arrival in LNK. As I gathered what little I had, memories of my first night in the tent dashed through my mind. Khan brought me a big trash bag. I threw my bedding and some small shit I had acquired during all my time into the bag. Khan watched, sadness vivid in his eyes. He was losing the only friend he had in the whole place.

I absorbed the weight of his sadness. I took my backpack and dropped it outside, and went back for my three original sea bags and took them out. When I picked up my footlocker, Khan came over and insisted on grabbing one end of it. We carried it outside. I sat on it and lit up again.

At exactly 2100 hours Bruiser pulled up in a gator. He didn't bother getting out. He just looked at me. I grabbed my gear, walked over to the gator, and threw it in the back. Khan brought the trash bag containing my belongings. I grabbed the bag and threw it in the dumpster. No need for the extra weight, I thought. Khan helped me carry my footlocker.

I turned to Khan, and he pulled me in for a bear hug. His belly shook. "*Khodai pa aman worur Rohām,*" he said in my ear as he held on to me.

"And may God protect you, Khan Sahib," I replied.

I climbed into the gator next to Bruiser. The tension between us was dense and palpable. Bruiser, the alpha male, oozed dominance while I tried desperately not to submit to his hegemony.

We drove through a chain-link gate into a compound surrounded by concrete T-walls. The gator stopped and we got out. I looked at my new home: four makeshift one-story plywood buildings and a tent.

"You'll stay in there." Bruiser pointed to the tent and walked away.

I grabbed my stuff and walked to the tent. There were no bunk beds, only a few cots. I pushed one into a corner, dropped my stuff onto the floor and went back to get the rest of my belongings. I spread my sleeping bag on the cot and shoved my footlocker and other gear to the side, then went out, sat on the ground, and lit a cigarette.

Someone approached. I stood up just in time to meet his hand for a handshake. My bones cracked under the pressure of the grip. "Hey, I'm Ski," the man said with a friendly smile. "You must be the terp."

Ski's face displayed a superficial layer of kindness, but he was all business underneath that thin coating. In his early thirties, about five feet ten inches of visible physical power. The popping veins on his solid forearms attested to his strength. He could have passed for a surfer dude with his wavy, unwashed, dirty-blond hair.

"I'm Sanjar Rohām." I smiled tentatively. "The Terp."

"Come. Let's meet the rest of the team." Ski gestured. "You met Bruiser already, right?"

"Yes, sir. His name matches his personality." I couldn't help to throw a jab in there.

Ski looked at me with a big smile. "His real name is Bruce Zerland. Bru-Zer. You get it?" The smile faded. "He can bring a world of hurt to the enemy—he is a BRUISER!"

We walked into one of the buildings. The room was furnished with two giant flat-screen TVs, a refrigerator, a pool table, old but comfortable couches, and a few mismatched chairs. A couple of guys were playing *Call of Duty* on one TV while a few other men watched an MMA fight on the other. I counted five guys altogether, including Ski.

"Gather around, everyone," Ski said.

Everyone turned and faced us.

"This is our terp. What was your name again?"

"His name is Mr. Terp, aka Sanj," Bruzer said as he walked in.

I hadn't been completely intimidated by Bruzer until I stood in that room among all the Alpha Males. That was when I realized that it takes a Hyper-Alpha-Male to lead such a group as the one before me.

"Mr. Terp here is responsible for three dead Marines," Bruzer said.

I stood motionless. I had no other option. My mouth dried up. My tongue felt like a piece of termite-eaten tree bark.

"The powers-to-be have determined we are best suited to execute our next mission with the help from Mr. Terp," Bruzer went on.

"So, we can call you Sanj?" asked a black guy as he walked toward me, holding a book in one hand. Built like concrete, he reminded me of the rapper 50 Cent.

"Yes, sir," I replied.

"I'm Littles." He stuck his hand out as he brought the book to his lips and kissed it.

It was a Bible. The sight of it relieved some of my anxiety, even though I had a healthy skepticism of religion.

We shook hands. "Welcome aboard," Littles said.

Another member walked over. White and bearded, not imposing in stature, but rock solid. "Killian," he said.

The next guy walked up. He looked mixed-race. Clean-shaven, jet black crew cut. The smallest in the group. What he missed in height he made up for in confidence.

"Correa," he said.

The next guy came over. White, massively built, the biggest in the group in every sense of the word. Jet-black hair. Knotted eyebrows. The type who never smiled. He stuck his hand out.

"Les."

I looked up as I reached to shake his hand. "If you're Les, then what am I?"

The others chuckled. Les didn't look amused. He wrapped his hand around mine and gave it a good squeeze. My hand felt puny inside his. I'm sure he saw the pain in my eyes. His smile quickly faded back into a serious expression.

"Briefing tomorrow morning," Bruzer said. "Ten hundred hours."

I stood there not knowing what to do.

"Hit the sack," Littles said. "Get some good sleep."

"Am I dismissed?" I asked Bruzer.

"Yes, Mr. Terp, you are dismissed."

I went back to my tent. Sleep eluded me the whole night. The thought of resigning and going home dominated my thoughts.

The next morning I washed my face and brushed my teeth outside the tent using bottled water. My stomach rumbled from hunger. I didn't know if I could leave the compound to grab something to eat, so I decided to stay put. Luckily, I had a few packs of beef jerky in my stuff. I had over an hour before the briefing so I grabbed my little MP3 music player, put on my cheap earphones, lay down, closed my eyes, and listened to music.

A violent jolt brought me back to reality and I sat up, somewhat shaken. Les stood at the edge of my cot, shaking it with one hand. He gestured with his head for me to follow him. I got up and swiftly walked after him.

The rest of the group sat facing Bruzer, who stood in front of a wall covered with pictures and maps.

Bruzer placed red thumbtacks on the map to identify specific locations. "Intel suggests that these are the subject's favorite watering holes." He pointed to a picture on the wall. "As you all know, Mullah ZiaUlhaq, or ZQ, is a high-value target." He pressed his index finger on the picture. "You can see what this ass-wipe is invo—"

"TIP, mostly children," Littles said aloud as he read from a paper.

TIP is Trafficking in Persons.

"The children are sold on the black market for a measly few hundred dollars." Ski looked up. "Most are used as sex slaves."

"ZQ is a bad actor," Bruzer said. "He's got his tentacles in everyone's pocket, including ours. Our guys believe he keeps his favorite stash of child sex slaves here." He gave me a hard, long stare as he pointed to the map. "The intel he provides the coalition is about his enemies. He uses us as his private hit squad."

"Cunning motherfucker," Les said.

"His top Lieutenant is Sher-Allah," Correa said. "He's in charge of the underground operations for moving IED-makers and bomb-making material around."

"This ass-fuck owns whorehouses in the east near the Pakistani border," Kilian read out loud. "He pimps out girls and boys as young as eight years old."

Everyone went silent as they read the intel on the target. I hadn't been provided with a copy of the intelligence everyone else was reading from.

"We'll be operating in rough terrain," Bruzer said. "A bird will drop us off at 0200 hours." His demeanor shifted abruptly from instructional to predatory. "This is a *kill* mission. Understood?"

Ski stood up. "We have both sigint and humint (signal intelligence and human intelligence). The bastard is there." He pointed to a thumbtack on the map.

"We're gonna be in no-man's land, the Durand Line." Bruzer traced the map with his index finger. "In gray neighborhood."

I raised my hand.

"Yep." Ski pointed to me.

"We'll be on the border with Baluchistan?" I asked.

"That's correct."

"That's a heavy-traffic area for drugs as well," I said.

"Yes, in addition to human trafficking," Ski said. "The Pashton tribes collaborate with the Baluchi tribes."

"What else do you know about this region, Mr. Terp?" Bruzer asked.

"The Baluch region comes under no government, neither on the Pakistani nor on the Iranian side. " I said. "They want their independence, and for the most part they are autonomous because no government dares to enter the region."

Everyone turned and looked at me.

"The Baluchis are extremely impoverished and are neglected by both the Iranian and the Pakistani governments. They're loosely connected with the Kurds who supply them with basic tactics and techniques, somewhat like what we do with the Afghans."

The group looked impressed.

"What else, Mr. Sanj?" Bruzer asked.

"The Baluch tribes are fierce fighters—even their women."

"Do you know anything about the target?" Bruzer asked in a sarcastic tone.

"I know his name is Arabic. It means Light of The Truth." I looked Bruzer straight on. "And *Sher-Allah* means 'Lion of God.'"

2100 HOURS / NOVEMBER 17, 2011

My placement with the new team wasn't without its perks. No one in the group smoked and this fact intimidated me greatly to the point that I didn't dare to light up in front of them. I went smokeless.

My new team furnished me with new equipment since most of mine had been destroyed. While I prepared for the mission I couldn't help but remember my first time out with Kent, Smitts, and Gospol. Once packed, I left the tent and sat on the ground in front of the tent in the cold. There was no luxury of running to the toilet this time. These guys meant business.

For the second time, I recited my father's Hebrew prayer:

B'shem Hashem, elohei Yisrael,

B'yumini Michael u-smoli Gavriel...

The intensity with which I prayed was core-deep. I asked God to protect us all and to give me the strength and courage to pull through this. No need to come back alive and maimed or with missing limbs; I much preferred death to those options. I had everything to lose but much more to gain. This was my salvation. My desperate need to redeem myself not only with the Marines but with myself sustained fragile mettle.

A van pulled into the compound and stopped. Les slid the side door open and we began loading in our gear. For some odd reason, I had Lynyrd Skynyrd's song "Sweet Home Alabama" stuck in my head. Quietly I hummed the song as I helped load the gear.

Unbeknownst to me, the others had stopped loading. They watched me and listened. *Why am I the only one loading?* I asked myself as I turned to face the group.

"What?" I asked. "Haven't you ever seen a raghead sing 'Sweet Home Alabama'?"

The group cracked up. Littles shook his head. Les snarled. Ski patted my back.

"Raghead," Ski said as he lifted a heavy bag. "Raghead."

We climbed into the van. Everyone looked calm and focused, except me. The team checked their weapons in silence. I sat next to Bruzer.

"Life is a lot like death row, Mr. Terp," Bruzer said as he checked his weapon. "It's only the length of the reprieve and manner of execution that's different for each." He must have read the fear in my eyes. He smiled wickedly. "*Omnia Vanitas.*"

"Means ALL IS VANITY in Latin," Littles said.

An MH-60M helicopter was waiting for us as we arrived at the LZ. The team geared up and we boarded. The side-mounted M134 guns stood ready. We took our seats and buckled in. Bruzer darted a look at me and then slowly looked away. Being bookended between Littles and Les failed to lessen my anxiety or settle my rattling knees. They exchanged a glance with one another. Almost in unison, each placed one hand on one of my shaking knees, and held them steady.

I looked at Littles, wide-eyed.

"God gives his toughest battles to his strongest soldiers." Littles nodded as if to say, you'll be alright.

My unnerved eyes turned to Les. He nodded as if to say, I got you.

There I was, older than all my teammates, yet feeling like an adolescent boy, insufficient, in need of guardianship.

We took off into the cold, dark, autumn sky. Watching the group calmly check and re-check their equipment provided some distraction. I wished I was like them, one of them. These purveyors of death didn't divulge the slightest hint of fear. Maybe they truly didn't fear death; instead, they embraced it.

The pilot, or as they're called, the Night Stalker, gave the signal to get ready as we neared the drop-off point. Soon after, we made a hard landing on a ridgeline. The gunners gave us thumbs-up and we quickly deployed.

The helicopter took off and melted into darkness, taking with it little fragments of my arduously-assembled courage.

It took us nearly ten minutes to get prepared before we marched off in search of ZQ. My rucksack weighed as much as the others, about sixty pounds or so, but I lacked a weapon. Instead, I carried extra ammo magazines. Balancing the rucksack was a struggle at first, especially when hiking on uneven terrain. But I managed.

"Keep up, terp." Bruzer smiled. "No shame in asking for help!"

Bruzer knew I was at the point of no return; there was no way I would fold or ask for help. He led the way, followed by Ski, Correa, and me. Killian, Littles, and Les brought up the rear.

We walked along the ridge. My teeth clenched to the point of fracturing, and my nostrils enlarged as I breathed heavily through my nose. Eventually, I came into good stride even though my quads and hamstrings burned from fatigue. We had to avoid detection, so our progress took place in the dark with the help of night-vision goggles.

When the sun began to rise we found shelter between some rocks and laid low. Les and I lay next to each other in a tight spot between two boulders.

"You know the rules?" he asked with his eyebrows knotted.

"What rules?"

"Pole to pole, hole to hole, never pole to hole."

"Pole to pole—hole to hole—never pole to hole," I repeated.

Les nodded. "Only face-to-face, ass-to-ass. No spooning," he said.

2207 HOURS / NOVEMBER 19, 2011

Two days passed. We were on the move. We all sported some type of beard. My backpack load felt lighter, but that only meant we had fewer provisions. I'd kept my end of the deal up until that point and earned the respect of my team members, except for one: Bruzer.

"What's a Pepperdine business grad doing in this shithole?" he asked.

"Does it really matter?" I said.

"Nope."

"Maybe I'm running away from my demons."

"We carry our demons with us just like we carry our fate. You can't outrun either!" Bruzer seemed to be speaking from experience.

2023 HOURS / NOVEMBER 21, 2011

We finally began our descent from the ridge. For the most part, my eyes looked down at where I was stepping, rising every few steps to measure the distance between me and Correa. Bruzer took a knee just as I looked up and gave the signal for all to get down. He pointed to a spot about 50 yards ahead and above our position. A small light flickered from a hole in the mountainside: a cave. Below, about 300 yards downhill from our position, huddled a cluster of mud huts.

"What do you think?" Ski asked Bruzer.

"Don't know," Bruzer said as he assessed the cave. "Two teams. I'll take the first from the east, you take the second from the north." He looked at Ski, "I want you on top of the cave opening."

"Roger that. Keep your eyes open for booby-traps."

The group huddled. I listened intently to the curators of justice and death. Each knew exactly what to do.

Ski reached in his rucksack and pulled out an M4 with a sound suppressor. "You know how to use this?" he asked me.

"You're giving me a weapon?" I asked, lifting my goggles.

"We need every man. Besides, you need to protect yourself just in case," Ski said, checking the magazine. "Do you know how to use one of these?" he asked again.

"Yeah, I know how to use it."

Ski handed me the weapon. The group checked their sidearms, grenades, and gear. I couldn't believe my circumstance. The demeanor of the group prompted a sense of boldness in me, forcing me to deliberately accept the reality of death. The sensation from the adrenaline rush set me ablaze, penetrating every molecule within me. Unlike all my other missions, this time it surged at a much higher rate. My heart pounded against my ribs, my jugular veins dilated, my ears burned, and my balls dashed halfway up my ass.

Bruzer looked at me. "You're with me."

"Shouldn't he go with us?" Ski asked, a bit concerned.

"He goes with me," Bruzer said firmly.

The two teams separated. Ski, Correa, and Les flanked the cave from the top as Bruzer, Littles, Killian, and I moved in from the east toward the opening. We proceeded slowly and methodically. I imitated my team's every stealthy move. We came to within ten or so yards of the cave and sat for a bit to see if there was any movement or sound. All was quiet. We slowly moved closer. Bruzer took a knee with his weapon trained on the opening. Littles and Killian crawled slowly to the entryway, weapons at the ready. Tightly squeezing the grip of my weapon, I moved in closer behind them. Meanwhile Ski, Correa, and Les took up their position above the cave.

Bruzer and the other two disappeared into the cave. I held my breath and waited for the fireworks. Nothing. In a crouched manner, I moved quickly toward the cave and went in.

A banged-up black pot cooked on top of a small wood fire inside the cave. Moldy naan sat on a dirty rag on the ground next to the fire. Bruzer, Killian, and Littles examined the cave fastidiously, slowly picking up dirty blankets strewn here and there. The flickering light from the fire reflected our distorted shadows on the stone walls. The moment felt primitive, like we were cavemen. The sweet smell of the boiling stew tickled my appetite as it mingled with the moldy smell inside the cave.

"Stay where you are, Sanj; let us clear the place first," Littles said.

I froze.

The other three members walked in. One stood watch at the opening. The boot prints on the cave's ceiling grabbed my attention.

"That means 'We're always watching you from above,'" Correa said.

"The Taliban try to spook us out with this tactic," Les added.

"All clear," Bruzer said.

I knelt next to the pot and looked inside. Orange-colored stew simmered. A half-dozen or so flies simmered along on top of the stew—fly stew. Having no idea what the rest of it was or contained, I reached inside the pot with the help of a piece of moldy naan from the filthy rag, removed the flies, and flicked them off. I took another piece of the stale, hardened bread, dipped it in the stew, and shoved it into my mouth. Hurriedly, I took a few more bites. When I looked up, my six companions were staring in disbelief.

"How does it taste?" Les asked.

"Great."

Les moved in, picked up a piece of naan, and joined me. One by one the others joined in; even Bruzer.

At about 2400 hours we slowly descended from the cave toward the mud huts, and hunkered down a short distance away from the compound.

"This is ZQ territory," Bruzer said in a hushed tone.

"I count seventeen motorcycles by one of the huts," Killian said as he knelt to join the rest of us.

"Taliban for sure, maybe even ZQ himself," Littles said.

Bruzer gave out orders. "Ski, Les, Killian, and the terp go with me. Correa and Littles, keep outside perimeter."

Everyone nodded.

"You sure you wanna take Sanj?" Ski asked once again.

Bruzer gave Ski a *don't-question-me-again* look.

"*Omnes Morimur.*" Bruzer gave me a sinful smile.

"All Men Must Die," Littles translated.

"Let's send this fudge-fuck to the real Light of The Truth," Les said decisively.

"Now you'll see why he's called Bruzer," Ski told me.

Faint music could be heard as we moved slowly toward the mud compound. Motorcycles leaned against the thatched wall. The closer we got, the louder the sound of laughter, clapping hands and music became. The team swept the perimeter and checked the rest of the huts to avoid any surprises. The mud huts were abandoned.

A beat-up wooden door was the only barrier between us and the unknown inside the music room. Bruzer took point position as the other three lined up behind him. I stayed a few yards behind. Weapons ready. The emissaries dispatched by the angel of death waited calmly before striking the heart of belligerence on behalf of innocence. The sound of laughter and loud conversation contradicted the intensity of the moment.

Bruzer kicked in the door and jumped through, the others just behind him. I hesitated for a split second but quickly followed.

The occupants of the room sat on blankets on the dirt floor with bowls of fruits and food in front of them. A radio played Pashton music. A boy of maybe nine dressed and made up to look like a girl danced in the middle of the room.

Time froze as the men on the floor exchanged befuddled looks, then they reached for the weapons next to them. Bruzer and the crew opened fire before the men could touch their AKs. The music played on the radio as the men on the floor twirled, twitched and danced to Bruzer and his disciples' sermon. Blood, chunks of flesh, bone, and ripped pieces of fabric flew everywhere. A macabre orgy unfolded before me. Everything moved in rapidly slow motion.

The firing stopped. Gunsmoke hovered. The smell of gunpowder, dust, blood, and lead permeated the space. Slowly, narrow streams of crimson began to flow from the bodies, meandering through the shallow crevices and pooling in small depressions in the dirt floor.

The little boy stood frozen in the middle of the room, urine running down his leg and onto the dirt floor. The fuckers had dressed the poor boy in a red girly dress and put lipstick and blush on him. This was a banquet of *Bacha Bazi* or Dancing Boy. The boy had been the entertainment for the evening. After his performance the men would take turns sodomizing him. Most likely the boy wouldn't survive the ordeal, which would be a blessing; otherwise he would face a similar nightmare over and over again until he could no longer deliver the same sensations as he had earlier.

The team searched the room, examining the bodies and looking for any ID and intel. I glanced around. These men had been alive just a few short seconds ago. Now they lay dead with bizarre, disfigured expressions on their faces. A sense of righteous debauchery traveled within me. I savored it.

"Bruz, you got that mugshot of ZQ?" Killian asked.

Bruzer pulled the picture from his flak vest and walked over.

"Fuck me." Bruzer turned and look at the others. "This is the shitsack, ZQ."

The others gathered around to double-check. Positive ID was made.

The one and only ZiaUlhaq was dead. The corpse of his loyal henchman, Sher-Allah, lay next to him.

I stood over the lifeless body of these Bastards of Perdition. Their soulless faces were deprived of slightest trace of kindness. I so badly wanted to empty my weapon into their carcasses.

Efficiently and calmly, the group took multiple pictures, measurements, and DNA samples from ZiaUlhaq and the others. Each knew what had to be done. Meanwhile I stood with the boy, who shivered from shock. He had witnessed something no nine-year-old should ever see. I held him close as I stroked his hair.

Tatatata. Tatatata. Tatatata.

Machinegun fire got everyone's attention. The team hurriedly grabbed all they could and ran out. Taliban were converging on the compound. Maybe they'd heard the commotion, though our silenced weapons hardly made a sound and the now-dead vultures hadn't fired a shot. Or maybe the new visitors were supposed to meet the others for their feast.

Outside, tracer rounds whizzed by. Small plumes of dust indicated how close the rounds hit. We had no idea how many enemy fighters there were, but the muzzle flashes from their guns indicated one thing: we were fucked.

I huddled behind a low mud wall, holding the little boy close. He must have been in complete shock, as he didn't make a sound, nor even the slightest reaction to what was transpiring. Bruzer and his operators engaged the unknown number of enemy coolly and calculatingly. Peeking through a hole in the mud wall, I decided to get a few rounds off. It was now or never.

My weapon's trigger response was smooth as I emptied a magazine in the direction of the tracer rounds. Reloading quickly, I waited for the right opportunity to shoot again. *Save the ammo for the pros, you idiot*, I told myself. I refrained from wasting precious rounds and kept one magazine aside—to off myself before I was captured, should it come to that.

"Grab the bikes," Bruzer yelled. "I'll provide suppressive fire. Let's go."

The team dropped back and one by one got on the bikes and hightailed it out the back of the village.

Meanwhile Bruzer engaged the unknown number of enemy fighters. He ran to my position and dropped behind the wall as the team pulled out. Only the three of us remained.

"You know how to ride?" Bruzer asked.

"Yeah."

"Grab a bike, take him with you," he said, referring to the boy.

"What about you?" I said in a quiet, urgent voice.

"I'll be right behind you," he said as he turned and fired a few rounds.

My mind said *go*, but my legs didn't cooperate. My physiological fight-or-flight circuit-board malfunctioned at the most critical moment possible. I looked over at the bikes but couldn't recognize any of the brands. Unique, United, Pamir. They didn't look to be more than 200 CCs.

"Go. Go. *Now*," Bruzer said forcefully.

I grabbed the boy by the back of his blouse and made a mad dash for the bikes. I jumped on a bike. It wouldn't start. It was leaking oil and gas. Bullets must have hit it. I ran to the next bike. It was also a no-go. My prayers intensified as the situation became more dire. I jumped on the third bike. Nothing. My choices were dwindling.

Fear has a distinct taste and smell that cannot be described unless experienced firsthand. For the second time in my life I tasted and smelled true fear. Then I thought of Bruzer, who didn't have the luxury of time as I did.

The fourth bike. The fucker started. I reached for the boy, but then I thought I should leave the bike running for Bruzer. Hastily, I jumped on the next bike over. Dead as a doorknob.

Bruzer was standing next to me before I could try another bike. He jumped on the bike that was running. "C'mon, let's go," he yelled.

Pulling up the boy with his blouse, I sandwiched him between us on the seat of the bike. Bruzer popped the clutch and damn near did a wheelie, almost throwing me and the boy off. My fingers clutched Bruzer with a death grip. The boy nearly suffocated, squeezed between us.

Bullets whizzed past, but the fear of what might be chasing us prevented me from looking back.

We rode across the bumpy desert terrain for some time.

"Do you see the team?" Bruzer asked over his shoulder.

The wind delivered a glob of his saliva onto my face. I hadn't thought about the team until Bruzer mentioned them. Time becomes meaningless when you're being hunted by a merciless enemy. I looked around the desert with my night goggles. No trace of the other team members. No sign of anyone chasing us, either.

"Slow down," I said.

Bruzer eased off the throttle and eventually stopped. We were in the middle of nowhere. I had no idea which direction was north, south, or otherwise. But Bruzer did. After a quick survey of the situation, we decided to head north. We had to find a place to hide from the Taliban by daybreak, when they would surely begin to hunt us down in greater numbers.

At 0300 hours we came upon a small cluster of a dozen or so mud huts.

Bruzer turned the bike off and we pushed it forward with the boy tracking along.

"Let's hide the bike somewhere and take shelter here," Bruzer said.

"How do we know this village is friendly?" I stopped pushing the bike. "We're fucked if they're not!"

Bruzer stopped, too, and contemplated my words. "Yeah, I guess you're right." He mounted the bike again. "Get on."

"And go where? We can't travel like this. We'll be spotted in no time."

"We don't have many choices—either hide here or take our chance out there." Bruzer pointed to the open desert.

I looked at the village again. *Fuck. What if I make the wrong suggestion and get us killed?* The memory of the fateful day dashed across my mind. I didn't want my name to go down as a soldier-killer.

My stomach tightened, and I had an uncontrollable urge to piss. I unbuttoned my pants and started pissing. The excitement of the firefight eased as I emptied my bladder. Bruzer followed suit as the little boy watched.

"So, what do you think?" Bruzer asked.

This was the first time he had acknowledged me in this way.

The clothes hanging on a line by the cluster of mud-dwellings got my attention.

"Leave the bike here." I gestured for Bruzer to follow me.

Bruzer looked perplexed as he came along, but when we got to the clothesline he looked at me as if to say *aha*. We grabbed a bunch of clothes and walked back to the bike.

"Let's change into local garb," I said.

We began to undress.

"Hey, wait a minute," I said. "We can't travel like this; your looks will give us away."

"I'll pull a cap over my head."

"Are you kidding? These fuckers will spot you in a second."

"What, then?"

Rummaging through the clothes, I pulled out a burqa and a kamis, the long trousers worn by women.

"Here, put these on," I said.

"You want me to put on a burqa?"

"Listen," I shoved the burqa and kamis in his chest. "You don't speak the language, but men here will not approach a married woman!"

"What?" Bruzer shook his head. "You want me to be your wife?"

"You have no choice." I pointed to the boy. "He'll be our son; it's the only cover we have."

I took a *perhan wa tunban*, a long shirt, pantaloons, and a *kufi* cap for myself.

Bruzer was still shaking his head. The "don't fuck with me" look I gave him established my dominance over him in these circumstances.

"Fuck." Bruzer angrily disrobed.

"Look at it this way," I said. "You can carry our weapons under your burqa!"

Bruzer gave me a "fuck you" look.

I grabbed our uniforms and threw them down the village well.

Bruzer climbed onto the bike. "Let's go."

"Go where?"

"Let's get the hell outta here."

"No."

"What do you mean, 'no?'"

"Women don't drive motorcycles here," I said.

"You mean *I* sit behind *you*?"

I just looked at him in his Blue and black head-to-toe tent of garments. He slowly slid back on the seat.

"Grab our son and cover your face, dear," I said.

"Fuck you. I don't remember you proposing."

"Ugly bearded wife shouldn't talk so much," I replied dismissively.

Darkness was on a steady march toward its demise, one tick at a time. We rode across the dark desert for some time. An assembly of lights shimmering in the distance announced the presence of a roadside *caravanserai*, a rest area.

"I think we should stop here," I said.

"Maybe there's a phone," Bruzer replied.

"We good?" I asked.

"We good."

A few KRAZ and ZIL Soviet-era trucks and old Indian-made Tata trucks were parked in front of the inn. I stood in the doorway and looked around a dingy café lit by sapless florescent lights emanating a hazy glow. A few customers sat on the grimy, timeworn carpet that lined the sides of the room. Some ate, some drank tea, some smoked, and some slept.

An old man approached.

"*Tasou de shpai lapareh otaq lari?*" I asked him. "Do you have a room for the night?"

"*Ho, otaq larom,*" he said. "Yes, I have room."

"We are hungry; please bring us rice, potatoes, and bread," I said.

I walked back to usher in my wife and son. "You're too tall; slouch, make yourself smaller," I whispered to Bruzer. "Look weak, meek."

We sat in a corner with the boy in the middle and Bruzer sitting on the extra fabric of the boy's garb to make sure he stayed put. We were both concerned about what the boy might or could do. Bruzer's sidearm was tucked into my pantaloons' waistband for quick access. He held two M4's under his burqa.

The old man brought naan, rice, and potato. I took the dish and with my filthy hands put some food on the plates for the three of us. The boy didn't touch his. Bruzer and I ate with our dirty right hands. Bruzer's manly hand was a dead giveaway so I shoved his plate under his burqa to keep his hands out of sight. We had burned many calories and needed replenishment. I took a piece of bread, grabbed rice and potato with it and shoved it into my mouth. You could say I bit off more than I could chew. The food got stuck in my mouth. With my index finger, I shoved and pushed the food around in my mouth until I was able to force it down my throat.

The boy began to fidget. Bruzer's ice-cold eyes looked through the mesh covering them as we exchanged tense looks. The boy fidgeted again. I whacked him in the back of the head. Other patrons looked at us, so I whacked the kid one more time.

The old man took us to our room, unlocked the door and let us in. I paid him for dinner and the room. The small room smelled musty. A pile of colorful blankets were stacked up under the window at the far end. The single light bulb inside was on its last breath and barely lit the place.

"I'm not about to sleep on those blankets," I whispered to Bruzer.

"I need to get some sleep," Bruzer said. "You should too."

We slept on the hard floor, pressed against the door to prevent anyone from entering. Bruzer and I each also put one leg on the boy to keep him from doing anything stupid.

The next morning we walked out of the room, sleepless. It was just after 0700 hours on the cold 23rd day of November. I looked around for a phone. None could be found. We hoped to see a NATO patrol or one of our patrols roll by, but no go. We finally got on the bike and rode down the dirt road.

The bike began to sputter as we reached the outskirts of a village with a small stream flowing adjacent to it. A gathering of trees provided gentle shade by the stream.

"I'll go into the village to get some gas," I told Bruzer. "Take the boy and wait by the river."

"Why not go together?" Bruzer asked somewhat suspiciously.

"Because I can go in and out!"

He hesitated for a moment before taking the boy's hand somewhat apprehensively and walking toward the stream. His walk couldn't have been manlier.

"Hey. Walk like a woman," I said in a loud whisper.

Bruzer began shifting his ass from side to side as he gave me the finger.

The bike made it to the edge of the village before it stalled completely. No gas. I pushed the bike into the village, my eyes scanning everyone with distrust. In a place where everyone is a potential enemy, trusting your own shadow could be a detriment to your wellbeing. How was I going to find gas there? This was what I'd learned during my time in the field: to gauge nuance and make what might have to be a split-second decision. Friend or foe? Life or death? Get help or be blown to bits?

The villagers watched me closely, too. An outsider had ventured into their tight-knit community. My unshaven, dirty face camouflaged my true identity. The hostile stares unnerved me but I knew I had to maintain an authentic front. I played possum, not looking or sounding threatening.

It seemed to work; I managed to get the motorcycle fueled and began riding it back to the river. But as I topped a rise close to the place where I'd left Bruzer and the boy, I abruptly braked. From my vantage point I could see Bruzer slumped against a tree, his body relaxed in sleep—but no sign of the boy.

I could also see something else: a small horde of men armed with AK47s, approaching Bruzer with clearly portentous intentions. The men could only be Taliban and Taliban goons, and they were no more than thirty yards from Bruzer.

Desperate, I pressed on the horn button, but the feeble bleat did not reach Bruzer. The distance was simply too great. I yelled, to no avail. Finally, I pulled the handgun from my waistband and fired two shots into the air.

Bruzer instinctively jumped to one knee and took cover behind the tree. At the same time, the disparate crew fired at his position. Bullets ripped into the tree Bruzer hid behind, sending chunks of wood flying. Bruzer returned fire.

Choosing reckless abandon over wisdom, I twisted the throttle of the motorbike and sped toward the firefight without thinking of what I would do once I got there. The bumpy terrain made it difficult to handle the bike at high speed, so I lifted my ass off the seat and stood on the pegs for better balance. The handgun dangled from my finger through the trigger guard. The wind made my eyes tear even though I had my glasses on. Still, I saw silhouettes drop to the ground. Had they been hit or were they just dropping to avoid Bruzer's bullets?

BOOM.

The blast turned me into a human projectile. I flew several yards through the air before landing hard on the rocky terrain. The impact knocked the wind out of me, and my body went numb as I startled between consciousness and oblivion. Moondust lined the inside of my mouth and nostrils, depriving them of moisture. I realized I had hit an anti-personnel mine in my rush to get to Bruzer. My glasses and my weapon had flown off to who knew where. My chest heaved as I tried to deliver oxygen to my lungs. My limbs did not respond to commands from my brain. The sound of an intensifying battle and the ill-defined figures coming toward me inspired awesome fear within me. My right arm was stuck under my torso and I couldn't move it. Desperate and in great distress, I mustered up enough energy to move my left hand around, groping at the immediate area for my sidearm so I could off myself before the Taliban captured me. No weapon was to be found.

The sound of small-arms fire was drowned out by the reverberation of the noise from heavy guns. *Oh fuck, they have big guns.* With much effort, I moved my neck to get a last look at Bruzer. I prayed for a quick death for him.

From my cock-eyed hazy vantage point, I saw a Blackhawk make a hard landing near the river. Special Forces immediately engaged the enemy as they deployed from the bird. This must be a hallucination. A part of me wanted to let go of consciousness, but a part of me fought to hold on. That part lost. Slowly, I faded.

A swift jolt and I went airborne. A dull bump pressed hard against my solar plexus under the flak vest. The specks of moondust in my slightly-open eyes blurred my vision. I was dangling over someone's shoulder like a rag doll; his clavicle dug deep in my stomach, further stifling my breathing. *This is it, the Taliban have me. Surrender to fate, whatever it may be.*

Images of my mom popped into my mind. Then complete darkness.

A chill settled within me as the strong, bitter wind cut deep to the bone. Had the Taliban slashed my arteries, draining the life out of me slowly? Was that why I felt cold?

A gentle stroke brushed against my face; it reminded me of the touch I'd felt just before the ladybug incident. Fearful of what I would encounter, I labored to open my eyes. When I did, I met a set of steely gray eyes.

Fucking Bruzer.

He was sitting on his knees as he held the side of my face. The wind came from the helicopter rotors. I tried to look around, but saw only silhouettes and heard only muffled sounds. I faded again.

1015 HOURS / DECEMBER 01, 2011

The face looking back at me from the mirror displayed fresh scratches and bruises. My body still ached from the force of the explosion, but luckily, I hadn't broken any bones or lost any limbs. I walked over to my bed and continued packing my belongings.

I was going home.

The immensity of my experience weighed me down. This should have been a happy moment for me. It wasn't. The idea of leaving presented next to no appeal. Often, freed prisoners want to go back to prison. Now I understood their dilemma. Coming to this place had been distressing. Leaving it was heartrending.

Ski, Littles, Les, Killian, and Correa entered the tent. They stood quietly. Emotions had robbed everyone of speech.

"We fucked up that night," Ski said with tension in his voice. "We lost you guys."

"Yeah, we searched for you," Correa added.

"We got picked up by a bird," Killian said.

"Fuck," Les snarled. "I'm just glad we got to you in time."

"God looked after you guys," Littles said as he held his Bible.

The unpretentious concern evident in the eyes of the unsung heroes standing before me was undeniable. I would have never met this bunch if I hadn't come to Afghanistan or toughed it out when my world turned dark. The closeness I felt to the group surpassed my feelings toward my blood family. I desperately wanted to hold on to them and not let go. This was another moment in my life that I did not want to run away from. It was my defining moment. I didn't want to break my connection with the team—and I didn't want to feel abandoned. They were my only link to Kent, Smitts, and Gospol. My only connection to myself.

"Thanks for looking after me," I said, choking up.

Ski took a step forward and put his hand on my shoulder.

Killian said, "You're part of the team."

Les nodded. "Bruz told us how you saved his hide."

We had reached the end of our chapter together. The guys huddled, surrounded me. We hugged individually, shook hands and said our good-byes.

Les damn near broke my hand with his grip. "You're the coolest rag-head that ever sang 'Sweet Home Alabama,'" he said with his eyebrows knotted above a snarly smile.

The team left the tent.

Random tears fell from my eyes as I continued packing what few possessions I had.

A strong presence made me turn around.

Bruzer.

We stood face-to-face for a moment, saying nothing.

"The only certainty in life is what happened yesterday." Bruzer dropped his head. "I'm glad to have met you."

I stood still, much as I had during our first encounter in Lt. Laramy's office.

"War is a machine and we're the fuel...." Bruzer went silent, trying to hide his emotions.

Wiping away a few tears with my sleeve, I said, "My self-loathing led me here, to this place. Did I even have any business being here?"

"Everyone has an emptiness deep within their soul. Some of us choose to acknowledge it." Bruzer hesitated as if recollecting memories. "That's why we're all here." He cleared his throat. "You rode faster than your guardian angel can fly; that's why I'm here today."

A calm pause lingered.

"Good luck, tiny husband," he said with a faint smile.

"Crappy luck, huh?" I said. "Never imagined having a bearded wife with balls."

Wicked grins appeared on both of our faces but quickly gave way.

"Never let the sum of your fears exceed your courage," Bruzer said.

We stood in silence again as I deliberated Bruzer's words. We had been complete strangers a handful of days ago. Now we were two beads on the same rosary, linked to one another by the invisible strands of fate and faith.

We hugged.

"Never forget," Bruzer whispered in my ear, and walked out.

Tears fell from my eyes faster than I could wipe them away. When I looked up, Lieutenant Laramy was standing in front of me holding a folder. An embarrassing moment. I didn't want her to see me crying, but the obvious couldn't be disguised as I wiped away my tears and made an anemic attempt to put on a solid face.

She smiled awkwardly, then held out the folder. "You've been cleared of any negligence or wrongdoing," she said. "Our Marines' death, while tragic, was an act of war. K.I.A."

My eyes locked with Laramy's. I let her outstretched hand linger without taking the folder.

"For what it's worth, I'm sorry," she said.

The barrage of emotions plundering my soul rendered me motionless.

"You didn't deserve what happened to you," she said. "There's such a thing as 'fog of war'. There's plenty of blame to go around. You're not to blame."

I wanted to respond punitively, but I couldn't. I searched her eyes as I harnessed my unrestrained thoughts. For the first time, I saw uncertainty in the same set of unyielding eyes that had beheld me with indifference for so long. Her gaze dismantled my anger.

I pointed to the folder in her hand. "Is that you talking, or the report?"

She shifted in place. Her usual upright posture slightly slouched. "Partly me, partly the report," she said as her face blushed.

"I hope mostly you," I said with a wishful smile.

Laramy's eyes softened. "I was intimidated by you." She looked away. "You're not like the others; I didn't know how to handle you. I tried hard not to like you."

I waited for her eyes to meet mine again. "There's not much about me to like," I said, reaffirming how I felt about myself. "But a hard-ass Marine afraid of a simple terp?"

Laramy smiled.

An awkward pause as we held each other's gaze, then Laramy extended her hand.

"Your hand is dirty," I said.

"But my heart is clean," she replied with a daring glare.

I reached out. Our hands dovetailed. Neither of us broke the contact. Heedfully, I took a step forward, closing the space between us. I put my arms around Laramy. She edged closer and slowly wrapped her arms around me, enfolding me close. As I breathed her in I felt the collapse of the wall she had put up between us. At that moment, I held the world in my embrace, and the universe, me in hers. Good energy flowed between us. A bittersweet feeling traveled from my head to my heart.

Too bad it had taken so long.

1126 HOURS / DECEMBER 05, 2011

A Marine helped carry my sea bags onto the helicopter.

As the bird took to the air, a thick layer of yellow-gray moondust hung over Leatherneck, reminiscent of my arrival.

The open rear gate provided me with an unobstructed view. Below, Marines played soccer. Soldiers and civilians went about their business. I saw my old tent, the plywood building where my hearing had taken place. I saw the ghosts of my three friends: Kent, Smitts, and Gospol.

Looking out at the khaki landscape through the open rear gate reminded me of a poem by John McCrae, a Canadian field surgeon serving during WWI:

"In Flanders fields the poppies blow
Between the crosses, row on row,
That mark our place; and the sky
The larks, still bravely singing, fly
Scarce heard amid the guns below.
We are the Dead. Short days ago
We lived, felt dawn, saw sunset glow,
Loved and were loved, and now we lie
In Flanders fields.
Take up our quarrel with the foe;
To you from failing hand we throw
The torch; be yours to hold it high.
If ye break faith with us who die
We shall not sleep, though poppies grow
In Flanders fields."

Fate had delivered a lost soul in search of forgiveness to the Marines; a band of young soldiers had rendered salvation.

1209 HOURS / DECEMBER 05, 2011

We landed at Kandahar Air Field, the out-processing portal for Afghanistan southern region. A van from Global Vigilance picked me up and dropped me off on the far fringes of the massive base in a small camp of some thirty-odd tents, all unoccupied. The only soul in the big-little emptiness was me. I situated myself in one of the tents and waited to be processed out to a U.S. military base in Kuwait before the next leg of my journey home.

My wait in the wintery unheated tent turned from one day to two, then three, four, five, six. My memories of the recent past kept me company. Aside from my two-to-three packs of cigarettes a day and my cheap little MP3 music player, only my internal communion provided a source of conversation.

KAF had a good personnel transportation system which I used to get to the nearest chow hall for my two daily meals. The rest of the time I sat in front of my tent with my broken heart craving rain for the city of nostalgia I'd left behind.

On the seventh day, I decided to go to my employer's office since I hadn't heard anything from them about my departure. Finding the office in the huge base proved to be somewhat of a task, but eventually, I found it and inquired about my departure date. Much to the site manager's surprise, and to mine, no one had any record of my presence in KAF.

1024 HOURS / DECEMBER 14, 2011

The commercial jetliner touched down in Kuwait, where the December desert chill was unusually bitter. Luckily, I had a warm sweater in addition to the pilot-style jacket in my backpack.

My time in Kuwait lacked the joy of looking forward to going home. My days were spent in either the warmth of the small USO movie theater or sitting in the open-air smoke pit situated next to the half-dozen or so "restaurant row" venues, smoking and freezing. On two separate occasions my employer drove me to Kuwaiti customs to get my entry/exit visa; the military-chartered commercial plane finally took off on the fourth day, carrying me with it.

DECEMBER 18, 2011

A company van picked me up from Indianapolis International Airport and drove me to Camp Atterbury, where I went through the same process I had when I'd entered Fort Benning over a year ago. This time, however, I was alone. Afterward the company driver drove me to a section of the camp lined with barracks and stopped in front of one of the buildings. The bastard didn't give me a hand unloading my bags; he just watched with a harried look on his face as if he had to run somewhere and take a shit. He got more and more agitated while I took my time hauling my bags out of the van one at a time.

I walked into the massive barracks to find out that I was the only soul in the 200-capacity building. The quietness of the snowfall outside did little to invigorate the stillness inside. For no particular reason, I chose the sixth bunk from the door, threw my bags down next to it and went outside. Chain-smoking a couple of cigarettes in the frigid December Indiana air failed to warm me up. The sprawling snow-covered grounds of the camp looked desolate. No traffic or activity anywhere. My surroundings reflected my dejected mood. I went back inside the equally-freezing barracks and searched for a thermostat to heat the place. No luck.

At night, being alone with the ghosts of all those who had passed through the place gave me the jitters. The frigid air inside added to my disquiet. Sometime in the middle of the night I got up and put my clothes and boots back on to stop the shivering and to warm up my frozen toes.

The next day, I took a quick shower in the equally freezing, eerie showers, got dressed, and headed out to find a chow hall. I stood on the deserted snow-covered road not knowing which direction to take. My body desperately craved a hot cup of coffee. The snow fell harder. My cold hands clenched inside my pant pockets as I began walking in one direction hoping to find something or someone.

A jeep pulled up next to me and the passenger window rolled down. "Need a ride?"

I looked over, and for a split second was reminded of Joe, Tony, and the dusty road.

The soldiers brought me to a diner/store on the base, two and a half miles away. The interior of the place resembled a wood cabin; it was a multi-purpose joint. One side served as the dining area and the other a store. Everything from souvenirs to risqué camouflage-patterned panties was sold in the place. I ended up spending the entire day in the cozy atmosphere. I had nowhere else to go. At least there I could watch TV and eat.

The next few days were spent returning the army gear that had been originally issued to me prior to my deployment, and getting my discharge medical exam. One result was learning I had contracted TB dormant. Panic settled in when I heard those words. The doctor reassured me my condition was curable but would require a nine-month regimen of antibiotics and monthly blood tests to make sure the antibiotics weren't destroying my liver, kidneys or any other organ.

Time spent alone in the cold, snowy weather provided ample opportunity for soul-searching and reconciliation between me and myself as my contradictory emotions waged a quiet war within me. I mourned the losses that had left everlasting scars on my soul, and at the same time, I celebrated the strength I had gained from the wounds.

10:36 P.M. / DECEMBER 23, 2011

The sound of horns from Sunset Boulevard were no match for the stillness of my internal dialogue. Unlike my last visit to Boa steakhouse, accompanied by three female companions prior to my deployment, I sat alone at the corner table. But feel lonely I didn't. I'd gone through a sort of baptism, and a different man I'd emerged. More confident, comfortable in my own skin even though my soul was chafed forever. My view of life had changed unreservedly. Events and people required a deeper perspective now. Many conversations around me seemed inconsequential. The people having those conversations lived in homogenized, protective bubbles. They had no clue what went on in the rest of the world. Life was no longer about what I planned for tomorrow, next week or next year, it was about taking my next borrowed breath, my next undaunted step forward.

I looked at the patrons in the restaurant, and took a bite of the medium-rare steak. I savored it. The sweet smell of blood reminded me of my naked bloodlust during my time in the Land of the Afghans. Destiny had presented me with an unnegotiable offer and I had no choice but to accept it. It was a lesson to be had.

Life is a sequence of transactions, some of which result in a draw, no winner, no loser. Most are win-lose; we win a few and lose a few. There is no win-win. But it is within those ruinous transactions that we find the riches hidden within. Treasures are found in ruins, after all.

A sip of the *pinot noir* doused my sweltering emotions as I recounted my unintended experience. The memory of the two little brothers, dead and dying in the field hospital, materialized in my mind. Hila's mesmerizing eyes, her plight, and her demise. Maddox and the eternal guilt we shared. Clover's last words as we said goodbye. The memory of my fallen brothers, the young Afghan NIU team, and Nuristani, the caged free spirit. My time with Bruzer and his warriors, and the sensation of my embrace with Lt. Laramy, the strong female warfighter, hastened through my thoughts. I remembered the part of my soul I had left behind in the Land of Tears. Those memories will constitute the secrets between the two dates on my tombstone.

LETTER OF ASSIGNMENT - LOA

LETTER OF AUTHORIZATION

DATE OF REQUEST	9/27/2010		
REQUIRING ACTIVITY	Army CONUSCOM	GOVT AGENCY POC	
GOVT AGENCY POC PHONE		GOVT AGENCY POC EMAIL	@us.army.mil
NAME (Last, First, Middle Initial)		SSN/FIN	
DATE OF BIRTH	7/17/1965		
HOME ADDRESS		CITIZENSHIP	United States
PASSPORT # / EXPIRATION	10/29/2019	DEPLOYMENT PERIOD START	10/2/2010
DEPLOYMENT PERIOD END	1/1/2012		
EMAIL	conusspol@	THEATER EMAIL	aconusspol@
CLEARANCE LEVEL w/ AGENCY	None	CLEARANCE DATE	
JOB TITLE	Translator/Linguist	SUPERVISOR/NON-SUPERVISOR	Non-Supervisor/Non-Manager
COMPANY (full name)		COMPANY POC	Employee Relations
COMPANY POC TELEPHONE		COMPANY POC EMAIL	conusspol@
CONTRACT NUMBER/ TASK ORDER	W911W8-07-D-0019/0051	CONTRACT / TO START DATE	9/23/2007
CONTRACT / TO END DATE	1/2/2012	CONTRACT ISSUING AGENCY	Dept. of the Army
NEXT OF KIN (NOK) NAME	Available in SPOT	NOK RELATIONSHIP	Available in SPOT
ASSIGNED KO		ASSIGNED KO TELEPHONE	
IN-THEATER CONTACT	Employee Relations	CONTACT'S PHONE	
CONTACT'S EMAIL	aconusspol@		
COUNTRIES TO BE VISITED	Afghanistan, Germany, Kuwait, Kyrgyzstan, Qatar		

GOVERNMENT FURNISHED SERVICES
- ☑ APO/FPO/MPO/Postal Services
- ☑ Billeting
- ☑ CAC/ID Card
- ☐ Dependents Authorized
- ☑ Excess Baggage
- ☑ Govt Furnished Meals
- ☑ Mil Clothing
- ☑ Mil Issued Equip
- ☑ MWR
- ☑ Resuscitative Care
- ☐ Authorized Weapon
- ☑ CAAF
- ☐ Commissary
- ☑ DFACs
- ☑ Fuel Authorized
- ☑ Mil Banking
- ☑ Mil Exchange
- ☑ Milair
- ☐ None
- ☑ Transportation

PURPOSE
This contract is contingency based and as such, the bearer is a Contingency Contractor, considered EMERGENCY ESSENTIAL.

FUND CITE w/ BILLING ADDRESS	DBA INSURANCE INFORMATION
Virginia - 22060 United States	Company Name: Zurich Policy Number: WC3995254-00 POC Phone Number: 866-828-6816

The government organization specified above, in its mission support capacity under the contract, authorizes the individual employee identified herein, to proceed to the location(s) listed for the designated deployment period set forth above. Upon completion of the mission, the employee will return to the point of origin. Travel being performed is necessary and in the public's service. Travel is in accordance with FAR 31 205-36 and the maximum per diem allowable under the appropriate travel regulations (Joint Travel Regulation (for AK, HI and outlying areas of the United States and US possessions), Federal Travel Regulation for CONUS and US Territories, and Dept of State's Standardized Regulations for OCONUS Foreign Areas designated by DOS).

Prior to issuance of a DoD Common Access Card (CAC), the government sponsor must ensure completion of the FBI fingerprint check with favorable results and submission of a National Agency Check with Inquiries to the Office of Personnel Management (OPM), or a DoD-determined equivalent investigation.

Emergency medical support will be determined by the appropriate supported commander. Contractor authorization aboard military aircraft will be determined by the supported commander. Necessary identification badges will be determined and provided by the supported command.

"MK0YA3"

CAMP LEATHERNECK

BASTION I, CHRISTMAS 2010
Pizza Hut with British Soldier Dressed as Female Santa

BASTION I, Coffeeshop

MY FAVORITE CHAIR
Empty Ammo Canister Wedged Between T-Walls

CHEERLESS SUNSET

FOB NOLAY
Destroyed APC - Plywood Outhouse on Right

RED DIAMONDS - Enemy Forces/Land Mines
BLUE CIRCLES - Friendly Forces
LIGHT BLUE CIRCLE - My Truck

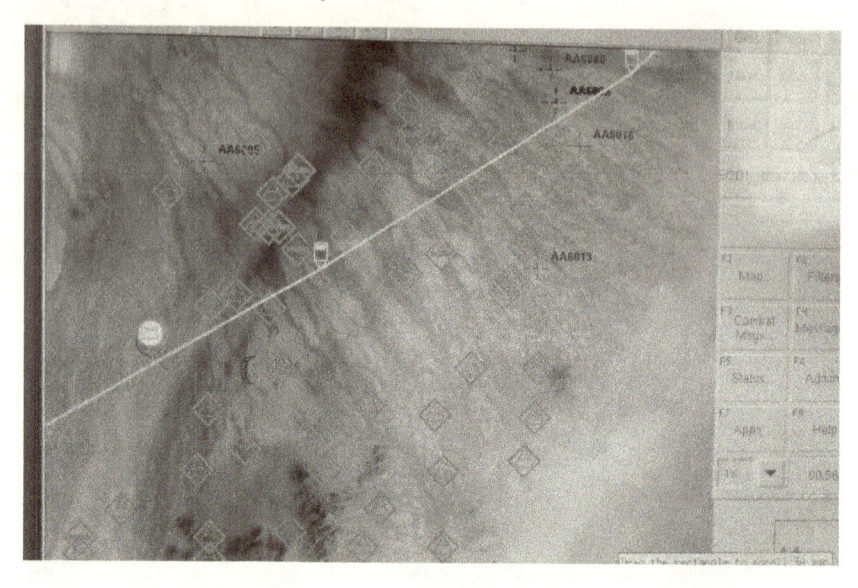

FOB NOLAY
Posing with Afghan Charles Manson Twin

FOB NOLAY
Morning after Air Drops - Observation Balloon Above in the Background

SLEEPING QUARTERS DURING THE MISSION
In 6x6 MRAP - In the Middle

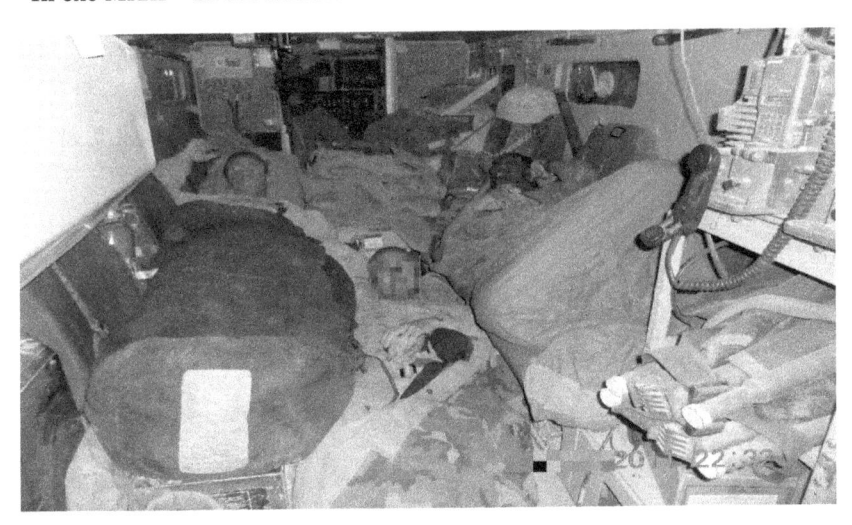

LATE NIGHT RETURN FROM A MISSION
Second from Right – MRAP 6x6

TRAINING DAY
Afghan National Army, Kabul

MUSA QALA RIVER

Sanjar Rohām

THE MARINES BBQ & TALENT SHOW
Camp Leatherneck

AFGHAN NATIONAL ARMY GRADUATION CEREMONY
US Marines Support Battalion, Kabul

LIGHTER THIEF

LZ, FOB EDI

PRE-MISSION BRIEFING WITH THE NIU TEAM

IN GREEN T-SHIRT WITH THE NIU TEAM

ON THE LEFT WITH THE NIU TEAM

LOCAL NATIONAL HIRES, LUNCHTIME ON A MISSION
Somewhere in Helmand Province

AUTUMN IN HELMAND PROVINCE

LOCAL BAZAAR

MISSION PIT STOP

PORTA POTTY GRIFFI ART

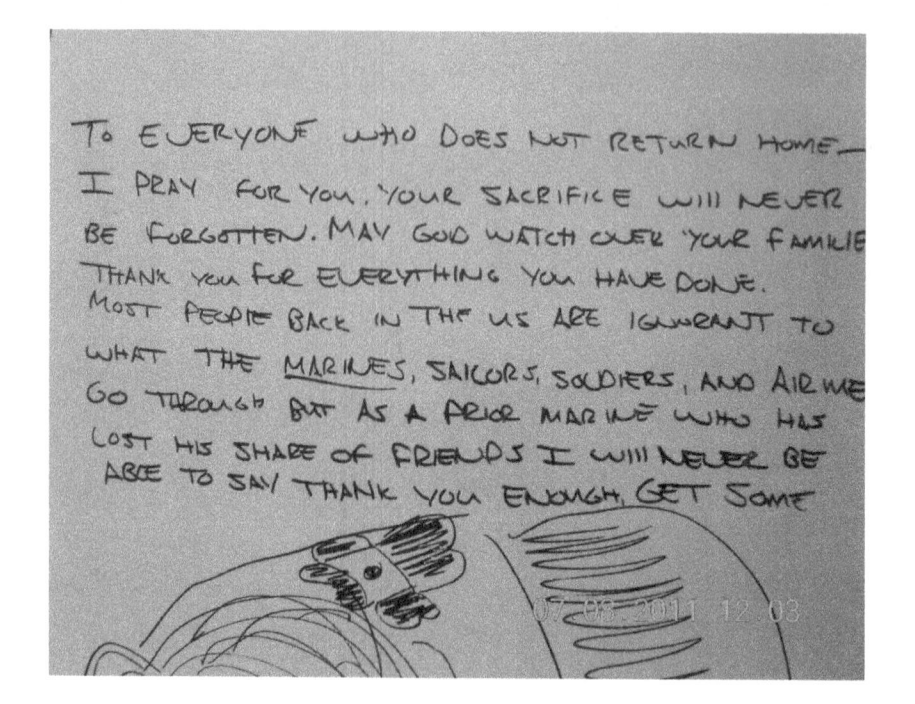

To everyone who does not return home— I pray for you, your sacrifice will never be forgotten. May God watch over your families. Thank you for everything you have done. Most people back in the US are ignorant to what the MARINES, SAILORS, SOLDIERS, AND AIR we go through but as a prior MARINE who has lost his share of FRIENDS I will never be able to say THANK YOU ENOUGH. GET SOME

Eat out of a bag
Shit in a bag
Sleep in a bag
Hope I don't go home in a bag

Rambo wuz ere.

To those who don't return,
we will meet again on the battlefield.

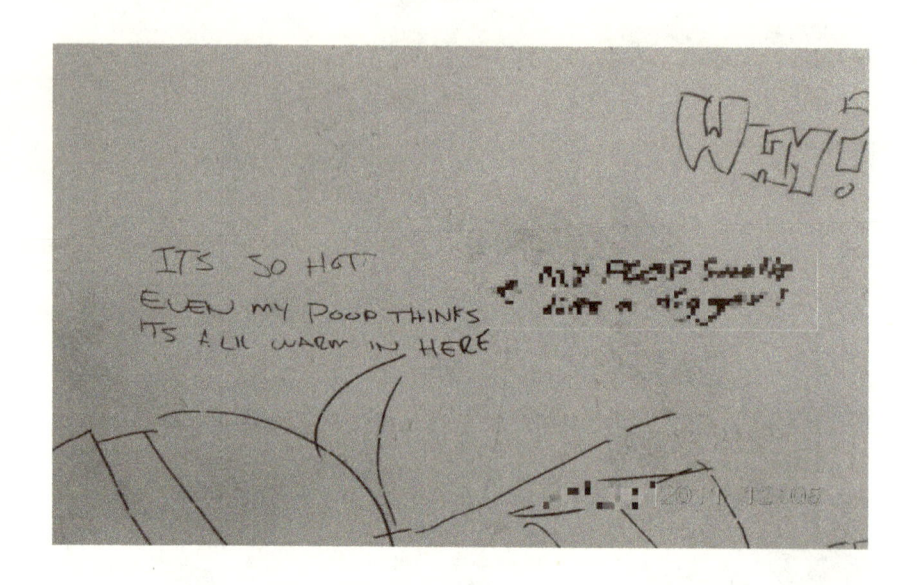

[Photograph: graffiti reading "IT'S SO HOT EVEN MY POOP THINKS ITS A LIL WARM IN HERE" with "MY POOP smells like a ———" and "WHY?" in the corner]

[Photograph: graffiti reading "STAY LOW, RUN FAST SAVE YOUR LIFE AND GET YOUR ASS BACK TO HOME TO SPEND ALL OF YOUR MONEY YOU EARN HERE. HAVE A SAFE TOUR. — 1/38 ASSAULT (R)...."]

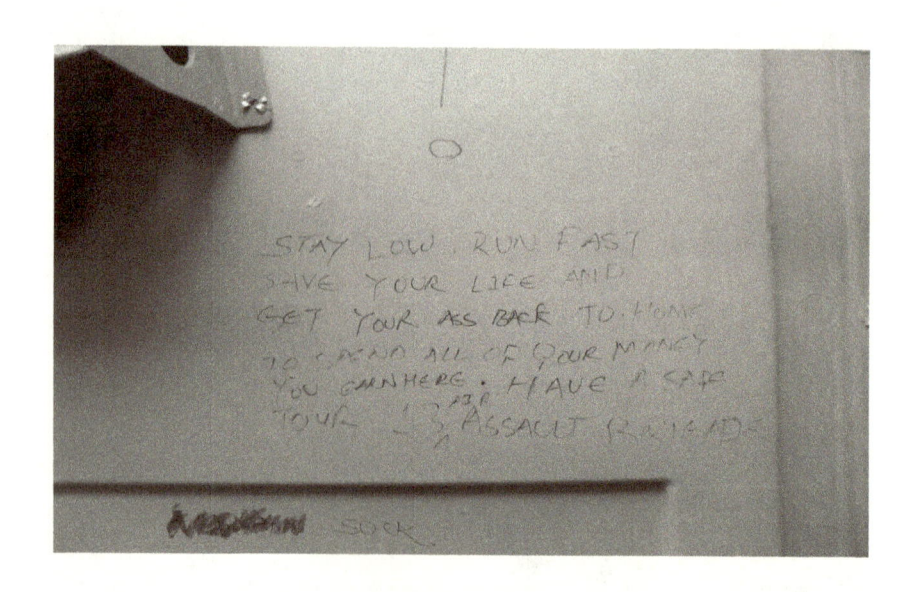

POG, FOR ALL YOUSE POG HATERS

I-M-P-E-D-E-D

U-T-U-T

R-U-N-T

← re-enlistment papers

Sanjar Rohām

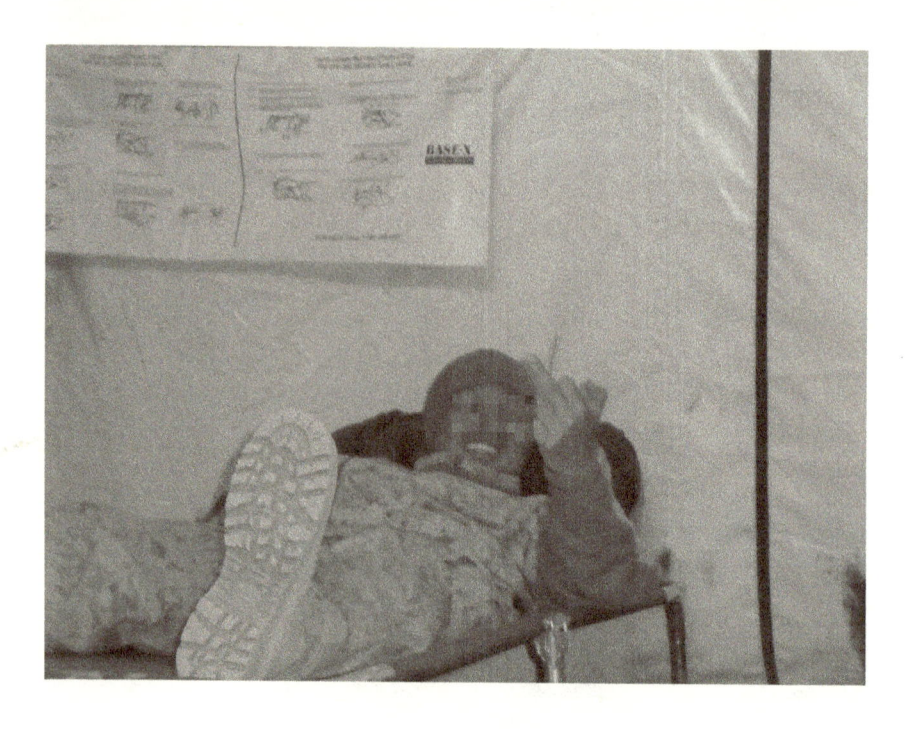

ACKNOWLEDGMENTS

Taking a moment to express immense gratitude and recognition to all those who have been instrumental in my journey. Firstly, heartfelt thanks to my mother for her unwavering support and encouragement that propelled me to venture into Afghanistan. I extend sincere appreciation to my family for their constant belief in me. Gratitude knows no bounds towards the Marines, and every dedicated service member of the U.S. Armed Forces worldwide, and their immeasurable sacrifices.

Special thanks to my literary agent Charlotte Gusay for navigating through the depths of my novice manuscript with patience. To Tracy Crow and the MilSpeak Foundation, thank you for the invaluable opportunity extended my way. Lastly, I offer my humble thanks to the divine for the blessings bestowed upon me.

ABOUT THE AUTHOR

Embarking on a new chapter of life in the United States from Iran at just twelve years old was an unexpected beginning leading to a remarkable journey. Little did Sanjar Rohām know that this land would become his permanent home amidst the winds of the 1978 Islamic Revolution.

The revolution not only tore apart the very fabric of the Iranian society but shattered the bonds within Sanjar's family. In the midst of the chaos, his father, a respected and accomplished businessman, found himself forced to make a harrowing choice. Faced with imminent danger and persecution, he made the gut-wrenching decision to flee the country, leaving everything behind, with only the clothes on his back as his silent companions. The events of the day unexpectedly altered the course of Sanjar's family's life. They were suddenly left to fend for themselves, faced with unexpected challenges that required resilience and unity. Overcoming adversity together strengthened his family bonds and taught him valuable lessons in perseverance. Faced with loss, financial hardship, and other challenges, his family discovered its true strength.

The pinnacle of Sanjar's aspirations was in 2005, securing an MBA from Pepperdine University, a feat he cherished deeply. Every twist and turn sculpted his path in unforeseen ways, unra-veling a tapestry of experiences that have shaped his identity profoundly.

Today Sanjar Rohām, a former in-demand business consultant from Los Angeles, is gearing up for his next assignment overseas.

Thank you for supporting the creative works of veterans and military family members by purchasing this book. If you enjoyed your reading experience, we're certain you'll enjoy these other great reads.

AMERICAN DELPHI
BY M.C. ARMSTRONG

During America's summer of plague and protest, fifteen-year-old Zora Box worries her pesky younger brother is a psychopath for sneaking out at night to hang with their suspicious new neighbor, Buck London, who's old enough to be their father. Their father, a combat veteran, is dead—suicide. Or so everyone thinks, until Buck sets Zora and her brother Zach straight, revealing their father as the genius inventor of a truth-telling, future-altering device called American Delphi.

SALMON IN THE SEINE
BY NORRIS COMER

One moment eighteen-year-old Norris Comer is throwing his high school graduation cap in the air and setting off for Alaska to earn money, and the next he's comforting a wounded commercial fisherman who's desperate for the mercy of a rescue helicopter. From landlubber to deckhand, Comer's harrowing adventures at sea and during a solo search in the Denali backcountry for wolves provide a transformative bridge from adolescence to adulthood.

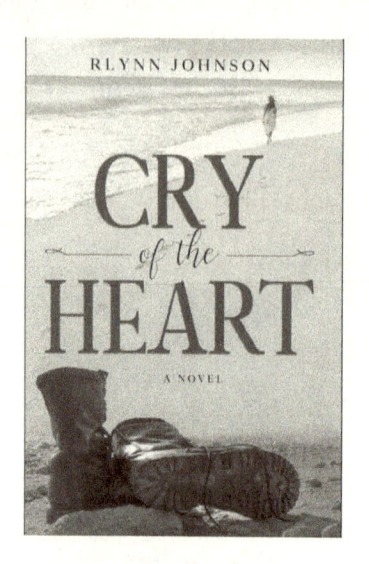

CRY OF THE HEART
BY RLYNN JOHNSON

After law school, a group of women calling themselves the Alphas embark on diverse legal careers—Pauline joins the Army as a Judge Advocate. For twenty years, the Alphas gather for annual weekend retreats where the shenanigans and truth-telling will test and transform the bonds of sisterhood.

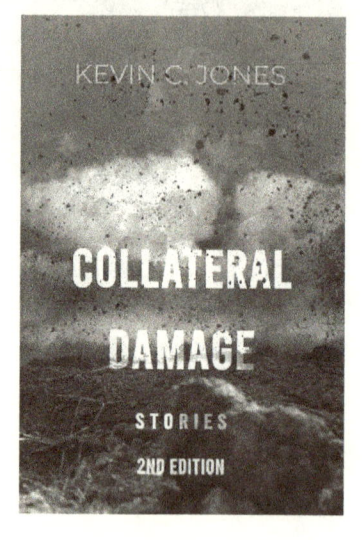

COLLATERAL DAMAGE
2nd edition
BY KEVIN C. JONES

These stories live in the realworld psychedelics of warfare, poverty, love, hate, and just trying to get by. Jones's evocative language, the high stakes, and heartfelt characters create worlds of wonder and grace. The explosions, real and psychological, have a burning effect on the reader. Nothing here is easy, but so much is gained.

—ANTHONY SWOFFORD, author of *Jarhead: A Marine's Chronicle of the Gulf War and Other Battles*

SUB WIFE
SAMANTHA OTTO BROWN

A Navy wife's account of life within the super-secret sector of the submarine community, and of the support among spouses who often wait and worry through long stretches of silence from loved ones who are deeply submerged.

BEYOND THEIR LIMITS OF LONGING
EDITED BY
JENNIFER ORTH-VEILLON, PHD

In America, WWI became overshadowed by WWII and Vietnam, further diluting the voices of poets, novelists, essayists, and scholars who unknowingly set a precedent for the sixty-two successive, and notable, war writers who appear in this collection to explore the complexity both of war's physical and mental horrors and of its historical significance in today's world in crises.

THE FINE ART OF CAMOUFLAGE

BY LAUREN KAY JOHNSON

A young woman's coming-of-age in the military against a backdrop of war, viewed through her lens as an information operations officer who wrestles with the nature of truth in the stories we hear from the media and official sources, and in the stories we tell about ourselves and our families.

THE SMOKE OF YOU

BY AMBER JENSEN

A young couple's love and marriage are tested during and after a military deployment with the National Guard to Iraq that results in a battle with chronic pain and the slow-burning challenges of married life. A story of selfless love and self-discovery, of hardship and hope, *The Smoke of You* will resonate with anyone who has ever suffered, and still bravely loved.

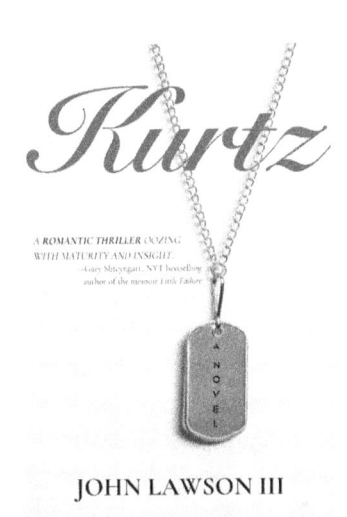

KURTZ
BY JOHN LAWSON III

Nick Willard may be three years her junior but he has pined for Annie Kurtz since they were both prep school students. However, after 9/11, Annie joins the Marines, eventually making a split-second decision her superiors never wanted her to make, and wrestles with whether she should have followed orders or her conscience. Nick—now a successful journalist—and Annie explore the tensions between love and friendship, even those between morality and law, as they come of age amid the psychological traumas that result when war makers sweep reality under a rug of ridiculous details.

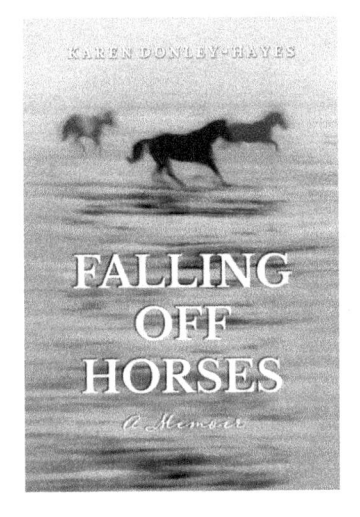

FALLING OFF HORSES
BY KAREN DONLEY-HAYES

A mutual love for horses unites two young women as teenagers who forge an undying friendship that will steady them after countless falls from horses, a roller coaster of love losses and triumphs, the emotional pitfalls of equestrian breeding and competing—and finally, through the heartbreaking diagnosis of a fatal illness.

THE WAITING WORLD
BY ANDRIA WILLIAMS

In 1929, two Irish housemaids, Nessa and Aoife, bonded through their journey to America, stumble upon and pocket a strange find on the shoreline of the home belonging to larger-than-life business magnate Titus McAvoy. When their path crosses a young white-passing British World War I veteran, John, who suspects the enormous worth of their find, the three friends forge a different life together—one free from the dark underbelly of how the rich treat the poor, and free from the pervasive rot of nationalist and racist behaviour, not to mention the injustices and dangers that too often befall women. But…nobody walks away from Titus McAvoy.

CELDAN HERESIES
BY MEGAN CARNES

A medieval fantasy world of heretics, led by young and brave Gaelle, rebel against a dark, militarized church after discovering a religion based in light. From Annie Dillard, Pulitzer-Prize winning author of *Pilgrim at Tinker Creek: An American Childhood*, "A work of startling imagination… a world both strange and deadly that feels at once feudal and extremely current, Carnes acquaints us with heretics, horse smugglers, poisoners, and church thieves—criminals…they are also wonderful company. Grab this book now. You won't put it down."

SHOALIE'S CROW
BY KAREN DONLEY-HAYES

A horrific fatal accident during an equestrian jumping event leads to the reincarnation of a newborn foal who discovers the only being who speaks her non-horsemanlike language is, of all things, a crow. Together, Shoalie and her crow-friend struggle to unravel a mystery that's leading toward another horrific fatal accident. (Published under our imprint Family of Light Books)

THE INDIGNITY OF KNOWING
BY AMBER ALBRITTON

From her lived experiences as the daughter of a U.S. soldier, Special Forces wife, and mother of a son in the military, Amber Albritton employs sound and lyricism in this hybrid narrative of poems and vignettes that examines the concept of ticker-tape patriotism and sheds light on the real lives of military families. From Albritton's special perspective, *The Indignity of Knowing* provides a testament of her multi-generational family for whom military service has become an ordained vocation.

Printed in the USA
CPSIA information can be obtained
at www.ICGtesting.com
LVHW092226250924
792123LV00004B/17